PEDRO ARRUPE S.J.

OTHER
APOSTOLATES
TODAY

Selected Letters and Addresses — III

Edited by Jerome Aixala S. J.

THE INSTITUTE OF JESUIT SOURCES
St Louis, 1981

in cooperation with
Gujarat Sahitya Prakash
Anand, India

Imprimatur

† C. GOMES S.J.
Bishop of Ahmedabad
January 8, 1981

2nd Edition, to be sold only in North America
Institute of Jesuit Sources
Fusz Memorial, St. Louis University
3700 West Pine Blvd.
St. Louis, Missouri 63108

Library of Congress Catalog Card Number : 81-80741
ISBN 0-912422-80-7 Smyth sewn paperbounnd
ISBN 0-912422-81-5 Clothbound

Edited by Jerome Aixala, S.J., St. Xavier's High School, Bombay 400 001
Published by X. Diaz del Rio, S.J., Gujarat Sahitya Prakash, Anand 388 001
Printed by S. Abril, S.J., Anand Press, Anand 388 001.

TABLE OF CONTENTS

v

JESUIT APOSTOLATES FROM PAUL III TO PAUL VI

The Formula of the Institute and the 32nd General Congregation

The Apostolic Letters of Paul III (1540) and Julius III (1550) recognize that the Society of Jesus was founded "chiefly for this purpose: to strive especially for the defence and propagation of the faith, and for the progress of souls in Christian life and doctrine, by means of public preaching, lectures, and other ministrations whatsoever of the word of God, and further, by means of the Spiritual Exercises, the education of children and unlettered persons in Christianity, and the spiritual consolation of Christ's faithful through hearing confessions and administering the other sacraments" as well as "in reconciling the estranged, in holily assisting and serving those who are found in prisons and hospitals, and indeed in performing any other works of charity, according to what will seem expedient for the glory of God and the common good."

(GC 32, Our Mission Today, n. 17).

*

Pope Paul VI to the Members of the 32nd G. C.

It seems to us that the originality of the new Society of Jesus consisted in having grasped that the times required people who were completely available, capable of detaching themselves from everything and of following any mission that might be indicated by the Pope and called for, in his judgment, by the good of the Church, putting always in first place the glory of God: ad maiorem Dei gloriam.

*. . . In the combination of this fourfold note we see
displayed all the wonderful richness and adaptability
which has characterized the Society during the centuries as the Society of those 'sent' by the Church. Hence
there have come theological research and teaching,
hence the apostolate of preaching, of spiritual assistance, of publications and writings, of direction of
groups, and of formation by means of the Word of God
and the Sacrament of Reconciliation in accordance with
the special and characteristic duty committed to you
by your holy Founder. Hence there have come the
social apostolate and intellectual and cultural activity
which extends from schools for the solid and complete
education of youth all the way to all the levels of
advanced university studies and scholarly research.
Hence the "puerorum et rudium in christianismo
institutio" which St. Ignatius gives to his sons, from the
very first moment of his "Quinque Capitula", or First
Sketch, as one of their specific aims. Hence the missions, a concrete and moving testimony of the 'mission'
of the Society. Hence the solicitude for the poor, for the
sick, for those on the margins of society.*

*Wherever in the Church, even in the most difficult
and extreme fields, in the crossroad of ideologies, in
the front line of social conflict, there has been and there
is confrontation between the deepest desires of man
and the perennial message of the Gospel, there also
there have been, and there are, Jesuits.*

(GC 32 SJ: pp. 301 and 305).

EDITOR'S NOTE

This third volume of Selected Letters and Addresses of Father Pedro Arrupe covers some of the main fields of apostolate of the Society of Jesus during this early period after the Second Vatican Council. The author has the experience on the subject gained through the years as Superior General of the Society, his five successive terms as President of the Union of Superiors General, and his participation in all the Episcopal Synods in Rome.

Many readers may have already seen the first volume of this anthology "Challenge to Religious Life Today" and the second on "Justice with Faith Today". One attraction this present volume should have — variety —, derived from the multiplicity of Jesuit ministries dealt with, and the different groups for whom the communications were intended. Some of the apostolates treated here are: Theological Reflection, Education, Evangelization, Social Communications, the Spiritual Exercises, Christian Life Communities, the Liturgy, Ecumenism, work with the Intellectuals, Youth, Workers.

There is no lack of variety either in the nature of the situations and audiences addressed by the speaker or writer. The pieces in this volume may be letters to the whole Society or some particular sections of it; addresses to the delegates of provinces in a Congregation of Procurators; homilies given during Eucharistic celebrations at the Gesù Church in Rome or in the Jesuit Church at Farm Street in London; talks to large groups of Jesuits or laymen in New York, Dublin, Bombay or Manila; conferences at international congresses of former Jesuit students or present presidents of Jesuit universities; an interview to Malcolm Muggeridge of the British Broadcasting Corporation, or a talk to lively Italian teenagers of the Eucharistic Youth Movement crowding the Basilica of St. Francis at Assisi; an address on the urgency of the apostolate of Social Communications to fellow Generals of Religious Congregations, or interventions at recent Synods of Bishops on the power of public opinion for Eanvgelization, on Catechesis and Inculturation.

x

I am indebted to those who helped in the choice of documents for this volume, to the staff of Anand Press and the Director of Gujarat Sahitya Prakash who undertook its printing and publication, and to Fr. Jean-Yves Calvez, General Assistant of the author and Assistant for France and Italy, who offered to write the following Foreword.

J. A.

FOREWORD

When Father Pedro Arrupe was elected Superior General of the Society of Jesus in May 1965, the Second Vatican Council was preparing its last session. Renewal and change were in the air in the whole Church. They were also in the air in the Society of Jesus. The 31st General Congregation which elected Fr. Arrupe stated: "Not a few doubts are being raised whether some of our works have become obsolete or are in need of a profound renewal at least in regard to the way in which they are carried on. On the other hand, new fields of apostolic labour invite us, fields which seem to be of very great importance for spreading the faith and imbuing the world with the spirit of Christ. We need to be more available to take on those ministries which answer the urgent needs of the modern Church and the special missions of the Roman Pontiff".

Precisely at the beginning of the 31st General Congregation a new Pontiff, Paul VI, had called the Society to such a special mission with regard to atheism. This too would mean change. As the Congregation stated it, "the mandate of resisting atheism should permeate all the accepted forms of our apostolate... We must also direct a greater part of our efforts, more than we have in the past, to non-believers, and we must search for and experiment with new ways of coming into close and more frequent contact with atheists themselves..."

Father Arrupe's task would be to guide this overall revision, renewal and adaptation of the apostolates of the Society of Jesus. He immediately launched in all the Provinces a general Survey of the apostolates as well as of the needs and of the context, human, social as well as ecclesiastical. In 1970, at a Congregation of Procurators, he was able to draw a list of our Apostolic Priorities — the first document contained in this volume.

The "Four Apostolic Priorities" were to make history, since about four years later the 32nd General Congregation (1974-1975), whose influence has been decisive on the apostolates of the Society of Jesus, resumed them in a synthetic way:

"— Research and theological reflection..., interdisciplinary and genuinely integrated with the culture in which it is done and with its traditions;

— Conscientization according to the Gospel of those who have the power to bring about social change...;

— Formation in every sphere of education...;

— Communication... (even) with those whom we cannot meet individually, and whom we can only help to the extent that we succeed in humanizing the social climate — attitudes and behaviour... In which regard the communication media would seem to play a role of great importance".

The importance of the Spiritual Exercises was stressed too. As a matter of fact they were not deemed important only as a particular ministry, but still more as a spirit and method — the 32nd General Congregation called it a "pedagogy of discernment" — which should permeate whatever apostolic contact a Jesuit has with his fellowmen.

Within that framework of Apostolic Priorities Father Arrupe would have to give orientations and guidelines all through the years for a variety of apostolates and ministries in which the Society of Jesus is active. This volume contains only a selection of them. It is however broad enough to serve — with the companion volume on Social Apostolate — as a handbook of Jesuit Apostolate today.

On the other hand many of the documents which are published in this volume are not merely Jesuit documents. Included are indeed some of Father Arrupe's contributions to the recent Synods of Bishops in which the apostolic mission and tasks of the Church were particularly discussed, especially those on Evangelization (1974) and Catechesis (1977). More generally speaking, the Society of Jesus in its apostolic activity these last years could not but share the concerns of the whole Church: justice, inculturation, ecumenism, faith and education in the faith, Christian Life. The reader will see here a reflection of the part — though modest and small — which the Society of Jesus may have had in the maturation of some ideas and initiatives of the whole Church.

The goal of the Society of Jesus is entirely apostolic. The letters, speeches and other documents of its Superior General show what a variety of interests and concerns are included in this goal. But still more they show what a degree of personal dedication to Christ and to His Mystical Body, the Church, is implied by such a pursuit. This shines forth in so many of Father Arrupe's statements: there is no christian mission to men that is not born out of Christ's love and out of our love for Him.

Rome
February 2, 1980

Jean-Yves Calvez, S.J.
Assistant General

ARRUPE THE MISSIONARY

Autobiodata in a Japanese Police Interrogation

In January 1970, Father Arrupe visited the Jesuits in England and Scotland. As there was no hall in the Jesuit Residence at Mount Street in London large enough to accommodate the number of Jesuits and many others who wished to meet Father General, a meeting was arranged at the nearby Piccadilly Hotel. This occasion was especially for the relatives and friends of Jesuits. Present were, besides the Jesuits from Southern England, Jesuits from Ireland, France, Poland, Malta, Canada, the U.S.A., Brazil, Peru, Rhodesia and Zaire. For over an hour Father General, exercised the apostolate of gratitude and friendship meeting people and then improvising this personal and informal address to parents and friends.

*

At this moment I am in an embarrassing position. I have no script and I have to reply to the speech given by Father Provincial in such wonderful English. To speak to you in my awful English will be just another in the series of humiliations which I have had during my life. You can offer the hearing of my English as a sacrifice for the Society of Jesus!

Many things happen during these journeys of the General. As you know from the dictionary, the word Jesuit means a deceitful person; so you can imagine what people think about the General! He mut be a terrible rogue — even Machiavellian. When he goes round the world visiting many countries, people think it must be some kind of political manoeuvre or scheme. When I answer the question, "Why are you coming to this country?", by saying quite simply, "It is a family visit, I want to meet my brethren the Jesuits", the reply is "Hmm, Hmm'. It does not happen in England — the press are extremely kind — but it happens in other countries.

I am accustomed to this sort of thing now. When I was Provincial and working in Japan I was put in jail as a suspected spy and interrogated by the Japanese police and the military who asked me:

"Why have you come to Japan?"

"To work for you and offer my work for you", I replied.

"Hmm" was the answer; they did not believe me.

"What are your diplomatic relations with your embassy?"

"I do not even know who is the ambassador."

"Oh!"

"Where is your money — in your bank?"

"I receive a little money every month, not as a salary but as a kind of gift; my provincial sends it to me so that I may be able to eat."

"Hmm."

Then the third question: "Where is your wife?"

A mystery! No money, no political action, no family. Well, I can tell you I was in jail for thirty-five days and I had thirty-seven hours of continuous questioning before the military tribunal. In the end they were convinced and when I thanked the commander for what he had done, he was astonished and asked me, "How can you thank me for putting you in jail?" I answered, "Because it was one of my greatest sufferings in life. I came to Japan to work and suffer for you, and you were, with the best will and intention, the cause of this suffering. I consider you one of my best benefactors." Then he said to me, "Father Arrupe, go away and work for us; this wonderful doctrine of yours could save Japan!" That was one of the most wonderful and precious moments in my life.

Therefore I have come here just to meet everybody — I am sure you will believe me — yes, just to meet and talk with our dear fathers and brothers who are working here. I cannot express adequately my emotions and deep feelings at this moment. This is the last public meeting of the tour. Father Provincial spoke very kindly about the inspiration my visit has given to the English Province — I think it works both ways — I myself have been greatly inspired by seeing the devotion, the sacrifice, the happiness of all those working for the Province and its missions.

Nowadays you hear so much scandal in the press about Jesuits. One Jesuit making some kind of statement to the press, another perhaps getting married and so on, but I can tell you that as I look from Rome I can see thirty-three thousand Jesuits all over the world who are really offering themselves for the Church and for the country in which they are working. To have personal contact with these men is a tremendous experience for me.

I would like to thank you all for your love and charity and affection for our fathers and brothers. After seeing the various works of the Society, I always come to the same conclusion — the Jesuits are working hard, but their work would be impossible without your cooperation. Therefore I thank you most sincerely and I hope in the spirit of Vaticau II more and more lay people will collaborate first of all with the Church, then with the *mínima Compañia de Jesús*, the little Society of Jesus, because the only purpose of our work is to offer ourselves for the service of the Church and for the people. Therefore I thank you because our work would be simply impossible without your cooperation.

Listening today to His Eminence Cardinal Heenan and talking with him privately, and also with His Excellency the Apostolic Delegate, I felt very touched with their understanding of and their affection for the Society. This is a guarantee for us that the representatives of God and of the hierarchy also appreciate the work that is being done by our fathers and brothers. I do not wish to speak too long, I just want to thank you and tell you how happy I am. I want to thank especially the benefactors here present and those wonderful people, the mothers and fathers of Jesuits and the wonderful families who give to the Society the best things they have.

We appreciate very much all kind of cooperation, physical, financial and collaboration of all kinds, but most of all we appreciate the great cooperation of the families who give us their sons. Sometimes I have the opportunity to talk with the mothers of Jesuits, in private, and I see the wonderful spirit of these families.

To appreciate a gift you must know the value of the thing given and the sacrifice that is involved. If one asks the mother of a Jesuit, "Well, when you were thinking of giving your son to the Society, how did you feel?" If she is sincere she will reply, "Father, I felt I was offering the best thing I had in my home — my treasure". "Fine, and was it easy for you?" Then one will see a beautiful smile and eyes looking into the past, and two tears in those eyes and hear her say, "Father, it was a terrible wrench". "Well, mother, are you happy now?" "Oh so happy — when I saw my son at the altar as a priest, or I saw my son as a brother taking his vows, that was a wonderful joy, just like being in heaven." Speaking as General and in the name of the whole Society I want to thank these mothers, these families who have given their treasure to the Society at such great sacrifice.

My dears, we need many more holy Jesuits. Perhaps some of the young men who are listening to me today or some of the young families may be able to help. There are few vocations today, we need many more. I am sure that you understand that a vocation is the gift of God but it is produced in some way by the hands of a mother and by the family. We now have artificial substitutes in industry, artificial fibres, plastics and many other things, but for the heart and the hands of a mother there can never be a substitute, never.

In urging you to give great thought to the needs of the Church and the Society, I will conclude with just two words which express the feelings of my heart — Thank you.

I

OUR FOUR APOSTOLIC PRIORITIES

Father General's Discourse to the Congregation of Procurators, 1970, communicated to the Provincials.

Rome
October 5, 1970

This address and letter on priorities of the various fields of our work represents Father Arrupe's thinking at the end of the Sociological Survey of the Society and at the conclusion of the Congregation of Procurators.

Interpretting the recommendations of the 31st General Congregation (decr. 21-22) that a commission should be set up to help promote a better selection of ministries and plan for the future, Father General saw the need for a thorough study of the actual state of the Society's apostolates. This study, he decided, should be along sociological lines that would relate it to the existential demands of the age in which we live, and its object would be a systematic collection of data bearing upon Jesuit activities and capabilities with reference to the needs and opportunities of each country and in each unit of the Order in the light of the new approach to the modern world heralded by Vatican II.

The sociological survey of the whole Society, which Father General set in motion in 1966, came to a conclusion four years later (AR XV, 1970, p. 538). Immediately after the Congregation of Procurators held in Rome in September-October 1970, Provincials received the following letter of Father General on "Today's Apostolate in the Society", which had been a crucial subject of the discussions of the

Delegates and the General. It was published in the 1971-1972 issue of the Jesuit Year Book for the information of relatives and friends also.

*

Introduction

In recent years some studies have been made to determine what works and ministries in our day can contribute more to the greater glory of God, in other words, to the greater service and good of our neighbour.

A sociological survey was conducted recently, and though of necessity it is subject to some limitations (not surprising for a project carried out for the first time in the whole Society), it nevertheless produced elements of great value for determining the actual state of ministries in the Society and indicated criteria and opinions of Ours on the choice of ministries.

Such a choice of ministries should be considered a more urgent necessity in the Society today. For the Society is essentially apostolic, and our true 'identity' ought to be manifested through the apostolate of the Society: the apostolic work of the Society is the visible form which expresses its invisible spiritual charism, while at the same time it determines the concrete life of each one of us.

Therefore, keeping in mind the Ignatian principles for selecting ministries, and taking into account the experience gained in these last years, especially by means of the survey, and considering the actual situation in the whole Society, I would have to make the following proposals to you:

I. THEOLOGICAL REFLECTION

In my judgment the first of all ministries that must be mentioned now is *theological reflection on the human problems of today*.

You know how important these problems are. The world does not know where to go. Notwithstanding the constant technological development, peace does not exist among men, nor justice between nations and social groups, nor equality between human households or between single individuals.

God, the alpha and omega, the beginning and the end, seems to be far away from human associations.

Besides, new methods of scientific development have been begun, there are keener demands in historical criticism, speedier means of human communication; international associations of peoples ask that concrete answers be given for new problems, which rest on fundamental human values, and which in the end open the way to God, the necessity of whom the men of today feel more and more deeply, though for most men it may still be a question of the "unknown God", whom they cannot find.

I would like to believe that the Society of Jesus can and ought to render this service to the Church and to the world. Furthermore this has been earnestly requested of us by the Holy See itself, by many Bishops, by many persons in different regions of the world. The very end of the Society demands this, desiring that in preference to others those ministries be chosen, which are directed to the greatest service of the Church and mankind.

And perhaps it should be said that the Society is more suitably equipped for this ministry of theological reflection, when we consider its many theological faculties, the large number of theologians among Ours, or even its broader competence in the whole range of human sciences.

But if this ministry is to be seriously understood and assumed, it is certainly necessary that the Society devote itself more earnestly day by day to biblical and strictly theological studies, and to a many-sided philosophico-theological investigation, through which divine solutions may be sought for the human problems and difficulties of today. It is necessary also that the Society devote itself to the fostering of those sciences which can open the way to theology, such as anthropology, psychology, sociology and others. These sciences of man and the human environment offer material for theological reflection, and along with theology can effect a certain substantiality in difficult questions, which greatly trouble all mankind today. And indeed haste is of the essence: we may not wait, for men are constraining us!

Only in this way, that is to say, by scientific competence, will the Society be capable of aiding the minds and thoughts of men in that arduous journey towards God. The publication of books, articles in magazines, scientific congresses, lectures in universities, personal conversations, all these will be so many means in this theological apostolate of our Society today.

I would earnestly ask all our young men to consider seriously before God their own responsibility on this point, and not hesitate to give their full attention and the whole man to philosophical and theological studies, since only by these studies seriously made will they be able to satisfy in their future ministry the expectations of men today.

II.   THE SOCIAL APOSTOLATE

I would say that the *social apostolate* comes second in the order of precedence among the ministries of the Society today.

This surely will need no amplification, since we have before our eyes not only that multitude of men, "which no one can count", that lack the means necessary to live a life worthy of man, but also the unjust oppressions, the defective social structures, the attitude of indifference of those who live in wealth, and finally the intrinsic difficulty of an apostolate of this kind, in which it is sometimes so hard to determine the limits between the economic, political or social field and the announcing of the Gospel.

Just as in the theological field, so too in the social field it will be the task of the Society, asuming serious and scientific preparation, to be of assistance especially to all those who seek the solution of these problems throughout the world, and at the same time along with them, to discover the nature of the humanism of the technical world, of the true social order, of the meaning of natural values, on which the well-ordered evolution of man is based, finally what is the meaning of the presence of the Church and the priest in the world today. But all these are the products of deep and accurate scientific inquiry; and the danger is present that we may be found unprepared to attain to that summit, where the learned debate, as something beyond our reach.

In the social apostolate it is not a question of some local problem, but of the truly universal problem of man living below the level of human dignity (who, we commonly say, are living a "marginal" existence), a problem which affects all nations, rich and poor, since everywhere is heard that cry, "much weeping and wailing", which rightly demands the advent of another better world, which can be truly said to be and actually be "a kingdom of justice, love and peace".

Our Society is bound to think this problem through, and seriously toil by its study, its industry, its influence on all those who govern nations and make laws, especially on those who take part in international organizations, also by its testimony of poverty, simplicity of life and generosity, by its sense of true justice and love towards the poor and the abandoned, sometimes even by its sharing in the labour, in the indigence, in the anguish of men: it is bound, I say, to toil seriously that the human condition of the whole world may become better day by day, and be transformed profoundly for the better.

This ministry of ours will be by no means easy, because it also demands great personal abnegation, but if the charity of Christ urges us, we will see more clearly than light its importance and its 'undeferable' necessity.

We have of course Social Centres in many Provinces: let us not readily think that the social apostolate is to be entrusted to them alone, since it pertains to each and every one of us. Indeed there are nations and peoples so poor that the work that must be done in them does not brook delay. But it can be said that an equal responsibility rests on the wealthy nations, which possess the power of finding true solutions for establishing economic equilibrium and for securing and attaining speedy development.

III. THE APOSTOLATE OF EDUCATION

So we come to our third point, which is the *ministry of education*. Today we need especially men endowed with strong willpower and solid preparation, men who are capable of spending their lives for others, of helping others, of directing others; men rooted and founded in the charity of Christ.

There will be no one who does not understand the duty and the importance of that true education. And the Society has been persuaded for centuries that the ministry of forming the minds of youth and fashioning their Christian morals is a most excellent one. Besides a large part of Ours devote their efforts to this ministry, and I have no doubt that from this ministry even now abundant fruits are gathered in the Society of the present day.

Still I would like to exhort all to subject to a close examination the new forms of education, which meet modern techniques, and for this reason tend to fashion men such as actual circumstances demand, capable of offering the service which the human family now urgently needs. Necessarily they differ in different regions. We must give them Christian principles that are not abstract and impersonal but concrete and of such a kind that they may attain to true religious experience. Their social consciousness must be enkindled and developed, and an authentic bond with other men in charity and justice must be inculcated.

For education such as this will not exist unless it touches the whole man, makes him a witness of the truth of Christ and renders him a useful worker in the new order. The new order in the world today must be effected by new men, who have been called for that reason to receive a new education. I know well how many of Ours, assigned to the ministry of education, are today concerned about the necessary adaptation of education to the new circumstances of present-day life, and to the new necessities that arise.

I would not wish to omit mentioning here how necessary it is that no labour be spared for this end, that in our Colleges and Universities, whether by help obtained from the Government or by other economic means that have been found, there exist no distinction between our students from an economic and social aspect. Nor is it advisable that we confine our educational work to our Colleges alone, but in so far as it is possible, we should spend ourselves in others also, either in those so-called official or national colleges, or in private colleges, that in this way the truth of our faith may reach more young students. Finally, we must not neglect any cooperation on our part in the study and preparation of those education plans which are being made ready now in so many nations for the purpose of meeting better present-day circumstances.

IV. THE MASS MEDIA APOSTOLATE

There is a fourth type of ministry, which we must say is at once a means of diffusing ideas and of promoting education in the world of today, and which now exercises the greatest influence on our contemporaries, and appears to be an excellent way of preaching the Gospel itself in a more effective manner. I speak of those so-called *Mass Media,* which exercise essential roles in all human association, and on which no small portion of mankind depends for information, entertainment, and their way of thinking and acting. The importance of this human invention escapes no one, but we must confess that we, as sons of the Society, have not yet become truly conscious of our undoubted responsibility in the face of this manifest reality. We have the means ready at hand whereby we can reach a countless multitude of men, if we know how to use it patiently.

In the sixteenth century our Society did not hesitate to adopt fully and use the culture and technical means of that age. Our Fathers and the schools of the Society fostered the humanities, oratorical skill, scenic representations, technical development of every kind in that time, rejecting nothing but rather using all means for the purpose of gaining the world for Christ. What Ignatius, Xavier and so many others of our Fathers did, we too ought to do.

Our Society ought to ponder this point seriously and diligently, that it may not so be weighed down by old practices that it loses the flexibility of its original charism.

To your consideration, my dear Fathers, and through you to the consideration of your Provinces, I would like to commit this solicitude of mine, whereby I would judge that we can accomplish much more for the service of souls if we learn how to use rightly these modern instruments of the apostolate, if we consider those Mass Media and all who toil in them as part of our present-day apostolate, if finally we offer our co-operation in preparing, aiding, directing those numberless men who devote their efforts to means of communication of this kind.

It does not escape you how useful these means can be for the formation and instruction of Ours, as experiments conducted in some Provinces clearly prove.

I know the matter does not lack difficulties and that it is impossible without careful study, but it is well known how rich are the rewards of this labour, provided only it is done in the right way and suitable means are used to pursue the purpose we intend.

*

These are the four ministries which seemed to me to be necessary at this particular time in the Society, and I would offer them for your consideration.

Theological reflection regards our priestly mission in the Church of God: the other three types of apostolate of which I wished to treat are urgently demanded by the very historical circumstances of the day, and imply our positive involvement in the historical reality surrounding us.

I judge them of such vital importance that I resolved, as you know well, to establish special Secretariates in our Curia for developing and coordinating the activities necessary in each of those fields of our apostolate: namely, a Secretariate of the social apostolate,a Secretariat of Education, a Secretariate of the Means of Social Communication, whose directors I ask to be willing to share with us this discussion of ours on the apostolate of the Society today.

Before concluding this allocution of mine I would like to mention also that precious instrument for forming Christian men, which we received from Saint Ignatius as part of the Ignatian charism. The *Spiritual Exercises* of Saint Ignatius are the most effective means of the apostolate and an excellent way to obtain more collaborators, who, forgetting the thiṇgs that are their own, seek those of Christ Jesus.

I was very pleased in this morning's session to hear you speaking at such length on the Spiritual Exercises. In them I put my confidence of our genuine renewal of the Society and of a total consecration to God, and I express the hope in behalf of Ours and of externs that they will obtain from the Exercises that manifold divine grace, which is necessary for us to attempt and perform so great a task as the Church of Christ rightly expects from our Society and from all our lay collaborators.

In this consultation, which for me is of great value, I look forward gladly to your suggestions on all these topics.

2

QUESTIONS ON POLITICS, MISSIONS, EDUCATION, RECRUITING, ATHEISM

Interview to Malcolm Muggeridge of the BBC

On the BBC London
January 25, 1970

Mr Malcolm Muggeridge, the BBC Television interviewer, started his career as a lecturer at the university of Cairo before taking up journalism. For some years he worked on the Calcutta "Statesman". In 1953 he became the editor of "Punch". His war service record as a Major in the Intelligence Corps was distinguished; he was awarded both the Légion d'Honneur and the Croix de Guerre. In recent years he has been known as a broadcaster both on television and radio. Among his many publications there is "Something Beautiful for God" on Mother Teresa.

The TV programme was apparently so successful that Mr Muggeridge asked if he might go to Rome later to make an in-depth programme with Father General. A few months later, a crew of technicians of the British Broadcasting Corporation were operating in the Jesuit curia in Rome to film a colour television documentary, lasting fifty minutes and titled "The Hated Society". The BBC later reported an unusually large correspondence in praise of the programme and some dissenting letters. Oliver Pritchett in "The Guardian" summed it all up: "Astonishing Jesuit villainies and amazing Jesuit achievements were chronicled by Macdonald Hastings with a sort of surprised admiration. A fascinating programme made with almost jesuitical panache. Which is a great deal more than you could say for the Conservative Party broadcast which preceded it."

*The text of the BBC-TV Broadcast of this Introduction
and Interview of Sunday, 25th January, 1970 appeared
in "Letters and Notices" of the English Jesuit Province
for July 1970.*

*

Introduction: *In "All Things Considered" this week Malcolm
Muggeridge talks to the man they call the "Black Pope". Last week,
for the first time this century, the Black Pope was in Britain. The
nickname comes from the colour of his vestments not his skin, and it
is applied to the most powerful religious order in the Roman Catholic
Church, the Jesuits. They were founded in the sixteenth century by the
crippled Spanish soldier Saint Ignatius Loyola as an almost military
body. Intellectually brilliant and aggressive, they have always been
controversial, sometimes they have been ridiculed, often they have been
hated. Sometimes they have been expelled for their political as well
as for their religious activities. Well, today the Father General of
these intellectual shock-troops of the Catholic Church is Father Pedro
Arrupe who is a former doctor and missionary in Japan. He came to
Britain to review his 600 troops in the English Jesuit Province.
Before he left, Malcolm Muggeridge took the opportunity of asking
him some questions why.*

1

Muggeridge: As I understand it, Jesuits traditionally have
mixed themselves up in *politics*, in the struggle for power
that's going on. For instance, they used to hear the confessions
of important people. Well, I don't suppose you will be able to
hear Harold Wilson's confession, though it might be rather
interesting and take quite a long time.

Arrupe: We never go into politics, never; politics as such.
It is true we try for instance today, in the whole question of
international justice, to help the underdeveloped countries
and so forth. We are for truth, for justice. If you call politics
this high idea of justice, fine. But if you speak of politics in the
sense of parties, or working for governments, we are completely out of this. We are evangelically universal.

2

Muggeridge: Well, Father, of course, a lot of the work of the Society has been *missionary work*, hasn't it?

Arrupe: Very much so.

Muggeridge: From Saint Francis Xavier onwards.

Arrupe: Yes, you see one of the goals of the Society is *Defensio et Propagatio Fidei*, therefore one of the essential points of the Society is the propagation of the Faith, the missionary work, to go to people who have no faith. Therefore Saint Ignatius sent the best man he had, Francis Xavier, just to India, to Japan, to the East.

Muggeridge: Now you've been to Japan yourself of course.

Arrupe: For twenty-seven years.

Muggeridge: As a missionary. Now how do you feel about that? Do you feel that today it presents itself in a different way to you in Japan, than it did to Saint Francis Xavier?

Arrupe: Oh yes, very much so, because the Japanese people have changed very much also in mentality. The best thing we can give the Japanese people is the Christian faith. But the way of giving will be different. We are convinced that we cannot go directly. We have to present the truth, as I told you before, just to present the truth — present our mentality from the *human* point of view. We don't start with talks about faith, we start with the human point of view and because the faith is the truth, naturally we speak with all sincerity in our, I say, detachment from every human element. The Japanese and other people in the East are very intuitive. Therefore they know right away if you are sincere, and that is a great, tremendous consolation for us — even if they are not converted, they will say, Father, we know you have the truth.

Muggeridge: So you feel that in your twenty-seven years you left them at any rate with some truth.

Arrupe: Oh yes, sure.

3

Muggeridge: Then, of course, another terrific part of the

Society's work has been from the beginning *education*, hasn't it?

Arrupe: Yes. We are still very much in this, because we are convinced that is one of the great contributions we can make, you see. We try to help humanity to form men and today more than ever. Because we have many machines and we have computers, we have all kind of jets, jumbos and everything. But we have no men of character, of principles, of energy, of involvement. Our schools are supposed to be "factories for producing men".

Muggeridge: But do you consider *that* purpose can be achieved by conducting your schools on the terms offered in a secular society?

Arrupe: By all means. That is *our* problem, How we can adapt *our*-selves, our values, to modern conditions. Therefore we are sure that the merchandise, the product that we are selling, that is education, character, human beings well formed...

Muggeridge: Love of Christ?

Arrupe: Yes, surely. But I would distinguish that again. Love of Christ, that is the last goal for us, but in Japan or in India, we cannot start with love of Christ. We have to start from human values, with what is called today "pre-evange-lization".

Muggeridge: Hoping that they'll lead up to love of Christ.

Arrupe: Yes. Because of course that its the preparation. We are *so* sure that the truth always leads to Christ that if we are presenting the truth we know, we are sure, this will indirectly or implicitly lead them to Christ. That is our conviction.

4

Muggeridge: I'll tell you another thing that I wanted to ask you Father General. Do you think that, making the *religious life* easier encourages *vocations*? Or the reverse?

Arrupe: You have to present the ideal, the tough ideal ... "*sine glossa*".

Muggeridge: Ask a lot?

Arrupe: Yes. But in the right way. If we ask young men to undertake this life of sacrifice in the old-fashioned way, it won't attract many; and that is the point. Sometimes we have the impression that religious life is going to be easier: perhaps this is an error in our appreciation. Religious life is changing, adapting itself to the mentality of today and therefore some of the old fashioned structures are gradually falling down. But the sacrifice is more demanding today than before, you ought to realize. Therefore I would answer your question by saying: if you want vocations, you have to demand very much of youth, but for a great, clear ideal, the right ideal and in the right situation.

5

Muggeridge: I read somewhere that you were given special orders from the Pope to *combat atheism*.

Arrupe: Yes.

Muggeridge: A heavy assignment Father!

Arrupe: Oh yes! something tough and very complicated! That was in '65 at the beginning of our General Congregation. The Holy Father asked us to face atheism. At that time I made a tremendous mistake. Afterwards, speaking on the Council, I said: "we will fight atheism". Which was not a good expression due to my lack of experience in the West. Our task is not to fight, it is to confront, to face, to try to study atheism. You say very well that it's complicated, because when the Holy Father asked us to do this task, he was thinking of atheism in a very broad sense, not only the militant atheism, not only the philosophical, even the actual secularism, all these problems connected with the modern "God is dead". Therefore it would take practically the whole Society of Jesus with activity in this line; we try now to study how to approach the problem of unbelief. And we are always making the distinction between the *ideology*, atheism (in which we have to present the arguments philosophical, anthropological, scientific, etc.), and the *atheist as a person*. As I told you before, we have to present it in a very human way, try to persuade him to see the argument in order to see that God is not dead. And God exists and is living, is very much a living person today, and present in all the events of the world. We have arguments good enough for every sincere man to recognize today more than ever that God is living.

*

Conclusion: Malcolm Muggeridge was talking to the General of the Jesuits, Father Pedro Arrupe, who incidentally was leading a mission in Hiroshima at the time the first atomic bomb was dropped.

3

RELEVANCE
OF THE SOCIETY AND ITS APOSTOLATE
IN THE WORLD OF TODAY

Talk of Father General to the Provincials and other 300 Jesuits of the Indian Assistancy

Bandra, Bombay
April 21, 1971

In April 1971, Father Arrupe came to India to participate in a meeting of the Major Superiors' Conference of India, held at Vinayalaya, Andheri, Bombay. This happy occasion coincided with the Bombay Province Renewal Seminar attended by over 250 Jesuits.

Present at the General's talk at St Stanislaus' School hall, Bandra were also the members of the Assistancy Commission of Studies and professors and students of various provinces of India and Sri Lanka who had come from De Nobili College, Poona and St Mary's College, Kurseong.

The text is substantially faithful to the tape-recorded talk. It is the spontaneous spoken word, poured out at times passionately and with a generous sprinkling of Latin or other phrases, minus the gestures and facial and vocal expression. It was later approved by the speaker. Captions have been added. The topics dealt with are some of those uppermost in his mind in that period of preparation for the coming General Congregation.

*

I thought you would like some information about the role and the apostolate of the Society today, something that might serve as an inspiration for your life and work as Jesuits.

1. A Moving Target

Today, as you well know, the Society is at a very important moment of its history. In the four hundred years of its existence this moment is one of great opportunities, when we can delve deep into the charism of Saint Ignatius and busy ourselves with its practical application. This is no easy task, because our target, though very definite, is not stationary but constantly moving. Circumstances of rapid change surround us on all sides, and so we have to reflect constantly on our course of action and the application of our spirit.

Saint Ignatius said that the Society was founded for the service of the Church — "*servitium Ecclesiae sub Romano Pontifice*" — and this remains true of the Society even in these times when the Church and the world are undergoing so much change.

Changes herald problems, and this is a good thing. Were there no problems in the Society, it would be a sign that it was a calcified body, a dead body. Today's problems need to be approached calmly, with a profound confidence in God who is leading the Church and the Society. The Holy Ghost is responsible for this. He inspired and directed the second Vatican Council, and this we know '*de fide*', and we in our '*minima Societas*' try to be part of the Church and work for the Church with a sense of dedication, knowing all the while that we are working with Our Lord.

Does all this smack of unwarranted optimism? Fr. General is optimistic, and there is a reason for it: we can count on the providence of Almighty God. We can be nothing else but optimistic, positive, trying to contribute to the glory of God and the betterment of the world according to our charism in the best way we can.

2. Ignatian Charism and Jesuit Identity

The question on the lips of many is "What is a Jesuit?" It is the question of the Jesuit's identity. We shall discover the answer by understanding the charism of Saint Ignatius.

Simple and sincere, Ignatius was a man who had received from God the special grace of grasping the mystical quintessence of the Gospel. The experience that Ignatius went through in Manresa, when he saw the world in a new light, can never be aptly and exhaustively expressed in articles or books. As the Apostles continued the mission of Christ, so the Society has inherited the charism given to Ignatius.

In the *Spiritual Exercises* we see that the motive force of our lives is to be found in the personal love for Christ. This personal love of Christ expresses itself in a total commitment "*sub vexillo crucis*", where one chooses poverty and suffering and humiliation rather than riches and glory. The evangelical attitude of the third degree of humility that is expected of every Jesuit coincides with the attitude portrayed in the third class of men. Compromise has no place here, and the Jesuit must, with a tremendous detachment, be open to the Spirit, always looking for God's will and His greater glory. This epitomizes our spirituality, and this is what the Society has to give to the world.

Christocentricism for a Jesuit means a personal love for Christ, for of this love comes true discernment and the vision of the world through the eyes of Christ. This must be the basis for building up a 'new world'. In the process of development in the world, the men of today may not be conscious of the 'inner' progress, and it is we who can make our contribution by stressing that "*charitas Christi urget nos*", by displaying an enthusiastic Ignatian 'indifference'.

The Society has a *raison d'être* in that it fosters progress of the world for the greater glory of God. And to the charge that the Jesuit has had his day, and that was in the sixteenth century, but that in today's democratic set-up he hardly has a place, I reply that the Society today has still the living spirit to move the world to Christ. The Society as '*defensor fidei*' has to defend the faith from all a-christian ideas that go counter to God's plans for man and the world, and to proclaim the Word of God to a society in which the Church is losing ground.

The real identity of the Society is crystallized in the Formula of the Institute and in the Constitutions, wherein is the spirit of the Good News understood radically. Ignatius was the first founder of a religious order or congregation to identify the apostolic goal with all perfection, and he did so from the very beginning. Explicit though he is about the scope of activities which the Jesuit may undertake, he often adds the remark that the local man in charge is to judge whether circumstances dictate another course of action. This embraces the phenomenon of pluralism. Just to give a small concrete example: one month ago I was in Holland, where I didn't see a single soutane. Here in India I see plenty of them! The external appearance may differ, but under it there is one and the same Society.

Saint Ignatius said that *unity* in the Society is of capital importance. We are a *"corpus universale Societatis"*; we are not a federation of provinces, as the Benedictine Order is a federation of monasteries. The symbol and bond of this unity, as set down in the Constitutions, is the General. Further, it is this unity that enables us to plan for the whole world and renders it possible and imperative for the Jesuit to move from one place to another according to the mission he receives. Provincialism simply has no place in the Society.

Our mobility is linked to our *obedience*, and for our obedience to be effective there is the *'ratio conscientiae'*, whereby each one's capabilities are correctly fostered so that these may harmonize with one's spiritual needs and aspirations. We are working in Congo and Alaska, in Russia and in Czechoslovakia, practically under every clime and government, and there is no condition in which the Society is a stranger. I challenge you, my dear Fathers and Brothers, to find a human structure more fundamentally suited for apostolic activity anywhere!

3. Apostles in a Secularized World

The Society can do something for the world. Starting from this conviction, we must study the concrete circumstances and discern how we may best spend ourselves for the world of today.

The world of today is secularized. And it is not only the Catholics who find it secularized, but also the Hindus and Moslems, the Buddhists and Shintoists. This secularization is a tremendous challenge to religion and we have to confront this challenge.

We Jesuits are supposed to be in the front line, we have to be in contact with the world of today; but before establishing this contact — before, at least, '*in signo rationis*' — we have to be in contact with Christ, put on Christ's mentality in a spirit of trustful prayer. If we do not, then we shall be carried away by the current. It is for this reason that hundreds of Jesuits leave the Society every year: they are not prepared to meet the challenge, a challenge that twenty years ago was easier to meet when we had so many structures to protect us.

We had, for example, the 'rule of the companion'; our houses closed at 8 p.m. In South Europe we used to have a very regular life: at 8.30 p.m. all were at home. The litanies were recited. Supper and common recreation followed, then a quarter of an hour of points and examen. The next morning, the bell would ring at 5. There was a visit at 5.25; then an hour's meditation and Mass.

Today this regularity is not observed — I don't speak about India now, I say this from my knowledge of the Society as General. Some Fathers have now to work late at night. Students and workers can be contacted by our Fathers only after 9 p.m. The Fathers return home at 1 in the morning. In normal circumstances a Father will need 7 hours of sleep and so he will not be able to be up before 8 a.m. Only the Father who has to say Mass for the working men in the morning need get up at 4.30 or 5. Now the question arises: Who controls the Father who returns home in the small hours of the morning? Nobody, except his conscience and sense of responsibility. Who knows whether he is working with his students and clients, or is not somewhere else? He alone knows. You can see that such a man needs a tremendous fund of virtue, he must be a man of prayer, or else after a while he will say, "Why am I a Jesuit?"

What I am trying to say is that if we must apply ourselves effectively to our apostolic tasks, we must first count on a solidly built interior life.

The great problem of the Society today is lack of prayer. Are we prepared with a life of prayer to challenge the world and still keep to our Jesuit way of life, not merely maintaining the '*status quo*' but drawing the world to Christ? This obliges us to a more intense life of prayer, a deeper love of Christ, a more profound spirituality. The Society has not to become secularized, it must apply itself apostolically to the secularized world.

You can see in the Society today *three groups*. One group is made up of the more traditionally thinking Fathers, Brothers and Scholastics, who say that the Society admits of no change, that changes are dangerous, that the outcome of this period of chaos will be a return to the sanity of the old times. This group forms a minority.

There are the others, mostly young men, who feel that the Society itself as also the 31st General Congregation are dated, and that charismatic processes point to a faster pace within the Society. Rules and regulations do not matter; the real experience of Ignatius is what matters.

Finally, there is the silent majority who persevere in their vocation and work amid the tensions felt throughout the Society.

4. Do we need a Congregation?

The Congregation of Procurators met and the question of *"cogenda aut non cogenda"* was placed before them: Should there be a General Congregation or not? Is today's Society in such a state that we need a Congregation in order to restore order and put things straight? The Procurators were not only to vote on the *"cogenda aut non cogenda"* issue, but also to discuss other questions of our life and apostolate. Some measure of the Society's thinking could be got from the fact that 65 provinces voted *"non cogenda"* and 15 *"cogenda"*.

There were also the issues contained in the Holy See's Instruction *'Renovationis causa'*, which includes formation and touches on matters which only a Congregation may deal with. The experiment with the new Assistants-General, with the periti, the new set-up in the Curia, are yet to be evaluated, which only the Congregation can do and then effect the necessary changes.

The 31st General Congregation had dealt with the question of Grades, but concluded that the question of the Brothers needed to be studied first. Would the question of the Brothers necessitate a General Congregation? Then, too, many are leaving the Society. Is this an indication of deteriorating standards in the Society, to remedy which a General Congregation would have to be called?

The issues raised by the '*Renovationis causa*' did not require a Congregation. The document insists on our going back to the Constitutions and applies to all religious institutes a number of points which were proper of the Society.

The question of the *Grades* has been studied for the past 5 years by a commission of five experts. And even though there are about 50 Fathers collaborating with them, the issue is far from clear since the historical significance of the Grades even in the time of Saint Ignatius is not fully known.

In the international *Congress of Brothers* we touched on a crucial point: Is the Society an '*ordo sacerdotalis*' or not? Is this an essential feature of the Society? Can Brothers be Superiors? What is the precise significance of Temporal Coadjutor, Spiritual Coadjutor, Professed, and so forth?

To study the question of the Society being essentially a 'clerical order', I called ten renowned Jesuit theologians. They had their answer ready in just 10 minutes: "Father, this is not a question of theology, it is a question of history, and history is clear on this point: the Society *is* a clerical order." From this it follows that we have to find out what exactly is the place of the Brother in this clerical order. A change in this regard must be considered as fundamental and can be effected only within a General Congregation and with recourse to the Holy Father.

After all these considerations, the Congregation of Procurators, with just 100 votes, voted thus: 91 for '*non cogenda*'; 9 for '*cogenda*'.

5. The Apostolate of the Society Today

The apostolate of the Society was to be discussed at the Procurators' Congregation, but it seemed evident that without a fair preparation the matter would take up several weeks. I therefore presented a little paper that was the result of prayer and reflection, the result of the general Survey and other documents concerning our ministries.

It seemed to me that there were four points to which the Society would have to pay special attention. The first was *theological reflection* on the human problems of today; the second was *social action;* the third was *education;* and the fourth was *mass communications.*

1. *Theological Reflection.* Consequent on the cultural changes and the technological progress taking place in the world, new problems have arisen to which few answers have been given. These answers have to be formulated in the light of a God-given faith. Knowing the divine response to these human problems will show us the right way to find solutions. But today we do not know this divine response. No single individual can discover the solution; team-work is needed. We need a combination of forces, we need the findings of anthropology, sociology, psycho-analysis, international law. The Society is particularly well equipped to help in working out such a solution. We are established in 80 countries; we have so many faculties of theology, philosophy, sociology etc., that on us hangs the responsibility of finding the Christian solution to world problems.

I was recently addressing a German assembly at the *Katholikentag* and I asked them the following questions: Who knows where the world is heading today? Who can discern humanism in our technocratic society? Who from among our leaders knows what is in store for mankind?

We have schools, colleges and universities in many countries. During the 10 or 15 most impressionable years or a boy or young man's life, we have the opportunity of forming the leaders of tomorrow, as we have done for the past 400 years. That is a heavy responsibility and a most precious opportunity.

Therefore, theological reflection is of primary importance; and at this point I address myself to the young Jesuits of India: please apply yourselves seriously to the study of theology and to the sciences of man and human environment which will open the way to theology. Today immediate results are looked for. But to grasp and solve a problem in all its varied aspects long hours of deep study are required, much effort and profound reflection. And so the Reader's Digest kind of theology or the demagogic articles on the theology of revolution will not do today. We have to sit down and study and proceed scientifically in our theological reflection.

2.   And now to the *Social Apostolate*. Justice and mutual collaboration are at a discount in this world. I don't know how far you will agree with me when I say that this 'third world' is the incarnation of original sin. It is egoism that has brought about the appalling differences in the world. Inspite of international meetings and conferences, the rich are getting richer and the poor poorer.

Is this not why young men speak about revolution, contestation, the unidimensional man? The young man wishes the present order to pass away and in his short-sightedness requires that all existing structures be discarded. He may be wrong, but he has a point. It is not enough to identify oneself with the poor man. It is not enough to change the role; we have to change or adapt the structures and for this study and reflection are necessary. Applying '*Populorum Progressio*' with a view to developing '*totus homo et omnes homines*' demands a change in the structures that obtain now in the world. It may also mean that we shall be considered Marxists or communists, whereas we are only putting into practice the teachings of '*Populorum Progressio*', '*Mater et Magistra*' and '*Gaudium et Spes*'.

3.   And then there is *Education*. If you can change Man, you can change the World. Our schools are very important. It is at times distressing to hear that the Society is no longer interested in Education but rather in the direct apostolate. The Society is interested in Education now more than ever, but in schools that are performing a real function within the context, not in museum pieces that are quite abstracted from the conditions and circumstances of today. And the same goes for education in general. Besides, there is the education of the masses to be attended to.

Taking the case of Latin America, who educates the millions upon millions in a population, 52% of whom are under 20 years of age? In India you have the same proportion; you will therefore be having more than 300 million people who are less than 20 years old. In Brazil alone there are at least 50 million under 20. Who educates them? The Governor of Sao Paolo told me that in that city the majority of school teachers were young girls with only 2 years of primary education behind them. And then there are the adults to be cared for!

4. And last but not least, *Mass Communications*. I am no prophet, but I can tell you that in another 10 years India's teeming millions will be reached only by TV. Today Delhi alone has television; here in Bombay you will have it soon. TV will be possible on a grand scale in about 2 or 3 years when you have your satellites as they do in Latin America.

You must prepare yourselves to turn this avalanche into a blessing. We know the awful waste of time that results from TV advertisements and cheap films in Europe and many other countries. The Indian Government will be ready to accept good programmes. The time to prepare for it is now. After ten or even five years it will be too late. We will have missed the boat! In a church you may have 2000 or 5000 people listening to you. On television you will be able to contact directly 4 or 5 million listeners and viewers whom you would never have been able to approach in any other way. And this is not wishful thinking but a fact of the very near future.

*

In conclusion, my dear Fathers and Brothers, let me once more express my intimate conviction that a Society faithful to the Ignatian charism, made up of men thoroughly dedicated to Christ, is highly relevant in our days and can do much for the Church and for the World. — Thank You.

4

PROGRESS REPORT
OF JESUIT APOSTOLATES

**Report on the State of the Society
Congregation of Procurators of the Provinces
September-October, 1978**

**Rome
September 27, 1978**

*The Congregation of Procurators of 1970 was the occasion
for Father General Arrupe to crystallize in his mind and
in his address (here on pp. 1-8) the great apostolic priorities
of the Society. Eight years later, in the following Congregation of Procurators, in his comprehensive report on the
State of the Society, he could give us a bird's-eye view of the
progress, not unhindered, of the varied activities of the
Society in recent times.*

Here is the corresponding section from the General's report.

*

. . . .

21. Calling to a shared and varied apostolate

During the past three years the Society's apostolate has
been clearly changing, though in different ways and degrees
in different Provinces.

The main agent of this change has been Degree 4 which has
brought about a distinct shift in our apostolate towards "the
service of faith and the promotion of justice" both in education
and pastoral work, social action, etc. The evaluation of our
works, which is being carried out at the moment, is being done
in the light of this priority.

This renewal continues in spite of the ambiguities and tensions characteristic of change: a ministry to the poor or to those who are socially and economically influential; a predominantly spiritual apostolate or one based on integral human development and liberation; a choice between objectives with short-term results or long-term ones; a parish ministry or a specialized one; an institutional or a personal approach; an apostolate using simple methods as a witness to poverty or one using costly equipment for the sake of apostolic efficiency, etc.

But since you have already received full reports on the different sectors of the Society's apostolate (atheism, education, social apostolate, etc.), here I believe I need only refer briefly to each and give you my personal assessment.

22. Social Apostolate

The social apostolate has undergone change in the past few years and gradually becomes a dimension permeating all our apostolic activities. We must admit, however, that its impact on our more traditional apostolic commitments is still limited and that, at Province or Assistancy level, it has not produced the basic changes we were hoping for.

In the social sector porperly so-called we see new commitments, both personal and institutional. The Social Institutes or Centres which played such an important role in the past are passing through a crisis in some places. They are trying to adapt to new needs by linking themselves more closely with those working at grass-root level and by co-operating with other sectors of the apostolate (educational, pastoral, theological and interdisciplinary reflection, etc.) and thus extending their field of action.

Directly social work is often conditioned by the social, political and cultural situation in each country. To the difficulties inherent in this type of aposolate and the strong hostile reactions it sometimes provokes, must also be added in some places a lack of preparation and of right criteria on the part of those engaged in it.

23. Education

Education continues to be the apostolate occupying most

Jesuits. Many doubts and discussions have been voiced whether we should maintain our educational institutions and whether other more direct apostolates and with poorer people should not take priority. Today its value is recognized but only on condition of a change in its goals, contents and methods.

Our universities are facing serious economic and staffing problems. In other instances the difficulties have to do with their independence. The Society cannot lack the juridical means needed to preserve the Ignatian characteristics of such institutions. I am aware that in some Provinces they represent a heavy burden calling for considerable sacrifices. But they are also nerve centres of our apostolate and important means for propagating it in the long term, so the Church asks us to continue providing this costly service. But the number of our universities is another problem: can we continue to maintain all we have at the moment in view of other apostolic needs, many of them new, and the lack of personnel?

One problem that has emerged in these last years and that is a matter of concern to superiors is that of the relationship of faculties of theology to the superiors of the Society. The status of the faculties, frequently, make it difficult for superiors to intervene, especially in academic questions and yet, if the Society is to continue to recognize them as its own, it must have the statutory ability to intervene when the occasion demands. The Statutes will have to be revised to insure that this possibility is safeguarded without any sort of ambiguity.

The colleges or secondary schools also continue to be an effective means of our apostolate. In many places they have become real educational communities which reach out to the lay teachers, parents and old pupils. More emphasis is placed on social training and religious education is taking new forms. The possibility of admitting all classes of pupils and thus overcoming economic obstacles is being followed up as fast as conditions in each country permit. There are many new schools for poorer students and the proportion of poor students in our other schools has increased. In many cases professional schools have been given top priority. The idea that we were educating the upper classes is disappearing.

Educational work in institutions, universities and secondary schools that do not belong to the Society is another service that is being offered generously and has much in its favour. But is has difficulties too, not only for those concerned but also for our own institutions which find themselves thus deprived of additional staff that is often highly qualified and sometimes badly needed. The apostolic mission of these men as such, must be carefully evaluated, as is true of the mission of everyone, and it would be to our advantage, if every kind of individualism were overcome and closer ties were established, on the basis of a common mission, among all members of the Society who work in institutions of higher learning that do not depend on the Society.

24. Intellectual Apostolate

I consider this one of the most privileged means for that defence and spreading of the faith mentioned in the first paragraph of the Formula of our Institute. Consequently I tried to dispel all doubts arising about the validity of this apostolate today by publishing a letter to the whole Society reaffirming its importance for the service of the Church and the readiness of the Society to undertake it.

25. Pastoral Work

Through the Exercises in particular there has been much development in our parish work, in Christian Life Communities, in rural apostolates, and in new types of ministry to youth, married couples, etc.

Bishops increasingly wish to hand over parishes to the Society and this sometimes puts us in difficult situations. On the one hand, a parish community provides an excellent opportunity for apostolic work and, in some countries, is a need that presses hard on the Bishops. On the other hand, this work can get in the way of others that the Church also expects from us and to which we give priority according to our charism. It is often very difficult to make a discernment here.

26. Means of Social Communication

We are putting behind us the days of the worthy self-taught

pioneers in unexplored territory, and we are now beginning to rely on men with good training suited to modern needs. Such men are, however, far from numerous. Still, a hopeful sign is the growing interest aroused by this apostolate, especially among the younger men who have been introduced to it in the course of their training. Allied to this is a very keen awareness of its far-reaching importance for the future, an importance denied by no one today.

Two problems in this area call for a speedy solution. one is the integration of the communications media into the formation of our men, and the second is the coordination of all our activities in the field of the communications media in order to achieve greater depth and wider apostolic outreach.

27. Evangelization in the "Missions"

This is one of the fields of our apostolate where change is remarkably swift and deep. A contributing factor is the development and evolution in the very theology of evangelization in what were formerly called the 'missions'. The movement of personnel is now less and at the same time it has become more diversified: young churches are now among those supporting those even more recently founded or with more pressing needs.

We do, however, find that we must re-assert our mobility and our universality, as in some places there are noticeable tendencies that may be called 'regionalistic' or 'nationalistic' which are clearly out of harmony with the total availability on which the effectiveness of the Society's apostolate must be founded.

The internationalizing of the 'missions' is going ahead successfully. But progress is still needed with regard to international solidarity both in the area of finances and in that of personnel.

The tension between evangelization and human development is approaching a point of integration and balance.

Inculturation is a dimension that we can in some respects regard as new. This holds at least in as much as we see it these days as something right, something we cannot do without, and something with untold apostolic possibilities. We see this especially, but not exclusively, where the Church is new and where the nation is developing. For this reason, in obedience to a charge from the General Congregation, I wrote a letter to the Society on the subject.

In the interests of brevity I should like to refer to page 6 of the statement on 'Evangelization and Missions' where there is a summary of the answers to the questionnaire issued in 1977. There you will find plenty of information on this topic.

The vision of the world as one vast mission field is becoming more common, and rightly so. It is also good that we are less inclined to distinguish between Christian countries and countries with the prefix 'mission'. This must not, however, lead to a loss of zest for spreading the Gospel and for apostolic endeavour in countries other than our own.

28. New Apostolates

Creativity is these days indispensable. It breathes new forms into old apostolates and brings to light apostolates that are quite new. In its path it must overcome uncertainties, insecurity, resistance of various kinds, and situations that are in a constant state of flux. This sort of thing leads some people into a state of chronic hesitation, a lack of self-confidence and a lassitude which can lead to passivity. We have seen innovation, and we continue to see it, for example, in "involvement", in the rural apostolate, in the means of social communication, in educational institutions, in education in outside institutions, in pastoral work and catechetics, in Christian Life Communities, and so on. There is, in fact, a great desire to open up new roads for the apostolate. But we must be careful not to fall into the trap of 'immediatism', that is, choosing the apostolate that demands no great effort on our part and yet gives us a feeling of satisfaction by quickly producing results that attract a certain measure of public attention.

But there can be no doubt that changing conditions often call for new apostolates or new forms of those already established. We must not only accept these but actively promote them, avoiding on the one hand a naive awe for something that is 'but the bloom of a day', and on the other hand an attitude of suspicion and fear that is without foundation.

29. A brief indication of other points that may be developed:

1, Collaboration with the hierarchy and our involvement with the diocesan clergy and other religious in 'shared pastoral work'.

2. Collaboration with the laity, to whom we ought to give an increasingly greater share of responsibility in our works, including structures of wider participation and joint administration in which the apostolic identity of our institutions is guaranteed.

3. Greater involvement with the people of God, with smaller communities carrying as much weight in our apostolic commitment as larger institutions.

4. Opening up of our retreat houses as houses of prayer and other kinds of apostolic encounter.

5. Opening of many of our theological faculties to seminarians and laity.

6. The "Workers' Mission" in various countries.

7. Theological reflection.

8. The press and publications.

9. The Apostleship of Prayer, etc.

(30 — 58)

5

THEOLOGICAL REFLECTION AND INTERDISCIPLINARY RESEARCH*

I — THE GREAT PRIORITY

1. Theology's answer to human problems

On various occasions I have referred to "Theological reflection" as one of the great priorities in the present apostolate of the Society. And by theological reflection I mean especially the need and urgency of an in-depth and exhaustive reflection on human problems, whose total solution can not be reached without the intervention of theology and the light of faith.

This does not imply that every theological investigation must have as its objective a mere human problem or one originating in the sciences of man or the natural sciences. We are all aware that the formal object of theology transcends by far this limited range of problems. The point I wish to make is that, given the gravity, the urgency and the multiplicity of the problems that vex mankind today — whether directly theological or ideological, scientific or moral —, we can not escape the recourse to the theological science as one of the aids to solve human problems.

The theological reflection will in its turn help us to delve more deeply into some points of our faith. If we are to offer the suitable answers which the world needs and expects of us today, we cannot be satisfied with a superficial theology or one that deviates into sociology or psychology under the camouflage of theology. It is necessary to penetrate into the depths of revelation and be illumined by the Spirit. We stand

*Translation from the Spanish by Jerome Aixala S.J.

in need of theologians and exegetes of the first rank. Who can not see, for example, the light that the labour of modern exegesis has shed to clarify a variety of modern concepts, and at the same time the light that exegesis itself has received from archeolgoical discoveries and from the findings of the natural and exact sciences?

2. An Attitude and its external manifestations

The concept of theological reflection may be considered in the broad sense of a permanent attitude of life, or in the more restricted aspect of a concrete act or manifestation of an inner disposition that casts light on life as a whole under the influence of faith and according to God's plan.

The permanent attitude of theological reflection is necessary for all, both for our spiritual life and for our pastoral ministry: this is what constitutes "the contemplative in action". The acts or external manifestations of theological reflection are manifold: one is the examination of conscience, a reflection on one's own most intimate feelings and state of mind; another is the spiritual discernment whereby we discover the spirit that moves us in our actions or brings about external events; a third one is the reading of the signs of the times whereby we interpret the phenomena of history and the world; again another is the choice of ministries to analyse the apostolic needs and find the ministry that here and now can render the greatest service to the Church and the greater glory of God.

Thus it becomes clear how useful the theological reflection can be for our work. A profound reflection, for instance, of the pastoral ministry under the light of faith can have a decisive influence on its planning and execution. For such a reflection will ever maintain the right orientation of our apostolic thrust and revitalize our work, will help us to avoid modern activism whilst giving us the depth and measure of our activity. It will also enrich us all the time, offering us new viewpoints and a capacity of adaptation, inspiring derivations and applications of the faith and Gospel, placing us in intimate contact with supernatural realities and with the depths of the problems of human souls whom we are endeavouring to help. This type of reflection leads us to view and interpret worldly and human events in the light of God.

Theological reflection properly so called is that whose direct object is the study of God and the divine mysteries : this constitutes the formal object of theology.

Interdisciplinary theological reflection, on the other hand, endeavours to find a solution to human problems: its object is constituted by concrete facts of life or the fundamental problems of mankind. It seeks to give an answer to problems in the field of human sciences — in various departments, pastoral spiritual, scientific, and at various levels, local and universal.

There are today in the world a number of questions of the greatest gravity and importance. Mankind, despite its technical progress has not succeeded in securing justice, equality and peace. There is a constant increase in the problems raised by the sciences, historical criticism, the rapidity of the means of communication, the phenomenon of the so-called contestation, the structures of the multinational companies and international associations, etc. In a world that grows secular at gigantic steps, God's absence is felt the more day by day.

These problems and many others of the world of today demand solutions which, on the one hand, rest on fundamental human values that will often have to be rediscovered, and on the other avail themselves of the data supplied by revelation and faith and which may offer very useful help in the very presentation of the problems and the search of reliable and viable criteria. Hence, if a fund of tested knowledge of human sciences is of primary necessity, a solid and inspired theology in the broadest sense of the word will also be indispensable.

A superficial consideration may lead us to think that the variety and extent of the problems is immensely vast. It is so indeed, but a deeper analysis shows that all this problematique converges towards one central focus — man. This anthropological convergence constitutes man as the centre, a sort of "problematized king" of the whole universe.

3. Revelation and History

Man can not be thought of as a merely materialistic immanentism; it is necessary to have recourse to the sense of the transcendent and to the science of the transcendent — theology. This proves that if we wish to reach the required solutions we must recur to a truly interdisciplinary study, taking this term in its broadest sense which includes also theological science. The objective consideration of things opens an avenue towards God, whose light is necessary to know the world, to find a solution to its problems and to discover the true path to progress and peace which many want to discover prescinding of God altogether.

This is the thinking of outstanding scientists today, men like Einstein, Heisenberg, P. Jordan and others. Research institutes as well as prestige universities re-introduce in their programmes the theological studies that were eliminated in earlier centuries but are now appreciated once more for what they are and enter the centres of learning "by the main gate".

The irruption of God into human history is an ongoing event. Without the theology of history the evolutive process in time makes no sense. If we prescind from God and the supernatural order, man and history become two abstractions of suicidal irrealism. In our own days we are witnessing how the world, that boasts of the progress achieved, has become the victim precisely of the tragedy brought about by what it considers progress but is the source of its disarray and slavery with the consequent loss of many specifically human values.

Here lie the roots precisely of human frustration and disorientation with its destructive manifestations. Insistence on the untouchability of human freedom, which is considered as the highest human value, tends to deny every transcendental value: there lurks the fear lest the intervention of a superior Being limit this liberty or the possibilities of progress. Those who act thus are not aware that in trying to do without God, they block the living springs of progress and eliminate the light of the most powerful and indispensable knowledge of man which rests in revelation and faith.

It is sad to see how man today believes that the objectivity and veracity of his planning and the solutions to the problems depend chiefly on the multiplicity and variety of accumulated data and the power to achieve quick results. The human brain can no longer face the multitude of data that have to be gathered or the speed at which information has to be combined, and has to have recourse to the electronic computer. It is an additional humiliation of "the king of creation", that he needs the machine to tell him the path to the future — the electronic determinism directing human freedom.

This consequence is but the logical result of the premises. If scientific materialism and materialistic dialect are applied to man in all their force, they drag him to self-destruction at the precise moment when he takes pride in his unbounded progress. Man's fundamental error consists in his dream to set up an earthly paradise, in which, once God is eliminated, there is nothing but fallen man. The solution is to be sought in the opposite pole: the faith in that God, who dying to raise fallen man, becomes through his resurrection the centre and goal of history, the indispensable road that leads to the heavenly Paradise after the happy passage through a just and human earthly pilgrimage.

II — AN INTERDISCIPLINARY TASK

4. More and more about less and less

Theology therefore has its proper place and role in interdisciplinary research. There is much talk today of interdisciplinary investigation and activity. The term has become fashionable, but ambiguous. Let us try and clarify the concept.

The tendency of scientific specialization is to create separate fields or compartments, smaller day by day and limited, with the purpose of going deeper and deeper in each discipline. This carries the danger of an atomization of science and of limiting our mental horizon to a bare minimum. The remedy against this fragmentization consists in creating a new category of researchers whose task is to be to offer a synthesis by developing interdisciplinary comprehension and creativity: "The unity of the science of man will be for them a state of mind and an orientation of the will, even before establishing themselves in the acquired knowledge." (George Gusdorf, *"Project de recherche interdisciplinaire"*, p. 38).

It is a matter, therefore, not of merely juxtaposed monologues of various specialists but of collaboration of the different branches of knowledge. The "interdisciplinary space" is made up of the sum total of the various specialities, it is the unified field of knowledge, the negation of intellectual frontiers.

No attempt is made at excluding the existence of true specialists in a very reduced field; these are more necessary today than ever before: but they alone do not suffice; we need besides men capable of selecting and utilizing the mass of knowledge contributed by the various disciplines and relating one with the others. The study that this requires surpasses by far any sort of universal encyclopedic knowledge, which is for the most part shallow and superficial. And the reason is that what is intended is not to sacrifice depth but to gain in interrelation and to broaden the horizonts. The creation of this type of research workers, who without loosing in depth may be able to correlate the various branches of knowledge, is one of the greatest services we can render to mankind today.

5. Need of team-work

Certainly it is no easy matter to reach this goal without lapsing into superficial mediocrity. Tean-work is essential among the best specialists in the subjects connected with the matter in question. Others must also collaborate whose task will be to interrelate the findings of the various disciplines to reach the conclusions which exceed the ambit of any single one of them, thus a constructive synthesis emerging through the previous analytical break up.

This method is especially applicable when the point in question is man, that unit metaphysical, psychological, sociological and personal, which on being subjected to the analysis of various sciences is liable to become reduced to a mere conglomerate of parts not integrated.

Human redintegration must in its turn be the task of a man, who aided by a working group, prepares the reflection and then effects the synthesis of all the elements. Those who contribute the initial material will be many, fewer will work out the synthetic presentation, whereas just a few will formulate the final grand synthesis. This will take the form of guiding principles and orientations which are to direct all the activities of man as a unit and individual.

The integrating total synthesis of the human problems acquires special and highly complex characteristics. It is an effort, in fact, to combine and relate elements so disparate in nature that their harmonization supposes the knowledge of God through revelation. The natural and supernatural, the immanent and the transcendent, body and soul, time and eternity, freedom and providence, the individual and the ecclesial society or mystical body — all these are so many elements whose reality, and even at times apparent incompatibility clamour imperiously for theology to supply the true solutions of the most profound and characteristically human problems of the contemporary world.

6. Priority and urgency of this attitude and ministry

The requisites for this type of reflection and its very complexity increase the difficulty and diminish the number of those who may become capable of effecting this synthesis in all its depth and requirements. This explains why such a ministry is at once highly necessary and extremely difficult.

Another aspect which we cannot afford to forget is the priority for a solution which these problems demand, since they are the fundamental issues and exert such an influence on the rest that, if left unresolved, the others can not be faced without the risk of the most serious errors.

The world moves at a dizzy velocity and the question on everybody's lips is: whither, to progress or to destruction? Who can give an unerring answer to this question; who can offer sure directives leading with certitude to the goal intended by man?

This ministry is besides highly proper of the Society, not only because it is attuned to its spirit but also because of its exceptional importance and the dearth of men capable of developing it in all its extent and diversity. If we apply to it the criteria for the choice of ministries bequeathed to us by St. Ignatius, we shall see clearly the preeminent priority it holds.

7. Objections and Possibilities

True, the problem thus presented may appear utopian, or
at least reserved for a few and extraordinary men. In the
foregoing exposition I have tried only to describe an ideal,
or at least a concrete field of action, the highest and most
arduous. But what is important and must be common to all
Jesuits, especially in our days, is the permanent attitude of
reflection in the light of faith. All our works are again to be
submitted to evaluation in the realism of faith and the present
order of things: education, social works, our pastoral enterprises, retreats, etc. Each one must cultivate this habit, so
typically Ignatian, of remaining in a constant examination or
discernment and choice of ministries, thus making concrete
the original idea of St. Ignatius who considered this ongoing
reflection so important in the Society that he priced it more
highly than mental prayer itself.

A consideration of today's secularizing world brings out
how necessary it is that we should maintain ourselves in this
attitude of illumining the whole of our life with the theological
reflection.

On the other hand, this ministry, and much more such an
attitude, far from devaluating other apostolates, animates
and strengthens them. For it imparts to them a profound
meaning by directing and inspiring them and by contributing
to the genuine renewal and necessary adaptation based on the
ideas of modern theology and pastoral.

Everyone has a place in this activity; not all can do everything but all of us can contribute to the enrichment of the
reflection. Science and experience, difficulties and problems,
viewpoints and practical solutions that have produced good
results: all these are of great value for the reflection and
may offer a concrete modality for its 'incarnation' and the
necessary base of realism.

Nor need we put off the exercise of the planning of these
ministries until such time as this reflection has produced its
fruit. For action ought to accompany reflection, and reflection
ought to vitalize action. Hence it is not a matter of a paralysing abstract study but, on the contrary, we are intent on
discovering how the most abstract and theoretical investigation

can be enfleshed without falling into the trap of an enervating irrealism, precisely at a time when the world stands in urgent need of immediate solutions to its most anguishing problems.

On the other hand, the Society is particularly well equipped for this task. First comes its spirit and the training of its men, who acquire an inclination to this continuous reflection and discernment, for which they were prepared in the school of the Exercises.

At the research level as a ministry, the Society is endowed also with the proper elements. There are the numerous Faculties of theology, the various centres of higher studies and research (universities, institutes, social centres, reviews, etc), and the Society's presence in so many and diverse countries of the world with its activities in a variety of works and ministries. In order to utilize all these factors effectively it is necessary to create an attitude of interdisciplinary work and reflection with cooperation at all levels.

Fortunately, today's situation is very favourable to convert this ideal into a reality: the new generations are better disposed for this type of intercommunication and possibilities of communication are also on the increase.

8. Some difficulties

There is no doubt that a work so vast and complex is bound to encounter not a few difficulties. The first hurdle to clear consists in the change of attitude required in the persons who have to carry it out, particularly at the highest levels. Often the planning of theological reflection does not attack human problems, and most research workers in the human and natural sciences are content with delving into their specific problems and seek solutions within the framework of their speciality, without attempting problems posed by philosophy and less theology. This change of attitude, which is so necessary, is not an easy one.

Another serious obstacle, and looking towards the future the greatest difficulty, is the scarcity of men capable of making a synthesis so complex in this field of investigation. Given the anti-intellectual and utilitarian trends noticeable among today's youth, if we are to attain the desired results, we require a comparatively large number of men who study these disciplines in depth and are possessed of the mentality demanded by the interdisciplinary work — men capable of achieving a comprehensive synthesis, as far as it is possible, without degenerating into a superficial dilettantism that deforms and falsifies. This labour requires that one keep pace with the latest scientific discoveries and developments, and then effect a synthesis which be at the same time an expression of the situation and offer a solution to the problems of man and society, according to the findings of the various disciplines.

What is needed is a new category of synthetic investigators, who, based on pluridisciplinary study at the highest level, be able to make the synthesis and infer the consequences that are to illumine the man of today in the orientation of his life. This kind of men hardly exists, but we should start training them. On the other hand, the few existing men of this calibre are generally so overburdened with other work, that they find it impossible to devote themselves to what is today still considered a marginal occupation.

It would be a sad thing if man had to entrust to a computer machine the profoundest deductions of his progress. It is man himself who, under the illumination of faith and as a result of a deep and serious study, is to work out his self-orientation in life and discover his own answers, the transcendental answers to the modern problems on which the future of mankind depends.

ROLE OF JESUIT SCHOOLS
AND THEIR FUTURE

**Address of Father General Pedro Arrupe
to the Board of Directors of the Jesuit
Secondary Education Association in the
United States of America (JSEA)**

**Fordham University, New York City
November 10, 1972**

*The Society of Jesus is heavily committed to the apostolate
of education in several countries, particularly in the United
States and in India.*

*During his visit to North, Central and South America in
1972, Father Arrupe delivered two key addresses to Jesuit
educationists. One was on Secondary Education in New
York City (AR XV, 1972, pp. 960-967), which we
reproduce here, and the other on Higher Education, delivered
in Jersey City (ibid. pp. 968-976).*

*The immediate audience of the following address was the
American Jesuit teacher and school administrator, but
the challenging questions and encouraging concern will
find resonance in the ears and heart of every Jesuit school-
man in other countries, not least of all in India, in their
search for the meaning of their school work.*

*

1. Jesuit Educators meet in U.S.A., India, Rome, Japan, Mexico

I am very happy to be with you today. Through such face-
to-face encounters we lift to a higher level of intensity the

dialogue carried on in part through exchange of letters and circulation of reports. In exchanging our reflections, we grow in the *"unio cordium"*, which St. Ignatius urged in season and out of season. In a sense we are contributing to a type of communal discernment for the whole Society on the meaning of the Jesuit apostolate in secondary school education.

I am not being merely courteous when I congratulate you on the outstanding work you have been responsible for during the past two years. I am genuinely convinced that through your many activities you are leading Jesuit secondary school educators to a truly penetrating study of the meaning of your work and its future. As you are surely aware, Jesuits in other countries are engaged in a similar search.

In May last year, for example, some 100 Jesuits from every part of India spent six days together discussing the direction their 85 secondary schools should take in the years ahead. The report of the meeting, *Not Without A Compass*, reveals that they tackled the toughest of questions. That they intended their deliberations to be of service to all educators throughout India is clear from the fact that they considered Jesuit education within the context of national development.

At the Jesuit Curia in Rome in September, 1970, we were privileged to host a meeting of Jesuit prefects or directors of study from most of the western European countries. Through four days they discussed what the future held for Jesuit secondary schools. Their reports on student attitudes in their different countries made it clear that European youth faces basically the same major questions in every country. It was striking to see, for example, that almost all were agreed that problems concerning personal faith, which a generation ago were widespread at the university level, are now quite common among secondary school students.

If we turn to east and southeast Asia we see that a small, resourceful group of Jesuits organized and helped direct a truly historic meeting for educators from some fifteen countries during the entire month of August, 1971. Held in Kyoto, Japan, this educators' social action workshop brought together approximately fifteen educators from each of thirteen east and southeast Asian countries to work out ways of incorporating in their educational systems the major provisions of the United Nations universal declaration of human rights.

This meeting, let me emphasize, was not a meeting of Jesuits. It was, however, organized by a network of Jesuits, known as the Committee for Development of Socio-Economic life in Asia (SELA) which for the past decade has unobtrusively been sponsoring think-tanks on major social issues.

Less than a year ago — in December to be exact — a group of Jesuits met for one week in Oaxtepec, Mexico, to explore a whole range of questions relating to education, both institutional and non-institutional. Their report has formed the basis for discussion on the part of Jesuits in almost all Latin American countries and will, I predict, generate several kinds of practical response. Its five major conclusions you will, I am sure, have no difficulty in resonating to. They are:

1) The basic criterion for the revision of our educational apostolate in Latin America is social and distributive justice, and in the measure that we give ourselves to these demands shall we be fulfilling the *magis* that our vocation requires of us.

2) We have therefore to shift the thrust of our labours from the products of our education to the producers of social change.

3) To achieve this new thrust we shall need both to train the young Jesuits going into education and to retrain the older ones already lodged in it.

4) The most effective school for this training or retraining will be the *schola affectus* of the Exercises and community discernment, wherein Christ is both the medium and the message.

5) No matter how valiant our efforts, they will always fall far short of national needs. All the more reason, then, why we should extend our collaboration to, and seek the collaboration of, other church and national bodies whose educational ideals we share.

Finally, I should like to mention briefly two seminars held in Rome to help the Superiors-General of major religious congregations and their councilors keep abreast of some of the more notable trends in education. The first, held in November, 1970, enabled us to hear and enter into discussion with Paulo Freire, whose works you are all familiar with, and with Maurice Strong, the organizer of the United Nations Conference on the Environment. The second, which took place in May this year, focused our attention on the role of education in the promotion of justice among men. Like the meeting in Asia I referred to, these two seminars were obviously not Jesuit affairs. But we made them our concern, and I believe we contributed to their fruitfulness.

2. Corporate Sense of Identity in Worldwide Movement

I mention these meetings not to feed a sense of corporate complacency but to strengthen your sense of identity with a worldwide movement of men asking themselves in serenity and seriousness how best we can serve our Lord. No less do I mean to assure you that your own contributions, through the presence of Father McDermott — both in India and at the Rome meeting of Prefects of Study — and through your publications, have been felt, deeply appreciated, and gratefully acknowledged.

I mention these meetings for yet another reason; namely, to make clear how important they are, and how important it is that their findings and recommendations reach down to the individual school, to the individual administrator and teacher. There are some who argue that our lives are cluttered up with meetings and that we gather largely to pool our bewilderment or ignorance. They call for a moratorium on meetings and for a return to the quiet of individual contemplation. It is easy to understand this line of thinking, for some meetings are unproductive, while the results of others are never felt. But the conclusion to be drawn from this is surely that we should be more conscientious in preparing, and leading to fruitful conclusions the meetings in which we do take part.

Who could doubt, for example, the worth of the meeting which issued in your *Preamble*, the April 1971 national meeting of your Association in Chicago, the June meeting of your Association's Commission on Research and Development, as well as those for teachers of religion and for presidents of your schools? Certainly the impact of your *Preamble* has been extraordinary, while the response to the CORD report, "The Jesuit High School of the Future", will, I predict, be gratifyingly enthusiastic.

So, let meetings flourish, I say, provided that they are solidly prepared, professionally conducted, stimulate responsible feedback, and issue in action responding to the needs of our time.

3. Possible Responses to Questioning on Role of our Schools

This demanding and at times painful work of self-study and projections for the future is all the more necessary now that in each individual community we are preparing for the forthcoming General Congregation. As we explore earnestly and serenely what the vocation, mission, and apostolate of *the Society of today* are to be, we are asking about *our* community, about *our* school, *our* place in the Society of Jesus, about *our* role in society itself.

Each day, the role of our schools in society comes under more strident questioning. One response open to us is to give up our work in order to begin something new; specifically, leave the educational apostolate and turn to more specifically pastoral works, especially such as bring us directly in the midst of the poor. Another response is to carry on what we are doing as in the past. A third response is to carry on, indeed, but to improve on past performance. This, I take it, is your response — a wise one indeed. You, it seems, are evaluating the criticisms so rampant today. You are not flinching from those which point to weaknesses in your own schools. You are uniting your efforts to share the best in each of your schools with your confreres in other cities and thus are making it clear that the "mindlessness" of which Charles Silberman accused American educators does not characterize your own efforts.

We are all, I am sure, at one in our conviction of the unique contribution of Catholic education to the community at large. It is not to sustain a minority culture. It is not to provide a competitive educational system in order to prevent the state system from becoming monolithic. Its unique contribution, as Dr. Mary-Angela Harper so well expressed it, *is its precise understanding of the human person as a God-related being and its explicit teaching and developing and implementing of the values that flow from this understanding, values that nourish and strengthen the entire public community. If we choose to dilute our identity as religious, value-oriented schools, we will have cheated not only ourselves, but even our fellow citizens in the civic sector.*[1]

This is extremely well said, an encouraging reaffirmation of your own views in your *Preamble* and in the CORD Statement. I know that you will study and discuss this Statement with the same enthusiasm that marked reflections on the *Preamble*, and that the parents of your students as well as teachers in many schools will draw enlightenment and strength from it. Let me draw your attention to its initial statement concerning three ways of viewing the Church as reflected in the documents of the Second Vatican Council and then suggest one or two lines of thought that you may want to develop further. We can understand the Church as the visible means of man's salvation instituted by Christ; as a kerygmatic event issuing in the People of God; and as a prophetic servant to all men. Each of these views reflects the wonderful richness of the Church from one particular angle. They are complementary, not contradictory.

4. Kerigmatic Apostolate and Prophetic Service

When we see the Church as kerygmatic event, we focus on Christ, revealed as Son and proclaimed as Lord, drawing all peoples into a community of believers, forming them into the People of God. When we see it as prophetic servant, we focus on it as pointing to the One Who is always coming yet already in our midst, reflected surely if obscurely in the faces of the scattered sheep of Israel. In our schools, does this not mean that we should strive to build a true community, one which becomes more and more aware of its identity as a recipient of gifts given precisely so that they may be shared? Our students are not to see themselves as isolated individuals learning how

---

[1] "Catholiç School — foiling the Gravediggers", *America*, Sept. 16, 1972. p. 173.

to elbow their way through hostile masses to positions of power and prestige. Rather, let them discover in ways they can never forget that they are brothers in a planetary village, fellow pilgrims on spaceship earth. Perhaps in the past we stressed individual achievement somewhat too much. Who can say with certainty? But now, let us be ingenious in educating our students — and ourselves — to *the joys and hopes, the griefs and the anxieties of the men of this age, especially those who are poor or in any way afflicted.*[2] As part of the People of God, let them experience that they are to be led by the Spirit of the Lord as they labour *to decipher authentic signs of God's presence and purpose in the happenings, needs and desires in which this People has a part along with other men of our age.*[3]

As the Church explicitates its mission, so should our schools work *to structure and consolidate the human community according to the divine law . . .* (and to) *initiate activities on behalf of all men.*[4] This emphasis on service for the human development of all people is the hallmark of the Church today. As I mentioned last year in my letter, "The Social Commitment of the Society of Jesus", we are called to this service, yet "there still remains a gap between the intentions publicly expressed and the reality of the apostolate".

5. Jesuit Schools' Global View

Let no one say that this mission of expanding the mind to global views and schooling the heart to a spirit of service is outside the scope of a Jesuit high school. If our faculties and students were outraged at injustice, zealous in study and service, experienced in doing without and yearning for contemplation, they would serve the Church today as Canisius and Regis, Bellarmine and Claver did in their day.

How, you may ask, can this be done in an educational institution? Through curriculum, I would answer; through educational theory and methods; through teaching and living Christian values; but most effectively through the type of

[2] Gaudium et Spes, 17.
[3] Ibid., 1.
[4] Ibid., 42.

education described by a brother Jesuit as follows:

> *...the 'new humanism' should place a counterstress on the more*
> *social virtues: sensitivity to human need; concern for the poor,*
> *the oppressed, the marginalized, not so much as objects of charity*
> *but as subjects of rights, as equals who must be helped to help*
> *themselves, so that by taking their rightful share of the cost of*
> *human development they may also take their rightful share of its*
> *rewards.*[5]

We show a genuine interest in combating injustice in the third world by respecting persons in our schools, by dialoguing with students, by encouraging interdependent activities among teachers, by individualized instruction, by social action as a constitutive part of a curriculum designed to promote reflectiveness, contemplation, meditation.

6.   Evaluation: Student, Teacher, Pedagogy

As Jesuits we are accustomed to examining ourselves daily. We are now corporately examining where we stand in today's world. For yourselves as educators I think this means that you will want to judge your effectiveness in meeting the educational needs of our time. This examination will lead you to look closely at the student, the teacher and the entire educational environment and technology. Let me comment briefly on each of these points.

Those who draw up criteria for judging the effectiveness of our educational programs today should situate the student in a *new stage of history*.[6] Historically our listing of educational goals tended to emphasize the *perennial* needs of all peoples. We must now recognize the urgency of responding to the *special* needs of each person in this special period of cultural change. *These changes recoil upon* (the individual person), *his manner of thinking and acting with respect to things and to people*.[7] The special needs of youth today are vastly different from those of students in a rural, pre-industrialized society. If we ignore this fact, we will be trapped into dealing with students

---

[5] Horacio de la Costa, "New Humanism" in *Let No Flame Be Quenched*, p. 14.
[6] Gaudium et Spes, 4.
[7] Ibid., 4.

in a regimented, routine-structured way that reflects nothing of the joy and confidence of *Gaudium et Spes* and *Octogesima Adveniens*.

I would like to invite each school to list the needs of their students today and to discuss them in relation to curriculum and the total school experience. Certainly these discussions will include such very practical matters as individualized learning, practice in decision-making, living experiences with those of other economic and racial backgrounds, service to others and, obviously opportunities to find God in private and public prayer.

Further, I hope that as you evaluate your schools you give much care to a description of a good teacher and his irreplaceable role in a school sensitive to individual needs, to the oppressed and to the special community we call the Church.

Your discussions will certainly lead you to deeper insights into the educational philosophy that is reflected in your institutions — especially in the United States, where you are flooded with pedagogical innovations of every kind, it is imperative that we have administrators and teachers truly competent in the field of pedagogy. It would be a most serious dereliction of duty if special help and guidance were not available to the over one thousand, one hundred Jesuits who are now working in your high schools. I urge every province to have some Jesuits thoroughly prepared in educational theory and practice so that they can help guide our schools in continuity with our best traditions through the unchartered educational seas of the 1970's.

7. Religious Education

I do not need to tell you that religious education today is not easy. The experience of every day brings home to you this fact. I do, however, want to urge all of you to examine carefully what kind of religious education is found in our schools today. In one of our better schools in another country I was told that some of the best students confided to a teacher-friend that they were atheists only during religion class. Such a remark should stir all of us to reflection. If during your review of the state of religious education in your school you find that you are not meeting the needs of your students, I know that you will avail yourselves of the experience and knowledge of your Commission on Religious Education. In this field, above all, I trust that we will all share with one another such experiences as can be mutually helpful. I trust too that your cooperation will extend far beyond your own schools and include brothers and sisters and lay teachers who, like yourselves, are laboring so tirelessly on behalf of youth.

In short, my dear brothers, as we draw together around Christ, we shall see indeed what our contemporaries see in the field of education: the beds that have borne only sixty, some only thirty, per cent of the hundredfold we confidently expected when we went out sowing. We shall see the patches of rocky soil which have long ceased to bear fruit at all. We shall see the clumps of thorns which have choked both the fruits of the harvest and the enthusiasm of some of the harvesters. We shall see all these, but we shall not be discouraged by them, for with Christ we have lifted our gaze and rearticulated our vision, as your CORD Statement so challengingly expresses it, to the rich promise that beckons and sustains the valiant laborer in his Lord's vineyard. Be assured of my prayers that your laborers be many and your harvest great.

OUR SECONDARY SCHOOLS: TODAY AND TOMORROW

OUR SECONDARY SCHOOLS TODAY AND TOMORROW

Concluding Address to the participants of a meeting on Secondary Education

Rome
September 13, 1980

From September 10 to 13, 1980, a meeting was held in the Jesuit Curia in Rome to discuss two specific issues in Jesuit Secondary Education: genuine collaboration with the laity, and the application of Decree 4 of the 32nd General Congregation (the service of faith and the promotion of justice) to secondary education.

It is the custom of Father General to attend all sessions of such meetings, and to speak at the beginning and the end of the meeting. As he explains in the opening paragraph, Father Genearl used this occasion to speak more broadly about Jesuit secondary education as an apostolate of the Society of Jesus. He spoke from his own outline.

After the meeting Father Arrupe revised and expanded on his address, in order to put it into a more polished form. The pages that follow contain his final revision, and their publication as an issue of 'Documentation' of the Press and Information Office was a means of providing to a wide Jesuit public thoughts of Father General on this important apostolate of the Society. It was suggested that the addres should find a place also in this collection.

*

1. I do not intend to cover the same ground as those who will publish the proceedings of this Symposium on the *Apostolate*

of the Society in Secondary Education. They will have their work cut out for them, given the wealth of experience, reflection and reports of pioneering efforts that you have exchanged during these past few days! I am not even going to enter into the two specific points which you have discussed in such great detail: lay collaboration in our schools, and education for justice.

I prefer, instead, to devote the time at my disposal to some considerations of a more general character concerning the apostolate of education, and, more specifically, concerning our Jesuit secondary schools. For many years I have been deeply convinced of the apostolic potential of our educational centres, and specifically of our institutions of seconadry education. And today, after hearing from you about the difficulties and the problems, as well as the possibilities offered by the new focus of this apostolate, both within and outside the institutions, my conviction about the importance of the secondary schools is stronger than ever — if that were possible! Both in themselves, and in their relationship to other forms of the Society's apostolate.

I. SECONDARY EDUCATION

2.   In contradistinction to primary and university education, secondary education gives us access to the minds and hearts of great numbers of young men and women *at a privileged moment* of their lives. They are *already* capable of a coherent and rational assimilation of human values illuminated by Christian faith. At the same time, their personality has *not yet* acquired traits that are so set that they resist healthy formation. It is especially during the years of secondary education that the mindset of young people is systematically formed; consequently, it is the moment in which they can and should achieve a harmonious synthesis of faith and modern culture. (Cf. GC 31, Decree 28, no. 17).

We usually define secondary education in terms of its educational content — sometimes too closely bound up with academic programmes — or else in terms of the age of the persons being educated. I would include in the category of secondary education the educational work which the Society is providing to adults in many different places: in literacy compaigns, or projects of professional or cultural improvement. This kind of work has many of the same goals (and therefore offers many of the same apostolic opportunities) that are characteristic of traditional secondary education. The adult student in such a situation approaches the teacher voluntarily, even eagerly, with a receptivity which is not generally true for his or her age level; this inspires the kind of openness to formation which we find in secondary school students.

3. The Society has taken giant strides in recent years in this type of education, especially in culturally depressed countries or regions. Inspired by the direction of the last two General Congregations, the Society has initiated an imaginative use of modern mass media of communication, creating *educational institutions of a new type*: radio, audiovisual, correspondence courses, etc. However, the characteristics, advantages, and limitations of this type of education — and of the institutions and structures which serve it — are not the theme which I wish to develop here. Nor will we analyze now the role which they have to play in the future. We must return to this theme on another occasion and with the depth which such an important topic deserves. But I could not let the occasion pass without at least mentioning this new educational reality, which so hopefully enriches and diversifies the Society's educational apostolate. What I have to say here with explicit reference to our secondary schools, established according to the traditional model in the Society, can and should be applied in an analogous way to this new kind of educational institution.

II. THE COLLEGE, AN APOSTOLIC INSTRUMENT

4. The basic idea behind all that I have to say is simply this: the secondary school is an effective apostolic instrument which the Society entrusts to a community, or to a definite group of men within a community; the purpose can only be apostolic. This commitment to such men and for such a purpose, is an authentic act of "mission." The secondary school is the primordial means of apostolate for that community. And that community, inasmuch as it is an apostolic group of the Society, must concentrate its activity towards attaining the greatest possible apostolic results from its use of this educational instrument.

Since the secondary school is an instrument, and an instrument for a specific mission whose nature is so clearly spiritual, it is evident that the instrument should be moved by God, the Principal Cause. That which joins this instrument with this principal cause is precisely the Jesuit community, to which the instrument has been entrusted. And the Jesuit community will use the instrument in order to achieve the predetermined goal: the spread of the Kingdom. The community which is dedicated to work in a secondary school absolutely must interiorize this outlook, and live out this conviction: The Society has given them a specific mission; and in order to accomplish the mission, it has entrusted to them this specific instrument. Any deviation from the mission, which would tend to diminish the value of its educational and apostolic finality — for example, by reducing it to a mere cultural or humanistic project, or even catechetic—, and any kind of abusive usurpation of the instrument — for example, by an inordinate attachment to it, with a consequent erosion of apostolic availability — will detract from the fundamental character both of the mission and of the instrument.

III. PRELIMINARY CRITERIA

5.   There are many criteria for deciding whether there should be an educational centre in the first place, and then for deciding what kind it should be, etc. The relative value of each criterion in different types of concrete circumstances will be conditioned and given a new meaning by many different factors. It would be a mistake to give absolute value to any one criterion, however pure it might seem to be. To take only one example, the secondary school needed in a country where Catholics are in the minority, but where the country enjoys a high level of technology and cultural refinement, such as Japan, can be very different from the secondary school in another country, say in Europe, where there are abundant opportunities for Catholic education, or, again, very different from a school in the developing world, where the cultural upgrading of the masses is an overriding concern of the highest priority.

This necessary diversity of criteria does not confer legitimacy on every institution simply because it exists; nor does it justify the excessive individualism of those who claim that "our situation is different" in order to resist any interference from outside, with no willingness to listen or to learn. Such an attitude of self-sufficiency, or even of superiority, is infantile and narcissistic, generally without objective foundation, and is contrary to the very nature of education, which is supposed to be a humanizing enterprise, fostering openness to others.

There is also the opposite danger, an even more destructive result of a false sense of superiority: the intolerant dogmatism that insists on imposing on everyone one's own concept of education, and of the proper kind of educational institution.

6. *Any Decision should be the Result of Discernment.* The nature of the institution, its location, the number of students, the formulation of objectives for academic quality or of the publics to be served, etc., are elements which diversify the instrument in order to adapt it to the circumstances in which it is being employed. Consequently, these elements should be arrived at by way of an Ignatian discernment in which, along with the usual criteria for the choice of ministries, account is taken of local circumstances as well as the comprehensive pastoral plan of the Province and of the local Hierarchy. In one place, the Church will need a centre which offers an option of high academic quality, that can compete with comparable institutions. Somewhere else, the need might be for a college geared to large numbers, as many as possible — in some cases with coeducation — in order to meet the pressing demand for schooling, or the specific needs of Christians, or in order to express an attitude of openness and invitation to an unbelieving world. In still other regions, an emergency situation — which, for St. Ignatius, can override all other criteria — might call for literacy education, or mass cultural programmes through the use of radio, records, and printed works. Each of these will be a form of education in support of evangelization!

The Ignatian criteria for selection of ministries are not absolutes. Before listing them in the Constitutions, St Ignatius, with his customary prudence, prefaces them with the caution: "When other considerations are equal (and this should be understood in everything that follows)..." [622].

7. *We are Committed to Educate any Class of Person, without Distinction.* It cannot be otherwise, because the educational apostolate (just as every other apostolate of the Society) bears the indelible Ignatian imprint of universality. To be sure, this total openness of the total educational work of the Society takes on — or should take on — individual characteristics according to local conditions. But what is never admissible is any kind of exclusiveness. Obviously, this total openness is joined to the Society's preferential option for the poor, an option which applies to every apostolate, education included. I think it is safe to say that there is no great problem in meeting the educational needs of the wealthier classes, and that there is a considerable problem — at times of tragic proportions — in meeting the educational needs of the poor. Although civil society has the prime responsibility to meet this social need, the Society feels an obligation, by reason of its vocation, to help to meet this human and spiritual need. It thus embodies the Church's right to teach in whatever way, to whatever degree, is necessary.

And even though the more comfortable classes have no lack of educational opportunities, there is a great need for evangelization among these people. And because instruction and education are most efficacious means of evangelization, the Society cannot limit its educational apostolate exclusively to the poor. Moreover, looking to the long-range interests of the poor and the disadvantaged, again using Ignatian criteria, the Society should actively promote the Christian transformation of other social classes. Nor should we lose sight of the silent middle class, also a part of the People of God, and so seldom mentioned when problems are discussed in terms of the two extremes.

8. *A Negative Criterion: Disavowal of Economic Discrimination.* Because the secondary schools of the Society are necessarily instruments of the apostolate — and are therefore subject in principle to the radical gratuity of our ministries, and to our poverty — their availability to students cannot be conditioned by ability to pay. This statement of principle is our ideal. I know very well that the reality is necessarily very different in various countries and in various kinds of institutions. But as

long as this ideal has not yet been realized, any Jesuit institution must live with the tension of striving to achieve a situation in which no capable student is refused admittance because he cannot pay. The recovery of genuine equality of opportunity and genuine freedom in the area of education is a concern that falls within the scope of our struggle for the promotion of justice.

9. *A Positive Criterion: Excellence.* Whatever be the other characteristics of a Jesuit secondary school, one trait should be common to all: excellence, which is to say, high quality. I am obviously not referring to structures and physical plants, but rather to that which specifically defines an educational centre and provides the basis for its evaluation: its product, the men and women who are being formed. The excellence which we seek consists in producing men and women of right principles, personally appropriated; men and women open to the signs of the times, in tune with their cultural milieu and its problems; men and women for others. Instruction, education, evangelization: these are three levels of operation which, in different countries and in different circumstances can have different priorities and degrees of urgency. But each one must be pursued with excellence as its goal, at least relative excellence. The true objective of a centre of instruction — it would be better to say of education — is in the area of the specifically human and Christian. And here I want to make a special point about the importance of academic excellence in our educational work in mission countries. It would be a mistake to sacrifice this — not only at the University level, but also in secondary schools— for the sake of other goals, which might be good enough in themselves and would claim priority in another type of institution, or simply in order to increase the number of students.

10. *Ignatian Education.* A Jesuit secondary school should be easily identifiable as such. There are many ways in which it will resemble other schools, both secular and confessional, including schools of other religious orders. But if it is an authentic Jesuit school — that is to say, if our operation of the school flows out of the strengths drawn from our own specific charism, if we emphasize our essential characteristics and our basic options — then the education which our students receive should give them a certain "Ignacianidad", if I can use such

a term. I am not talking about arrogance or snobbery, still less about a superiority complex. I simply refer to the logical consequence of the fact that we live and operate out of our own charism. Our responsibility is to provide, through our schools, what we believe God and the Church ask of us.

IV. THE STUDENT WE ARE TRYING TO FORM

11. Here, I take for granted the academic and educative aspects of the School. I want to concentrate on other aspects of the integral formation that we should be giving to our students.

a. *Men and Women of Service, according to the Gospel.* This is the "man or woman for others" that you have heard me speak about so frequently. But here I want to rework this idea from a new viewpoint, especially for those among our students who are Christians. They must be men and women who are motivated by a genuine Gospel charity, which is the queen of the virtues. We have spoken about faith/justice so often. But it is charity which gives force to faith, and to the desire for justice. Justice does not reach its interior fullness except in charity. Christian love both implies justice, and extends the requirements of justice to the utmost limits, by providing a motivation and a new interior force. All too frequently, we pass over this basic idea: faith must be informed by charity, faith is shown in works that are inspired by charity. And justice without charity is not evangelical. This is something we must insist on; if we are to understand our fundamental option correctly, and make use of its tremendous potential, we must understand and assimilate this basic point. It can lead to a holy respect, and a tolerance, which will temper our impatience for justice and the service of the faith. Especially in non-Christian countries, we must accommodate to possibilities and look for ways to insert those Christian values which are also human values and recognized as such.

12. b. *New Persons,* transformed by the message of Christ, who will be witnesses to His death and resurrection in their own lives. Those who graduate from our secondary schools should have acquired, in ways proportional to their age and maturity, a way of life that is in itself a proclamation of the

charity of Christ, of the faith that comes from Him and leads back to Him, and of the justice which He announced. We must make every effort to inculcate those values which are a part of our Ignatian heritage. We can even pass them on to those who do not share our faith in Christ, if we translate them into ethical and human values of moral uprightness and of solidarity, which also come from God.

The really crucial question is this: If the finality of our education is the creation of new persons, men and women of service, then what are the *pedagogical* repercussions? Because, this really is the purpose of the education that we are giving. It is a different kind of focus, at least to the extent that it gives priority to human values of service, of anti-egoism. And this has to have an influence on our pedagogical methods, our educational curriculum, our extra-curricular activities. A desire for Christian witness, service of one another, cannot thrive in an atmosphere of academic competition, or where one's personal qualities are judged only by comparison to those of others. These things will thrive only in an atmosphere in which we learn how to be available, how to be of service to others. We need to rethink our educational methods in the light of these objectives: how to form the evangelical person, who looks on every other man and woman as a brother or sister. Universal brotherhood will be the foundation of one's personal, family, and social life.

13. c. *Men and Women open* to their own times and to the future. The students that we are leaving our imprint on day after day, that we are forming at a time when they are still more or less receptive, are not "finished products" that we launch out into the world. We are dealing with human beings, who are in constant growth. Whether we like it or not, they will, throughout their lives, be affected by all of those forces through which they will influence the world, or through which the world will influence them. The result of this struggle will determine whether they continue to live a personal life that is evangelical, a life of service, or whether they will live a kind of neutral apathy, overcome by indifference or unbelief. For this reason, perpahs even more important than the formation that we give them is the capacity and concern to continue their

own formation; this is what we must instill in them. It is important to learn; but it is much more important to learn how to learn, to desire to go on learning all through life.

What I am trying to say is that our education, in its psychological aspects, must take this future into account. It must be an education which will be the seed for further personal growth; an open-ended education; an introduction to a basic thrust which will continue to be operative throughout life: continual formation.

Among other things, the formation we give must take into account the kind of civilization that we are living in, and that our students will be called on to live in for the rest of their lives: the civilization of the image, of visualization, of the mass media transmission of information. The revolution created by the printing press at the beginning of the renaissance is child's play compared to the revolution being produced by modern technology. Our education must take this into account! We must use it, and help our students to get accustomed to it.

14.   d.   *The Balanced Person.*   Perhaps I am asking for too much, after all the things I've already mentioned. And yet, this is an ideal that we must not give up. All of the values already mentioned: academic, evangelical, persons of service, of openness, of sensitivity to the present and to the future — these are not lost, but rather are mutually helped, when they are combined together in a balanced way. The ideal of our schools is not to produce little academic monsters, dehumanized and introverted. Neither is it to produce pious faithful, allergic to the world in which they live, incapable of responding to it sympathetically. Our ideal is much closer to the unsurpassed model of the Greeks, in its Christian version: balanced, serene, and constant, open to whatever is human. Technology threatens to dehumanize man; and it must be the mission of our educational centres to safeguard humanism, without at the same time renouncing the use of technology.

V.   THE EDUCATIONAL COMMUNITY

15.   This is a concept which has undergone great change. The traditional *"Ratio Studiorum"* of the Society, and I include

the revised version of the last century, has many merits which have been recognized throughout history. But it could do not more than reflect the restricted notion of a pedagogical community that was known at the time. The changed conditions of our own times have forced us to make generous use of the faculty foreseen in the Constitutions [457], to have collaborators who are not Jesuits. But this gives us a new responsibility: we must take whatever means are necessary to ensure that the formation given in our secondary schools continues to be a Jesuit formation, such as I have been describing.

The educational community is made up of: the Jesuit community, the lay collaborators, the students, and their families. And also, remembering that the school is the first stage of a formation that will continue throughout life, it includes also — and must include — our former students.

16. *The Jesuit Community.* The mission of the Society is entrusted, in the first place, to the Jesuit community; to it is entrusted the secondary school, as the apostolic instrument through which this mission is to be carried out. The Jesuit community, therefore, must be the primary source of inspiration for the educational work. Even in those cases in which lay persons have been appointed to administrative offices — for it is clear, in principle, that they must be persons who are in full harmony with the principles which guide our mission. And we must make special efforts to ensure this in the new structures, in which financial responsibility, maintenance and business affairs, and even the academic administration of the school have been transferred to an association or board, of which only a part is Jesuit.

The Jesuits of the secondary school must be seen to be a united community, one which is authentically Jesuit and easily recognizable as such. That is to say: they should be a group of men with a clear identity, who live the true Ignatian charism, closely bound together by union of minds and hearts *ad intra*, and similarly bound, *ad extra*, by their generous participation in a common mission. The Jesuit community will examine itself regularly, evaluate its apostolic activity, and use an ongoing discernment process in order to decide which from among the available options will best accomplish their mission.

This religious community will be the nucleus of the larger educational community, binding it together and giving it meaning. If the Jesuit community in the school is divided, then those who collaborate with them in the school will also be divided, and the secondary school will fulfill the dictum of St Ignatius: if it is not united, the Society not only cannot function, but it cannot even exist. (Const. 655).

17.   The inspiration that the Jesuit community brings to the school will consist, first of all, in its specific application of the Ignatian vision to the educational apostolate. Concretely, this means that the Ignatian vision is evident in the objectives of the school, in the type of person we are trying to form, and in the selection of the means necessary to attain that end.

Here I would like to add a word about the priestly activity of the Jesuits who are engaged in the educational work of our secondary schools. Teaching is surely a fully apostolic work; so is administration, or any of the other types of work necessary for the well-being of the school. Nevertheless, every Jesuit priest should also be engaged in some priestly activity in the strict sense of that term. This can be in the school, or outside of it. Within the school, it could take the form of a sacramental ministry, preaching, spiritual counselling, or the pastoral direction of different kinds of groups. Outside of the school, it might mean regular or occasional help in parishes, convents, hospitals, prisons, other institutions for the needy, Christian movements, etc. Such work could be daily, on weekends, or more occasional, even limited to vacation periods. What is important is that we keep alive in ourselves our priestly identity, and have other people see us in this way. To unite ourselves to Christ, to share in His priesthood, His mission of redemption and sanctification: this was the ideal that drew us to the Society, and it is the only ideal that will preserve us in it. I am slow to accept the excuse of "lack of time" as a reason for total withdrawal from specifically priestly works. Such a situation would seem rather to call for a reordering of other priorities. Experience has shown us that total withdrawal from all priestly activity, over a period of years, can lead to the loss of a sense of priestly identity. And this is especially the case when the priesthood is not exercised in the early years after ordination. From there, it is a short step to a loss of Jesuit identity. And the consequences of this second step are easy to predict.

18. In the second place, the Jesuit community should be the source of inspiration and stimulation for the other components of the educational community (the lay collaborators, the students, the families, the former students), and this through the testimony of its life and its work. *The witness of our lives is essential.* If what we are trying to form in our students is the whole person, and not just the intellect, then we have to do this with *our whole person*, and not just through our teaching. The students, their families, our colleagues, all have a right to see us as integrated, to see no division between what we teach, what we say, and how we live. And we have an obligation to respect this right. We are being hypocritical if we warn our students about the consumer mentality while we live lives that are secure and comfortable. And what I said above about priestly identity applies also here: a lack of priestly identity can lead to a secularized way of life — in the bad sense of that word — and perhaps rather easily in an educational institution (though not just there, of course). Style of dress, behaviour, use or abuse of property, the way we speak, etc., all these form a part of our witness and, consequently, of our educacional activity. Young people are not yet able to make mature judgments based on profound values; for them, these are often the basis for making judgments about individual Jesuits, and about the Society. We need to think about our responsibilities in this area, and about the relationships all this may have to the problem of vocations.

19. The witness of our lives includes also the *witness of our work.* I know that some of the men in our secondary schools are overworked: because of the reduced numbers of Jesuit personnel, some individual Jesuits have taken on unreasonable workloads. Does this sometimes lead to less excellence in our work? Could it lead to a lessening of inspiration in our mission? Are we working at times when we ought to be reflecting? Are we burdening ourselves with administrative details, or management that could be more easily delegated, and failing to do those things which cannot so adequately be done by others?

On the other hand, the opposite danger also exists in every institution, large or small. Have we become immovable, untouchable, even though we are turning out work that is hardly satisfactory, work that suffers in comparison with that of other members of the educational community? Do we resist any change in the order of the day, any attempt at evaluation, any request that we help out with priestly or extra-curricular activities, or anything that might fall outside our "professional responsibilities"? It is up to Superiors to make sure that our educational institutions do not become havens for the underemployed, the unavailable, the immovable. Frequently, the best solution would seem to be to assign such a man to a new type of work, in which his priestly and apostolic zeal can be restimulated. Preventing this type of parasitism is especially important in secondary schools where, more than at the University level, we are engaged in forming adolescents, especially sensitive to the influence of witness. What I am saying here has nothing to do with the presence in the community of older Fathers and Brothers, who continue to live in the school after a lifetime of hard work there. These men bring the example of their goodness, of their presence, their sense of tradition, a sense of being a family, to the educational community.

With regard to the question of the relationship between community and work, the separation of the place of residence from the place of work is, in itself, neither a necessary nor a sufficient solution. There are cases, however, where it might be a necessary first step.

20. *The Lay Collaborators* form a most important part of the educational community. In this regard, the Society has made great progress. I have already indicated how the Constitutions admit the possibility of collaboration as a substitute, when there are not enough Jesuits. It is suggested there that the contributions of the laity should not exceed the limits of teaching. But this thinking was a reflection of the times; it was based on a concept of the role of the laity in the Church that was widely held until quite recently. Since Vatican II, the role of the laity has been reassessed; the place of lay people in the mission of the Church is now recognized explicitly. Then why not their role in the mission of the Society? This means that it

is no longer the lack of Jesuits that determines the number of lay collaborators in our secondary schools, but rather the profound conviction that lay people have an invaluable contribution to make in our apostolate; they help us to extend the apostolate almost without limit. In former times, it was possible to find a community of fifty Jesuits engaged in the education of two or three hundred students — in a boarding school for instance! Let us frankly admit that this was disproportionate; and if we look to the needs of today's world, such attention would even be called unjust, or showing partiality. To maintain such a Jesuit-student ratio today would be a scandal in the Church. It is wrong to regret this situation of former days.

21. Today we need multipliers, and that is what our lay collaborators are. This under one condition, naturally, and that is that we esteem in fact their ability to be integrated into our apostolic educational mission. This means that we do not regard them as salaried employees, hired to do work under a master's supervision. They are not that! Their salaries should be adequate to relieve them of preoccupation with economics; they should be freed to dedicate themselves to full-time work, with complete dedication, without the need for an additional job. If they work with a divided spirit, they will almost of necessity become incapable of becoming real educators, and even good teachers.

But there is much more. What we truly need are not just teachers. We need *responsible collaborators,* who share in the fullness of our mission. This is how we must accept them. And we need to learn from them; learn about the specific charism of the laity in the furthering of the work of the Church. This is the only way that their integration into the educational community can have any meaning; this is the only way in which they will become true multiplying agents.

There are two things implied here: first, that they *assimilate the Ignatian principles* that give inspiration to our mission; and second, that they become *a part of the decision-making process,* with positions of responsibility in which their educational potential can yield its maximum fruit.

With respect to the first, it is clear that just as we ourselves needed a formation in order to assimilate and put into practice our Ignatian vision, so the lay collaborators must receive a formation from us — a formation adapted to them. Constant attention must be given to this; it must be an ongoing process, with due respect for the individual personality of each one. Even when they are not Christian, as will necessarily be the case in many countries, we can learn from them, and allow them to share, according to their own capacity, in those values of our mission which are universal. However, those who are incapable of appreciating our vision of man and of gospel values are not suited for education in a secondary school run by the Society, whatever academic and teaching qualities they may have. I am not talking here about forming mini-Jesuits! What we need to form are persons who are lay, but who also resonate with Ignatian ideals. To give this type of formation requires time and money. But it is an investment which will yield great dividends for the ends that we are seeking. And we can hardly neglect necessary formation of our collaborators and at the same time expect them to share in our mission wholeheartedly!

Concerning their integration into administrative positions in the school, what I have in mind is more than just a type of partnership. I assume that much! What I am talking about is offering, to those lay persons who are well prepared, not just administrative and managerial assignments, but the very highest levels of educational responsibility, and to do this with full confidence. This includes even the direction of the school (as principal or headmaster), when it is necessary or useful. We reserve to the Society only its essential role as the animator and inspirator, as I have explained already.

For many of our schools, participation of competent lay people is the only way to survive, if we wish the school to go on being a place of Ignatian education in spite of the impossibility of allocating the numbers of Jesuits that would be required. Bur for all of our secondary schools this collaboration with the laity (so long as they share in our mission, and do not just function as hired teachers — for, ultimately, teaching by itself is not the most important element) is absolutely indispensable in our day, when the influence of the Church and of the Society need to be multiplied.

22. *The Families.* We know that families have ultimate responsibility for the formation of their children. But this is just one more reason why we should *also* be working with the families. We should cooperate with them in the work of education, especially in those very frequent situations in which the married couples are hardly prepared to form their children. I want to give special praise to those organizations — associations, journals, formation courses — which promote the educational formation of the parents of our students, to prepare them for a more effective collaboration with the secondary school. Also, the school can and must function as a catalyst between parents and their children, to bring about unity. One of the evils of our time is precisely the disintegration of the family: not just of the marriage, but also of children with respect to their parents. The school is a privileged place for a real encounter of parents with their own children; there they can come to appreciate their interests. It is important, then, that families have contact with the school, participte in its life, and cooperate in its cultural, social, extracurricular and other activities.

23. *Former Students.* I have dealt with this theme many times in recent years, and I don't want to repeat myself here. I would only reiterate one point: the ongoing formation of former students is an obligation; it is a strict responsibility which the Society cannot ignore. It is a work that only we can do, practically speaking, because it is a question of redoing the formation that we gave twenty or thirty years ago. The person that the world needs now is different from the persons we formed then! It is an immense task, and well beyond our own abilities; we need to seek the help of lay people who can help to bring it about. But this, of course, assumes that we first form such lay persons! The Provincials need to provide for this by assigning to Associations of Former Students a sufficient number of Fathers who have both the aptitude and the time to devote to this work. If we do not do this, the Associations will languish, and the reeducation of our former students will not take place.

24. *Present Students.* The students are the centre of focus, the principal component of the educational community. I

have talked about them quite extensively in these pages, and there is no need to repeat what I have already said. I would only like to add one additional point: how much our students can teach us! We have to be in close contact with them. Because in dealing with our students, we can learn so much. We learn patience by encountering their impatience; we learn generosity by seeing their capacity to make sacrifice; we learn to be men for others by seeing how much they can give of themsleves if only we stimulate them with the right motivation! Through these young people we contact a civilization from which we ourselves will be excluded: in them we see the society of tomorrow; through them, we have a glimpse of the future. This is why it is impossible to educate the young from a guarded distance — living outside of their milieu, in antiseptic isolation, filled with academic dignity (and perhaps also with inferiority and timidity). This is not the way to get abundant vocations; and this is not the way to encourage young people to know the beauty of our Ignatian ideal: life in the service of Christ.

VI. THE SECONDARY SCHOOL: OPENNESS AND INTEGRATION

25.   You have been very clear on this point during your meetings these past few days. The secondary schools of the Society cannot remain in "splendid isolation" from the Province or from the local Church. It may well have been true in the past that some of our schools, because of their size and academic reputation, were ahead of their times and became pioneers for the city or the region, leading to a certain amount of isolation from the other schools. But this isolation, conscious or unconscious, wherever it exists, must disappear. Besides the fact that there have been profound changes in a very short time, we are part of the Catholic Church; we are part of the Society of Jesus. The secondary schools of the Society must take common cause, *form a united front,* with other educational institutions of the Church. They must participate in the different types of organizations which have been formed: professional, trade union, apostolic. This is especially important in those countries in which liberty of teaching, equality of opportunities, financial support, and other similar

issues are hotly contested by opposing ideologies.

But the more fundamental reason why our secondary schools must have this openness and ongoing contact with others is this: we need to learn, and we have an obligation to share. There are enormous advantages to be gained through collaboration of every type. It would be foolish to pretend that we have nothing to learn. It would he irresponsible to think only of ourselves in our planning, without considering the need to cooperate with other secondary schools, whether religious or secular — in the areas of elective subjects, for example, or specialized studies, or in teaching standards, courses for teachers and parents, etc. This articulation of concrete needs with similar educational institutions in a local, regional, or national ecclesial setting, will make us more effective apostolically, and will at the same time increase and strengthen our sense of being a part of the Church.

The secondary schools must also be integrated into the Province; their development must fit into the overall apostolic planning of the Province. Their relationship with other apostolic works in the Province must be fruitful. The schools are one segment of the individual unity of the "mission" of the Province, and they must be harmoniously joined to the other segments. I am not just speaking about a polite interest in the work that others are doing, or in cordial fraternal relations. I mean something much more specific: real collaboration! The pastoral aspects of the educational apostolate provide secondary schools with opportunities for cooperation with other Jesuit works which can be of benefit to all. Other Jesuits, for example, can help out in the extra-curricular pastoral activities for the young people; they can help with spiritual care, the Exercises, Christian movements, etc. And the Jesuits in the school community can help out in the parishes and residences at the times of greatest demand. And, when distance and time permit, our scholastics and young priests still in studies could also share in this fraternal collaboration. These activities will introduce the young Jesuits to the apostolic activities of their own Province, bring home to them the wide range of possibilities, and at the same time bring to light their abilities and interests. Both of these are important when the time comes for young Jesuits to receive a definitive mission.

Such opening up will benefit both the Jesuit communities in the schools, and also the students. It will keep Jesuit teachers in touch with the activities and needs of the Church and of the Society in other areas — and this is a valuable psychological preparation for the day when some from among them, for whatever reason, must begin a new line of work. These men will not be entering an unknown world. As I have already indicated, a certain amount of priestly activity in addition to one's primary work of education is an important means, at the personal level, for personal development of an attitude of sharing. The students will have their own horizons opened up by such contacts, by the opening up of the school. From their young years, they will become accustomed to the ecclesial and social dimensions of their lives. I wonder whether some of the hostility to Christian commitment or to social commitment, apparent in some of our former students, may not be at least partly due to the hothouse atmosphere of some of our secondary schools in the past.

26.   Openness and institutional contacts must be complemented by a radiant *apostolic energy*. Every centre mantained by the Society is a platform for apostolate. The parish, the hospital, the prison, the radio station, the social centre, the aid centre connected with it, the barrio, and so on... so many other places where Jesuits and Jesuit students should engage in some type of apostolate. Do not these places need an apostolic presence? But we have a greater need to provide it. Even more. I would venture to say that if the excuse for omitting all exercise of priestly and apostolic zeal is too much work and the fatigue that follows from it, then we shall have to discern whether it would not be better to suggest — or gently to impose — a quantitative readjustment of our labours (even at the cost of hiring additional personnel), which would enable us to make a qualitative shift to a life in which activity that is directly priestly and apostolic formation of our students are clearly present.

Would it not be possible to do more than what is being done, directing our service to parents, alumni, students, the good people of the neighbourhood... I am thinking of areas of service such as opening up our installations, making them available for night classes, literacy programmes, basic and continuing vocational and professional courses, social activities, sports, artistic or recreational programmes, meetings of neighbourhood communities, human development projects, etc. Is it not to some extent a continual scandal — and unjustifiable in terms of sound investment policy — that our plants are not effectively utilized more than eight or ten hours a day during the brief two hundred days of the academic year, i.e., about 20% of the time, when they could be so useful for so many projects and for the benefit of so many people? Would not this be an application of our teaching on the social function of property?

VII. TO WHOM THESE PAGES ARE ADDRESSED

27.   I want to conclude where, perhaps, I should have begun: by speaking about those to whom these pages are addressed. I am *not just speaking to you,* the fifteen Jesuits who have come from so many different parts of the world in order to participate in this seminar; you are not the only ones I have in mind. During these days we have had lengthy discussions, and you already know my thinking on all of these issues. I have prayed with you to Him Who is the Only Master: the Light, the Truth, the Way. I have listened to your experiences, your reflections, your preoccupations, your hopes. In your notes, and in the documentation which will be the result of your work during these days, you will find more than enough material for reflection and for inspiration concerning the future or your secondary schools. I am sure of that. And so I would say, rather paradoxically, that you are not the ones that I am really speaking to! You are not, perhaps, the ones who most need to hear all that I am saying.

28.   I am thinking, first, of the *communities of Jesuits presently working in our secondary schools*. These men, priests and brothers, have given themselves to a work that is very often hidden; the schedule they are subjected to — for the day and for the year — is very rigorous; often enough they are overworked.

And their personal austerity is sometimes obscured by the apparent opulence of the institution they are working in. I confer on these men, once again, the mission that they have already received from the Society. I repeat, once again, that the Church and the Society of Jesus hold the educational apostolate in the very highest esteem. And I encourage them to go on doing their work with dedication and enthusiasm.

And at the same time, I caution these men about the danger of inertia. It is absolutely essential that they become more aware of the changes that have taken place in the Church and in the Society, and aware also of their need to keep pace with these changes. If some of our secondary schools, at least those which have the reputation of "great old institutions" have become apostolates that are little appreciated by different groups of Jesuits, perhaps we should admit that the disenchantment of the younger, dynamic generation of Jesuits may be due in part to the failure of these institutions to adjust to the new demands of today's Society, Church, and society at large. That Jesuit community which believes that its school has no need to change has set the stage for the slow death of that school; it will only take about one generation. However painful it may be, we need to trim the tree in order to restore it to strength. Permanent formation, adaptation of structures in order to meet new conditions, these are indispensable.

29.   The second group that I wish to address is *our younger men*, or perhaps the not-so-young, whose apostolic impetuosity makes them look on our educational institutions — and perhaps the very apostolate of education itself — with distrust, with low esteem. It is hasty to indiscriminantly label all of our secondary schools, and especially the more "affluent" ones, as centres of power, symbols of a disregard for the poor, as countersigns to our fundamental option for the poor. Often enough, is ignored the real spirit of sacrifice that is needed to live and work in the school. I know that such a spirit is not always there; and I never stop urging the men in the schools to a greater personal and community austerity, just as there are other aspects — sometimes more important ones — that I have to insist on in other apostolates.

But the apostolate of education is absolutely vital for the

Church. So vital is it that educational work is the first, and often the only, work prohibited to the Church by certain political regimes. And this is enough to ensure the de-Christianization of a nation, without bloodshed, in the space of a few generations.

Education is absolutely necessary. And it cannot be done on the scale, and with the excellence, that I have been referring to unless it is carried out in some type of an institution. At the beginning of these pages, I have already talked about different kinds of possibilities. I have alluded to the fact that we need to educate the total person. In a social body, we cannot limit ourselves to education of the hands or of the arms; we must also educate the head. The training of future leaders is important, and Ignatian criteria are in agreement with this. Therefore, in order to promote the necessary renovation that can only come through the introduction of new blood, I urge our scholastics to consider the apostolic value of our educational works in a realistic way, and to offer themselves — or accept cheerfully — an assignment to these works with the evangelical and priestly attitude that I have already described. Let us not fall into the injustice of reproaching our educational centres for their immobility, and then at the same time deny them the means for moving forward! The solution is both "*ab intus*" by encouraging those already in the schools towards a personal renewal, and "*ab extra*" by renewing these Jesuit communities with new recruits.

30. Finally, I am thinking about *Superiors, Provincials, Regional Vice-Provincials, Commissions on Ministries,* and all those who do the apostolic planning for the Provinces. They must see whether the number and type of existing educational institutions is justified by the real apostolic needs of the area; they must see whether the present apostolic works are responding to those needs, or whether new apostolic works should be begun. Which ones, where, with what characteristics. They must work towards a more perfect coordination of the educational apostolate with the other apostolates of the Province, and develop our educational apostolate in accord with the needs of the local Church. They must stimulate Rectors to the type of renewal that is needed in order to go forward. They must support the Rectors in their efforts to call the members of

the educational community, especially the Jesuits, to a renewal of their academic and evangelical training. They must strengthen the faculties, as far as this lies within their power, both by the assignment of generous young men, and by the reassignment of those men who are still in the schools, but lost their effectiveness in teaching and evangelization, to other more appropriate apostolates.

31. Concretely, I suggest the necessity of *preparing young Jesuits specifically for the educational apostolate*. The reduced time given to Juniorate studies and to the period of regency in many Provinces has resulted, among other things, in a poorer training in the humanities and a weaker remote preparation for the educational apostolate. The Province should have a number of men who are experts in Pedagogy (with the appropriate academic degrees), a number proportionate to the number of its educational institutions. Finally, I commend the regional and national efforts that have been undertaken to promote the continuing education of personnel, both Jesuit and lay, often in conjunction with other religious and secular groups.

32. I realize that, in spite of the length of this address, there is much more to be said. As a matter of fact, for each of the topics that I have treated, a veritable library exists! It was not my intention to say everything, but only to recall to your minds some of the matters that I consider *more urgent or important*; matters that you yourselves have suggested to me. I ask you to carry back to your Provinces a message of my heartfelt encouragement and my constant concern for your fellow educators, and for the work they are doing in education. The words of one of our most famous Jesuit educators remain true today: *"Puerilis institutio est renovatio mundi"* — the education of youth is the transformation of the world! (Juan de Bonifacio, 1538-1606; cf. *Mon. Paed.* III, 402, note 15.)

THE JESUIT MISSION
IN THE UNIVERSITY APOSTOLATE

Inaugural Address of Father Pedro Arrupe
to the Convention of Jesuit Academic Directors
of Institutions of Higher Learning

**Rome,
August 5, 1975**

Early in 1975 Father General Arrupe planned to call for different meetings throughout the Society to discuss, assimilate and implement the decrees of the 32nd General Congregation as they apply to our Jesuit life and apostolate. The international Federation of Catholic Universities had scheduled a meeting in Delhi from August 12 to 16, and the International Association of Universities a meeting in Moscow immediately thereafter. This provided the occasion for calling a meeting of Jesuit University Academic Directors in Rome just before the Delhi meeting which several of them were to attend.

On August 4, the day of the assembly, Father General welcomed some 70 Rectors, Presidents or Principals, along with Provincial Representatives from Asia, Europe and the Americas, 2 Presidents of Jesuit Educational Associations, and some 20 men from the Curia staff including Assistants and Counsellors.

On the second day the group was addressed by Cardinal Garrone, Prefect of the Congregation for Catholic Education and were later received in a special audience by Pope Paul VI, who after a formal allocution had a word with each participant.

We here publish Father General's opening address on the

capital importance of the University apostolate for the Church and the Society today.

*

I. IMPORTANCE OF THE APOSTOLATE OF INSTITUTIONS OF HIGHER LEARNING

1. Unique Occasion

Just five months ago I looked out over this hall, to say my final words to the delegates to the 32nd General Congregation. Already at that time they and I were wondering how we could interpret to the entire Society the rich and profound experience of the preceding three months.

What better way for me to carry further the work of the Congregation than to use every occasion to meet with various groups of Jesuits and discuss with them the orientations which the Congregation has opened up for us? So you can imagine my joy when I learned of the meetings in Delhi and Moscow to which many of you were planning to go and when I saw that without imposing too much on you I could invite you to stop in Rome. That joy has fairly brimmed over, now that you are here. Not thirty or forty of you, as at first I thought might be able to free yourselves to come, but seventy!! Almost all of the directors of our institutions of higher education in Latin and North America, Europe, and East Asia, along with a strong representation from India.

Never before in the history of the Society of Jesus has such a large group of directors of our universities and colleges assembled!!

It is most fitting that it is with you, directors of the extremely important apostolate of institutionalized higher learning, that my staff and I hold the first large-scale meeting after the Congregation. Fitting, because the educational apostolate has been close to the Jesuit heart from our very origins (cf. *Const.*, part 4). Fitting because you may have doubts about the importance the Congregation attached to this apostolate, since it prepared no statement pertaining exclusively to it. Fitting too, because it is in and through the institutions from which you come that the Society inserts herself into that world of learning which, for good or bad, feeds the citizenry of every nation with the ideas and preconceptions which help to determine norms of judgment and action. Fitting finally, because "the Catholic university has a distinctive vocation in modern society" and to work for its development "is to carry on an ecclesial task, both urgent and irreplaceable," for "the Catholic university is a necessary element of the Church, living in and at the service of the world" (Paul VI, in *L'Osservatore Ramano*, Nov. 27-28, 1971 and Dec. 12, 1972).

How can we best use the limited time at our disposal? First of all, I would say as "men of prayer, of the evangelical mission of Christ, endowed with a supernatural spirit" (Paul VI, Allocution to members of the General Congregation: December 3, 1974). Secondly, in a communitarian way. Many of you are meeting for the first time and discovering that, though from very differing parts of the world, you are nodes in that net which is the *communitas dispersa* of the Society in the world of academe. You will see that you have not only common concerns, but also common challenges and opportunities.

Our prayerful openness to God in a spirit of fraternal sharing will lead us, it is clear, beyond the Society of Jesus. It will situate us ecclesially, *within the Church*, which mediates to us our mission of service to men in their quest for faith and in their promotion of justice. In these four days, let us with all the vigour at our command make the concerns of the Church our concerns, her needs our needs, her frailties our common burden.

Finally, let us ask the Father of Jesus to draw us to His Son, *to place us with His Son*, to be "propitious to us in Rome" as he was to St. Ignatius, following his vision at La Storta. God's arm is not shortened.

2. Why is the Apostolate important

The theme that I propose to discuss this morning is that the university apostolate *is* of capital importance for the Church, and therefore for the Society, and this for many reasons. You are more familiar with these reasons than I. Let me, nonetheless, select two and briefly develop them before looking more closely at the prophetic role of the Catholic university.

— The teaching of our blessed Lord is for all men, including specially the "wise of this world." Now the wise of this world are to be found, if not exclusively, certainly in strength, in institutions of higher education. These institutions, then, merit an important place in our apostolic planning and labours.

— Our Lord's teaching is to be the salt that penetrates and sustains the vitality of human cultures. Now human cultures, specially in the modern, technological world, are shaped in institutions of higher education. In these institutions, then, we are offered an unrivalled opportunity, where the graces of civilization flourish, for the grace of God to abound the more.

(a)   *The Wise of this World*

My first statement, that the teaching of our blessed Lord is intended in a special way for the "wise of this world", may come as a surprise to some. Did not our Lord Himself say that it has pleased His Father to reveal to the unlearned what He has hidden from the wise and learned (Luke 10:21)? And has not the Church in recent years, through the Holy Father and the bishops interpreting the Gospel for today's world, guided us very explicitly to be concerned, more than in the past, with the poor, the outcast, the marginados?

Paradoxical as it may seem the "wise of this world" have often to be ranked among the impoverished, the marginados, suffering from the isolation which is the special mark of the outcaste. They are often out of contact with the light and saving power of the Lord, shut up in a world of values that excludes the personally Transcendent. This isolation is often the greater, the more advanced the research on which their lives are centered. They have not encountered Christ, because — to give one reason — they have never met the modern equivalents of Justin, Irenaeus, Augustine, Bonaventure, Aquinas, Ricci or de Nobili. But if the "wise of this world" become wise in Christ, their influence will be enormous, like a lamp set upon a stand and bringing light to all in the house (Matt. 5: 14).

How will they become wise in Christ, if Christian scholars are not present in their world of contemporary philosophy, science, or art, and at home, even more so, in that world which evoked Paul's lyrical cry, "How great are God's riches. How deep are his wisdom and knowledge." Who can explain his decisions? Who can understand his ways?" (Romans 11:33).

As we look at the Jesuit community and then at the large number of lay professors and administrators at our institutions, what do we see? Are they — are we — distinguishable from our peers at other institutions? Has a "dominant secularism" become our native air, so that God is effectively absent from our world? To what extent have we internalized that judgment on the situation of today's world expressed so incisively in *Jesuits Today,* namely that "the prevalence of injustice in a world where the very survival of the human race depends on men caring for and sharing with one another is one of the principal obstacles to belief: belief in a God who is justice because he is love?" (*Jesuits Today,* no. 7).

(b) *Christification of Cultures*

I turn now to my second consideration; namely, that our Lord's teaching is intended to permeate human cultures and vivify them from within. It is not only for all men but also for the total culture which every human community builds in our different countries. Our cultures, ideologies, and structures are shaped by cultural, political, and economic leaders, who in turn draw their views about man and the world in part from the "knowledge industry", at the heart of which we find the university.

It was not always so. But today, man's growing awareness of his own cultural identity, the rise of "new" nations with their own cultural values, the ecological and population problems and the crisis of values triggered by the technological revolution of the last few decades have enhanced the need for universities, where such huge questions can be systematically studied in interdisciplinary fashion. From the viewpoint of rural-urban relations, we can say that the movement of peoples and the shift of power bases from rural dispersion to urban centres leads almost inevitably to strengthening the position of the university. It becomes the point where men in quest for knowledge and understanding give that quest a local habitation and a name.

Such convulsive changes bring us face to face with the question of inculturation in the true sense of the word; namely, the Christification of cultures. Clearly, this touches not only the "new" nations, with their subcultures based on different tribal and ethnic origins, but also the industrialized nations of the technologically advanced world with their sub-cultures and social strata. To understand what it maens to be a person, precisely in any particular culture or sub-culture demands experience, reflection fed by the contributions of many disciplines, and the light of faith illuminating all reflection.

Inculturation, then, is the incarnation or enfleshing of the Faith and Christian existence in each and every culture so that people can genuinely express them in ways with which they feel confortable. Thus they will be able to develop and deepen as well as transmit *their* faith in their own language (*ecclesia localis*), through concepts derived from their own culture (*inculturatio philosophica et theologica*), in accord with their own spiritual and religious tradition with the values proper to it (*inculturatio vitae spiritualis*). This process is to go on without any deformation of the Gospel, since it is only in the light of the Gospel that cultural and human values can be supernaturally judged and evaluated. How appropriate for our institutions of higher education is the study involved in such an enterprise, where history, anthropology, linguistics, sociology and other disciplines all have their place.

It may be argued that the advanced research institutes of governments and industry or popular programmes for millions of television and radio audiences both generate and popularize new values so that the institution of higher education is no longer so important. Undoubtedly, it is no longer without rival, as perhaps it was until the most recent past. But if we ask where the research workers of specialized institutes and the writers of television programmes have been educated, are we not directed back to our institutions of higher education?

Certainly the General Congregation was convinced of the need for "a profound and academic formation of its future priests". Consider from the viewpoint of higher education its strong words on this subject.

Thus the Society has opted anew for a profound academic formation

*of its future priests — theological, as well as philosophical, humane,
and scientific — in the persuasion that, presupposing the testimony
of one's own life, there is no more apt way to exercise our mission.
Such study is itself an apostolic work which makes us present to
men to the degree that we come to know all...their cultural milieu.
Our studies should foster and stimulate those very qualities which
today are often suffocated by our contemporary style of living and
thinking: a spirit of reflection and an awareness of the deeper,
transcendent values... (Formation of Jesuits, Decree 6, no. 25).*

3.   Our bonds with our Students and Lay Staff

Now what we say about younger Jesuits holds true in its
own way about young men and women in general. Those
particularly, who spend anywhere from 3 to 10 years in institutions of higher education are called on to develop that
"spirit of reflection and an awareness of deeper, transcendental
values" which will enable them to unify various branches of
study into a living synthesis of knowledge to be used for their
own true good and that of their fellows.

Let us not be too easily persuaded that students are developing this spirit of reflectiveness and synthesis merely because
they study at *our* institutions. On the other hand, let us not be
so obsessed by the difficulties as to assume that all that our
students seek is a degree or certificate to enable them to find
more profitable employment than their contemporaries.

Through the *students,* then, who choose our institutions,
our Lord's teaching is to penetrate human cultures and vivify
them from within.

Perhaps as you listen you are thinking of your institution:
the small number of Jesuits, the growing number of lay
professors. Perhaps you wonder if I am thinking of a model
that no longer exists — the small college of less than 1,000
students with an almost exclusively Jesuit staff. No, let me
assure you, I am thinking of *your* institutions, both the smaller
ones and those of five, ten, fifteen thousand students, a Jesuit
staff whose average age is considerably above where it stood
ten years ago, and a lay staff anywhere from 2 to 20 to 40
times as numerous as the Jesuit.

Considering these institutions, is it not clear that we have a special responsibility to strengthen our bonds with *lay professors and administrators?* Perhaps no single question is as important as this in almost all of our institutions. I will not go into detail on this point, but I would ask you to view your institutions from this point of view and ask yourselves some very practical questions, like the following.

(i)   What is the *general* spirit among the lay professors? Do they view the "Jesuit" university as part of themselves? Do they have opportunities for learning, discussing and explaining Ignatian values which have given birth to and are supposed to permeate the "Jesuit" university?

(ii)   Are Jesuits available for apostolic planning with lay professors? What concrete results have such plans led to?

(iii)   In the very delicate matter of selection of new professors, does your institution have a plan for emphasizing certain qualities of instruction and certain sectors of research, in the light of which it makes its selection?

Our former students too — are they not also part of our institutions? Are we really interested in them? Do we keep in touch with them, with a purpose larger than raising of funds? I will not go into this question in detail, but I do refer you to my views on this important matter. (AR XV (1968) 341-347).

4. Shaping of Opinion and Conscience

Finally, I would like at least to mention an enormous force for good at *your* disposal, one often overlooked or neglected. I refer to the making of *opinion* and the indirect formation of conscience implied in it. You may recall what I had to say on this point at the Episcopal Synod last year.

The Church cannot ignore this phenomenon which constitutes a real "sign of the times". Formation of public opinion and its freedom from forces which would suppress or distort should constitute one of the prime objectives in the evangelization of the Church today.

A proper formation and expression of public opinion is necessary for the integral human development which evangelization seeks to promote. Therefore, as the Second Vatican Council put it: 'Within the limits of morality and the general welfare, a man should be free to search for the truth, voice his mind and publicize it...and

...have appropriate access to information about public affairs (GS n. 59).

The two principal elements which in fact form and limit public opinion are: on the one hand, the information which is published concerning facts, ideas and the historic reality in which we live; on the other, the values, mental sets and attitudes which condition the reception of this reality and at times distort it.

To do the work of evangelization is to exert a force so that public opinion is not manipulated but formed in an objective and impartial manner, and so that this information can be received and interpreted in the light of a Christian vision of the world, man and society.

We are all aware of the enormous power of television, newspapers, and films to channel the mainstream of public discourse. If we are to play our part in directing this influence wisely and fairly, it is not so much the question of further information we should be concerned with. It is, rather, the image, the presuppositions, the angle of vision, the frame of reference, the symbolic presentation of values.

The university looks to the *total* development of people — intellectual, artistic, moral, religious — and to the issues of values, both personal and social. In what ways, we might ask, do our institutions contribute to the forming of the values which underlie social issues and community programmes? In what ways do they explore the deeper religious and spiritual values of human experience and thus, in line with their own finality, assure that they will have their place in the formation of public opinion?

I do not exaggerate when I say that few if any groups in the Society enjoy the opportunities that are yours to bring the wisdom of the Gospel to the councils of men. Your outreach into your local and even national communities may even frighten you; for you know that when you speak it is not as an individual Jesuit that you are heard but as the president of an important institution. You may recall the story of the illustrious president of Harvard University, Charles W. Eliot. His secretary was told that the then president of the United States, Theodore Roosevelt, was on the phone. She bade the caller wait and then after locating Dr. Eliot said to him: "President Eliot is ready to talk to Mr. Roosevelt." You may smile, but you know there is some measure of truth to the story, for bearers of political and economic power are aware that men like yourselves help shape the values of youth and of entire communities.

II. PROPHETIC ROLE OF CATHOLIC UNIVERSITY

5. Witness and Prophet

Our Lord's teaching, as we saw before, is for the "wise of this world." It is intended to permeate all human cultures and impregnate our institutions and structures. It is also intended to provide a bridge between what is and the shape of things to come — the *nova et vetera* of the good householder. Is not the Jesuit institution of higher education a privileged place for mediating between the set of ideas and views which hold sway in today's world and that divine wisdom which both participates in the folly of the Cross and is itself a sign of the "Behold I make all things new?" Is it not called to exercise a *prophetic* role?

Let me make clear what I do not mean, and what I do mean, with that word "prophetic."

I do not mean the angry, facile denunciation of a particular evil. I do not mean a proclamation which, while purporting to liberate the weak and powerless, instigates them to a self-righteous exaltation of their own virtue and to hatred and scorn for those who are not of their number.

I use the word *prophet* here in a biblical sense: one who is entrusted with a spiritual mission, that of bearing witness to the power and love of God towards men. By *prophetic* I mean the persevering, fearless speaking forth on the issues of the day by people whose views are rooted in Christ's teaching, clarified through discernment with their community, and consistent with their own total dedication to Christ. The prophet "speaks God's message" (1 Cor 14-24), not only when it is willingly accepted but also and especially when it is seen as a "hard saying", painful to all-too-human ways of viewing what God expects of man in history. The prophet has let himself be steeped in God, with the result that he is free interiorly and pure of heart. He is sympathetically critical of all movements and institutions, many of which are of course excellent, but all of them limited.

6. On the border line of Church and World

The prophet's role is to relate the living God to his creatures in the singularity of their present moment. But just for that reason, his message looks towards the future. He sees the future coming with its twin aspects of judgment and salvation. He judges the human situation with total freedom and reads the passing moment with the aid of a special, God-given light, which enables him to penetrate deeply into the meaning of events. The prophet knows that the judgment he pronounces comes from the God of salvation and is intended to "build and to plant" (Jeremiah 1:10). When the "wise of this world" must be silent out of ignorance of the profound meaning of events, the prophet speaks out. We can understand in this sense why Father Przywara says that "the Jesuit lives on the border line where the Church meets the world and the world meets the Church... It is the function of the Jesuit to interpret the Church to the world and the world to the Church. The border line is ever shifting. Our first task therefore is to locate it." (Quoted in John Courtney Murray's, "*The University in the American Experience*", New York: Fordham University, 1966, p. 10).

Was it not this which our Holy Father had in mind in his memorable allocution of December 3 when he addressed us as follows:

Wherever in the Church, even in the most difficult and extreme fields, in the crossroads of ideologies, in the front line of social conflict, there has been and there is confrontation between the deepest desires of man and the perennial message of the Gospel, there also there have been, and there are, Jesuits... You are at the head of that interior renewal which the Church is facing in this secularized world, especially after the Second Vatican Council. Your Society is, we say, the test of the vitality of the Church throughout the centuries; it is perhaps one of the most difficult crucibles in which are encountered the difficulties, the temptations, the efforts, the perpetuity and the successes of the whole Church. (Allocution of Pope Paul VI to the Thirty-Second General Congregation, Dec. 3, 1974).

These words mean that if we want to continue in our apostolic and prophetic role, according to the best traditions of the Society, we must remain at our post on that border line between the Church and the world of non-belief, between the forward leaps of science and the reality of everyday life, searching for solutions to the most pressing problems and in the process stirring up others. Firmly grounded in a solid and genuine tradition, and *therefore* progressive as are only those who are most driven by the inexhaustible desire of the *"magis"*.

In the sense just described, the Jesuit communities of which you are a part, and yourselves as leaders in the university apostolate, are called to be prophetic. You have not sought this burden. The Society, acting as part of the People of God, has missioned you to it, whatever the precise form in which you have been appointed.

7. Risk and Courage

To be a prophet in the sense just described and in the measure marked out for us by the 32nd General Congregation will not win us first place in popularity contests.

To live as a prophet demands integrity and spiritual energy far beyond the average. Now, even more than before the 32nd General Congregation, are we in need of that integrity and energy, for we have been called to make the service of faith and promotion of justice the centre of our lives. Given the demands of this task, I recalled to the members of the Congregation early in the discussion on justice the following grave words from *Octogesima Adveniens*.

> *Let each one examine himself, to see what he has done up to now, and what he ought to do. It is not enough to recall principles, state intentions, point to crying injustices and utter prophetic denunciations; these words will lack real weight unless they are accompanied for each individual by a livelier awareness of personal responsibility and by effective action.* (AAS, 1971, 437-438).

I went on to ask in my own name this series of questions, not drawn out of the air but deliberately chosen to assist us to foresee where our decisions might lead us.

> *Is (the Congregation) ready to accept this responsibility and to*

carry it through to the final consequences? Is it ready to enter on the sterner way of the cross, that which brings us misunderstanding from civil and ecclesiastical authorities and our best friends? Is it ready to give witness not only through decrees or statements which would put into words the sense and meaning of all the members or of a large part? Is it ready to give practical expression to its witness through concrete decisions which will necessarily modify our way of life, our style of working, our field of endeavour, our social and personal contacts, and finally our image and social standing? (Cf. *News* of the General Congregation, no. 6, December 20, 1974, p. 4).

The Congregation's response, we know, was the decree on our mission today and thereby the commitment of the entire Society. So, we cannot avoid asking ourselves in utter sincerity whether we have sufficient resources to bear the prophet's burden. We will indeed experience extra-ordinary power and authority if we say yes, but great sacrifices will be asked of us, both in what concerns us personally and in our relations with men who up to this point were counted among our defenders, our friends.

It is we who must decide. Do we want to play our apostolic-prophetic role with all that it demands, or be satisfied with a comfortable mediocrity?

From your strenuous efforts to maintain a Jesuit identity and spirit in your institutions despite ever mounting obstacles, from your prompt and generous response to my invitation to this meeting, from your evident determination to be faithful to your Jesuit vocation to the *magis* for Christ, I have no doubt about your answer. True enough, we cannot decide of ourselves to be ministers of prophecy. Prophets are God's creations, made not born, responding to specific needs. Nonetheless, as I said earlier, the prophetic spirit is to be found not only in individuals, but in groups and communities as well. We are called to be in some way prophets because we belong to the Church and because we are religious. The Church is a prophetic body. Religious communities, too, have a prophetic function. It is in this sense that Ladislas Orsy, SJ writes: "The purity of religious vocation consists in the purity of prophecy by word, deed and daily life." (*Open to the Spirit*, Washington: Corpus Books, 1968, p. 21).

III.   EXPRESSION OF PROPHETIC CHARISM

8.   Research, Teaching, Service

This charismatic-prophetic spirit should express itself in every aspect of our daily university life, be it research, teaching or service to our community. Generally speaking, the qualities that should distinguish these activities are insight, clarity of vision, sincerity, authenticity, fortitude in facing difficulties and in seeing our undertakings through.

It is these qualities that will determine the kind of *research* we undertake: our short- and long-term projects; the problems we decide to study, including some which others might not dare to treat; the aspects of them we focus upon. In this connection, I would like to cite the wise observations of Father Bernard Lonergan on the Jesuit approach to world problems.

If I am correct in assuming that the Jesiuts of the twentieth century, like those of the sixteenth, exist to meet crises, they have to accept the gains of modernity in natural sciences, in philosophy, in theology, while working out strategies for dealing with secularist views on religion and with concomitant distortions in man's notion of human knowledge, in his apprehension of human reality, in his organization of human affairs. ("The Response of the Jesuit As Priest and Apostle, in the Modern World", in *Studies in the Spirituality of Jesuits,* Vol. II, no. 3, p. 109).

Acceptance of gains along with a spirit of critical evaluation of their meaning and use: let this be our formula, if formula we seek.

Our *teaching* will be directed towards forming the new man, the man for today's world, and we will seek out the most efficacious means to accomplish this; greater emphasis, for example, on training in the use of freedom, and on the development of an integrated personality, instead of the customary maimed, one-dimensional products of our cultural technology. We shall foster an eagerness "to learn how to learn" which is at the heart of what is called Continuing Education. We shall build up Men for Others, men whose ideal is that of service; who enrich their own personalities for the enrichment of others; whose horizons stretch out to their fellowmen across the farthest national and international frontiers. It is our charismatic insight, our prophetic vision that will spur us to discover pedagogic principles, and diversify their application, in order to achieve goals that lie beyond the reach of purely human or rational considerations.

In our *service*, we shall be unremitting in our search for the truly important kind of service and the form that we should give it.

Some of the challenges we shall face will stretch almost as wide as the world itself: the massive phenomenon of unbelief in its theological, pastoral and other aspects; the fundamental basis of moral values; business ethics; the problems of ecology, lodging; inner city problems; the exploitation of the poor and defenceless; famine and drought; inadequacy of resources to population. Others will vary from region to region, from country to country. However, the principles that should guide us in confronting these challenges will be common to us all, for they derive from the one spirit that animates us and directs us to the end for which Christ called us to his company.

9. Interdisciplinary and International Approach

All this calls for men of extraordinary sensibility and spiritual discernment on the one hand, and of outstanding, unswerving fidelity to the Church on the other; men who are in continual contact with the world of science without losing touch with the world of the spirit, for their decisions do not always flow from certain rational deductions but also from a profound understanding of all the elements involved in a particular situation, and this can be very involved indeed.

So involved, in fact, that no single individual however learned, no one institution however resourceful, can hope to solve the problem unaided. The approach has to be both interdisciplinary and international. *Interdisciplinary* first; many of today's urgent problems are multi-dimensional in the sense that they call into play different areas of competence and have a social, political, economic, psychological, philosophical and religious aspect. The approach to solving them must be an interdisciplinary one if a truly balanced solution is to be found. Here the university is in a privileged position. Isn't a Catholic university really a corporative resolve to achieve the interpenetration of religious, humanistic and scientific experience?

Then because in today's world no man, no country is an island, but all members or parts of a global village, the solutions we forge must be *international* as well. This is being increasingly recognized by research scientists in industry, food and health. What we Jesuits have not perhaps appreciated sufficiently is that we have at hand the international network that these others have to strive so mightily to establish. Your presence here today from 70 scattered centres of higher learning across the world is sufficient indication of this tremendous advantage we enjoy but do not, I fear, adequately employ.

10. Fruits of pooling and cooperation

Among the fruits to be reaped from this coming together of ours from the four corners of the world, I hope two will hold an important place in your thoughts. The first is that while our deliberations will help each of us to a deeper realization of our responsibilities and opportunities in our own particular situations, they will also enable us to *expand our vision*, so that we can see our labours in relation to the Society's apostolate, see ourselves as members and representatives of that Society. We not merely belong to a world-wide organization; we form part of a global community (*unum corpus*); *communitas dispersa*, it is true, but *communitas vera* nonetheless, deployed across the world in the service of the universal church.

A second fruit to be hoped for is that we shall take full advantage of this occasion to *deepen the bonds of brotherhood between us*, so that in the years ahead we can work as a *communitas*, and that our institutions become in truth sister institutions. I hope we shall be able to get down to some very practical projects, seeking and sharing the information we need from each other in order to plan together, exploring ways whereby we can form national, regional, continental units for mutual assistance and cooperation, and recommending how I and my Curia staff can facilitate your task. We all need to communicate more one with another: presidents among themselves;

within the Society, as you are doing here; without, as you will be doing in Delhi and Moscow. Far from adding to your burdens, this sharing will lighten them. Then, because your labours represent but one apostolate of the Society, you need to be in touch with the superiors who coordinate all the Society's apostolates. And finally, because you are on a mission of the universal church, you have to make sure that you are interpreting that mission aright.

With these considerations, I draw my opening remarks to a close. I hope that they have helped bring out the capital importance of our corporate apostolate in higher education. More than ever do we need to strengthen that apostolate today, not for the credit of a great name upon earth, not for the power or influence it may give us in the councils of nations, but purely and solely for love of God our Lord in Whom we find all the treasures of wisdom and knowledge. May He in His overflowing generosity lead us unto Himself so that with His mind we see this world, and with His heart embrace it.

9

EDUCATION FOR FAITH AND JUSTICE

MODERN LESSONS FROM AN OLD ALTAR

Father General's Homily
at the Concelebration with University Rectors

Church of the Gesù, Rome
August 5, 1975

*Early in August some 70 Jesuit Rectors and Presidents of
University Colleges from all over the world (there were 6
from India) met in Rome and were addressed by Pope Paul
VI, Cardinal Garrone and our Father General. Each day
of the conference had its concelebrated Mass, usually in
language groups. Two concelebrations for the whole group at
which Father General delivered homilies were held; the first
at the altar of St. Ignatius in the Gesù, and the second
at the altar of the Chair of St. Peter in the Vatican.*

*Here we have the homily given by Father Arrupe at and on
the altar-tomb of Saint Ignatius. Roman guides say that
this is the richest altar in Rome. The general composition
of this masterpiece—of rare marbles and precious stones,
silver and bronze, fluted columns, pedestals and pillasters,
statues and reliefs and foliated ornaments, niche and
urn—is the idea of Brother Andrea Pozzo (1642-1709)
the painter of the vault and simulated cupula of the Church
of S. Ignazio. This precious altar has very precious lessons
to teach today's Jesuits.*

*

I am sure you share with me a deeply moving sense of joy
in this Concelebration that has brought us together before the

altar of St. Ignatius. We are paying a visit to our founding
Father, to be renewed in his spirit, to spur ourselves to greater
fidelity as his sons, to receive a deeper imprint in our hearts
of the image of the Society which Ignatius has traced in the
Constitutions under the inspiration of his mystic insights and
of the personal experience which he shared with his first
companions. This same image has been presented in contemporary terms by the 32nd General Congregation, with these
words: "Today the Jesuit is a man whose mission is to dedicate
himself entirely to the service of faith and the promotion of
justice, in a communion of life and work and sacrifice with the
companions who have rallied round the same standard of the
Cross and in fidelity to the Vicar of Christ, for the building up
of a world at once more human and more divine." (*Our
Mission Today*, no. 41).

May this Concelebration lead us to a thorough renewal of
spirit; the circumstances are definitely in our favour: the
Holy Year holds out an invitation to a renewal in depth; the
recent General Congregation made the renewal of the whole
Society its one concern, and in these very days a providential
concurrence of events has brought together almost all the
presidents of Universities in the Society, who represent in their
person one of our most difficult and responsible apostolates.

This altar, a gem of the baroque style—the finest in Rome,
according to Moroni, so that whole hours would be needed
to take in all its artistic merit and material value — this altar
I regard as the symbol of the life of Ignatius, of that soldier,
so dissolute and vain, who nevertheless surrendered himself
totally to the service of the Church under the Roman Pontiff
for the greater glory of God.

Below the table rests the body of our holy Founder and
Father; a little above, cast in bronze, is a series of scenes from
his Life, surmounted by the motto that reveals the secret of
that life: "*Ad Maiorem Dei Gloriam.*" Raising our eyes higher
still we find the statue of the Saint, measuring some $9\frac{1}{2}$ feet,
vested in priestly robes to remind us of the countless divine
favours that Ignatius received in the Holy Sacrifice for the
founding and the government of the Society; so we see, at
the foot of the statue, an angel holding up the book of the

Constitutions. Two other angels raise aloft the crest with the holy Name of Jesus; and at the very crown, in a glow of clouds and shining rays, is the Blessed Trinity, gazing with redeeming love at the human race, represented by the handsome globe of lapis-lazuli.

The whole altar thus puts before us the life and mission of Ignatius: here is that body, weak and worn, that seemed to be "entirely an obstacle", weighed down with long and weary toil, aflame with zeal for the glory of God, so active in those priestly ministries and apostolate which he describes in the Constitutions as a legacy to his sons, so taken up with one ideal—"to be placed with Jesus" and to serve him, the Eternal King and Universal Lord of the Spiritual Exercises, sent by the Father to redeem the world.

If we turn our gaze once again to the altar, beginning now at the top and taking in every feature with open eyes and open heart, we may be able to grasp in all its dimensions the mission of Ignatius, which springs from that dialogue within the Trinity where the Son offers himself to the Father: "In the scroll of the book it stands written of me: God, here I am! I am coming to obey your will" (Heb. 10, 7; Ps. 39, 8), and finds its consummation in the redemptive work of Christ, which is carried on through the ages by means of weak human instruments. Our Lord welcomes Ignatius as his servant and showers on him special graces which remain with us in the Constitutions, making them the firm foundation of a new religious, apostolic and sacerdotal family. Jesus himself will be the ideal, the distinctive mark, of Ignatius—a Jesus whom he imitates with the greatest generosity in his labours for the greater glory of God, till he is consumed like Jesus in the perfect sacrifice of the *"Consummatum est"*.

This magnificent urn of gilted bronze is a symbol, both beautiful and precious, of the earth in which the grain of wheat must fall, so as to die and bear much fruit. The "old man," the man of the world, the dissolute and vain soldier that Ignatius was, died quite definitely in Loyola and Manresa, that there might rise the man of the Church, the tireless apostle, the Founder of the Society of Jesus. And the "new man" in his turn, the man of the Church at the service of God and his people, was gradually consumed in the blaze of an inner mystical flame, till his worn out body yielded its last breath in circumstances very different from those which this imposing sepulchre might suggest. Ignatius died almost alone, without the last sacraments, in the sole company of Fr. Frusius, who used to cheer him up with his clavichord in moments of sadness. He died as might die any common man of humble means. Polanco tells us: "Though he knew his end had come, he wished neither to call us for his blessing, nor to name a successor—not even a vicar, so that we must elect one—not to put the last touches on the Constitutions, nor to give any sign, as some servants of God have done in these circumstances; he just passed away in the ordinary manner of this world."

This contrast of cross and resurrection, of death and new birth, of wealth in art and poverty of life, presents a vision of Ignatius that is both impressive and true to fact. We could not grasp it in all its significance without a visit to the little rooms, the *camerette*, in which Ignatius spent his hidden life of prayer and work, in which he received such abundant mystical light, as can be seen from a mere glance at his spiritual diary. This Church of the Gesù, archetype of so many other churches of the Society, this magnificent altar, symbolic of the life of an exceptional Saint, cannot be fully understood apart from the *camerette*, in which are recorded the events that they witnessed: "Here Ignatius received wonderful revelations from the Blessed Trinity regarding the Institute of the Society"; "Here, as he was writing the Constitutions, he became aware of the Blessed Virgin giving her approval"; "Here died Ignatius of Loyola, Founder of the Society of Jesus".

From such an interior life, as intense as it was hidden, from such divine illumination, comes the great work of Ignatius, which we all admire today and to which we feel we belong as sons of that prolific family which had so humble and obscure a beginning. In his famous funeral oration of 1600, Baronius said: "We see the foliage, the fruit, the trunk which is the Society of Jesus but the root is buried in the soil; and who is that root but the Blessed Ignatius who lies hidden here?"

The mystery of the life of Ignatius invites us to reflect on our own life. For our life, too, and the vocation of each one of us, enshrines a like mystery. God grant that we experience in our last hour the transformation of the grain of wheat, that dies that it might profit others and is thus the source of an abundant harvest of glory to God.

Every Jesuit who enters this Church of the Gesù, even though he may not feel—as the Roman faithful according to Moroni—that this is the very "antechamber of paradise," is nevertheless moved with a deep sense of reverence and devotion, in this place and before this altar where rest the remains of our holy Founder. In this context of reverence and devotion let us pause a moment to reflect on what our work as Presidents of Universities means in the concrete, in a world that is so like that of Ignatius because of the period of rapid transition through which we are passing, and yet so different from his. Let us imagine that we pick up the book of the Constitutions from the angel on the altar, and open it at Part IV to read the words of Ignatius: "Care should be taken that the rector be a man of great example, edification, and mortification...discreet, fit for governing, experienced both in matters of business and of the spiritual life. He should know how to mingle severity with kindness at the proper times... and finally, be one in whom the higher superiors can confide ...The function of the rector will be first of all to sustain the whole college by his prayer and holy desires..." (423, 424). This is not a mere job description for a board of directors but rather an application of the great charter of the Society.

Let us beg St. Ignatius, who had such high regard for universities, that he give us the light to understand what is the particular significance for us, as Jesuit Presidents of Universities, of the special marks of our vocation, of our charism, of our function in the Church of today. May he help us to penetrate the meaning of being a Jesuit, as expressed by the 32nd General Congregation:

"What is it to be a Jesuit? It is to know that one is a sinner, yet called to be a companion of Jesus as Ignatius was.... What is it to be a companion of Jesus today? It is to engage, under the standard of the Cross, in the crucial struggle of our time: the struggle for faith, and that struggle for justice which it includes" (Jesuits Today, *nn. 11,12*).

In this Holy Eucharist, let us all ask one for another that we may daily become better Jesuits, more truly companions of Jesus, in the position in which Divine Providence has placed us for the service of God and of his Church. Let us aks that at our hands the Heavenly Father may receive this Sacrifice of his Son in the name of our many thousands of students and collaborators in the Universities of the Society.

10

DIALOGUE WITH FORMER JESUIT STUDENTS

Interview with Father Pedro Arrupe for the Meeting in Ghent of the World Union of Jesuit Alumni

Ghent, Belgium
August 18, 1979

Nearly 400 delegates of Associations of former Jesuit students from countries of western Europe met at Ghent, Belgium, August 20-24, 1979, to explore "Christianity and the Future of Europe" in the fields of ethics, economic and social life, formation and politics. This congress was followed by another meeting of some 50 representatives of National Federations of the World Union.

Father Arrupe, who was at the time in Latin America, sent to the Congress a taped message of proposed guidelines in the form of an interview. He stressed the need of acquaintance with the documents of Vatican II and the directives of Pope John Paul II, and the need for a deeper life of faith and prayer which is demonstrated in dedicated work. Some of the questions proposed to him earlier touched the problems of loyalty to the Holy Father, unbelief, ecumenism, human rights, and social communications.

The present text is as abridged and edited for the East Asia publication, "Asian Report".

*

1

Q: *Father Arrupe, we'd like to interview you for the summit meeting of promoters of the Jesuit alumni movement. We recall* *your presence among us at Padova two years ago and the two memorable talks you gave there. We know that your heavy schedule precluded your coming to Ghent, but we thought we might transport your voice there, if not your presence.*

My first question, Father, may seem a strange one, for it concerns a picture; namely, the picture of yourself, kneeling before Pope John Paul II to receive his blessing. People visiting the Jesuit Curia in Rome see that picture prominently displayed just after they enter the door. Many Jesuit houses have the same picture in a parlour or public place. I have even heard that you sent out individual copies to Jesuits throughout the world.

A: The picture is perhaps unusual but not the attitude it portrays nor my motives for distributing the picture. For, as you know, loyalty to the person of the Holy Father is one of the distinctive marks of the Jesuit Order. Loyalty is the "principle and foundation" of our very existence as a religious congregation. Those words are from St. Ignatius himself, and they well up from the spirit of the Spiritual Exercises.

So, the attitude of listening very carefully to the Holy Father and receiving from him, either directly or indirectly, the sense of what the Church wants—"mission" in the broad sense of the term—is at the heart of Jesuit life and apostolate.

My motive in distributing the picture widely is simple; to keep before the eyes of Jesuits throughout the world what should be our fundamental stance vis-à-vis the Holy Father, and to highlight our unconditioned readiness as apostolic body to respond to his calls and appeals.

2

Q: *Would you care to go into any further detail on this matter, Father, keeping in mind that most of us live in a pluralistic world and that we have many responsibilities in our family and in our work? I think we all want to do our share in building a world in which our families can live in peace and in which human dignity and personal rights are vindicated for every man, woman, and child. But the obstacles are enormous, and our strength is so little.*

A: Yes, that's right: obstacles are enormous and we may feel rather powerless. But let us not underestimate the power we do have. Remember that cynical question of Stalin, "How many battalions does the Pope have?" Stalin was thinking in terms of guns and bombs and the like; admittedly, the Holy Father on that plane is nothing. But think of the meeting of Jesus in the Garden of Gethsemane with the soldiers sent out to capture Him. His "I am he" spoken with divine strength and authority was enough by itself to make the soldiers fall back in fear.

I think the Holy Father is reminding each of us—indeed, the whole world — that there are ways of confronting the powers of darkness, those within and those outside of us. Consider his trips to Mexico and to Poland. Did he not show that by expressing publicly our belief in God we make it easier for others to believe and express that belief? In so doing, he helped the peoples of Mexico and Poland—not to mention those of other countries—counteract the conspiracy of silence about God and His world, which has thrown a pall over so many people. In effect, he said in the market place as well as in the church, "God lives, His name is love, His desire is to save. He has designs on you and even more than you He wants you to grow, to become what you are called to be."

So, concretely, I would say: let all of us give ourselves in creative fidelity to the God Who has given us life. Let us not be afraid to be generous with Him. Let us really take seriously what we pray every day in the "Our Father." Let us live in such a way that others will be heartened to say "Our Father" and mean it.

3

Q: *But, Father, pardon me if I say that that is beautiful and true. But it's somewhat up in the air. Could you be a bit more specific, keeping in mind that you are speaking to lay men and women with all of our own concerns.*

A: Yes, I was a bit "in the air," I guess. So now I will descend from the air and from the broader view that being up there enables one to have. Let me ask some very concrete questions.

a) How many of our Jesuit alumni have really read and meditated on the documents of Vatican II? Excuse me if I ask such an elementary question. I do so, because one who does not take that Ecumenical Council with utmost seriousness is not "thinking with the Church" and cannot understand what the Holy Spirit is trying to effect in our times.

b) How many of our Jesuit alumni have tried to explain the teaching of Christ to those with whom they live and work when they are asked or when there is an occasion to explain? Have we, perhaps, without being aware of it, tacitly agreed that the time for Christ is Sunday—and then only an hour—and that the rest of the week is for more "serious" matters?

c) Are we trying to grow in a spirit of prayer? From the very beginning of His active life, our Lord stressed over and over again that prayer is the air of any serious spiritual life; that unless we pray we become entrapped by our own selfishness and by the desires of the world. The Lord has sown the seed. Where has it fallen—in my life? On the hard earth? By the wayside? Among thistles? On good ground?

d) Are we shocked by the fact of Christian dis-unity? Do we see it as a scandal? Are we trying to diminish it? What means have we taken to promote that unity for which Jesus prayed at the Last Supper?

e) Pope Paul VI gave a special mission to the Society to study atheism and to play an active role in work with atheists. Are we aware of the importance that this vast problem has today? In many sectors of life, God doesn't count, He is looked on as a "useless concept" meaningless for modern man. And in our own life of every day, is God not absent in practical ways? Is there anyone among our relatives who has lost the faith? What is our reaction to such a situation?

4

Q: *Father, let me interrupt. But you mentioned something about an "important development in the government of the Society of Jesus". What do you refer to and how does it affect us as alumni?*

A: Thank you for reminding me. The development is this. We are rediscovering that the Jesuit mission is universal, wherever the apostolic needs are greater, and we can help in a significant way (*"magis"*). This means that we have to think and plan to respond to more universal needs—or more urgent, burning needs and that our structures of government must help the greater mobility and flexibility that this implies. So, we now have in most countries a provincial who looks to national, rather than more local needs, while in Europe, Africa, East Asia, and the Americas we have more frequent meetings of national provincials to look precisely at apostolic needs that transcend national boundaries. These groups of provincials are beginning to spell out their priorities, which should be taken to heart by all Jesuits in that area.

First of all, a *deep personal conversion* on the part of all Jesuits and those with whom we work, including our former students. By "conversion" I mean an unflagging inner process in which we mold our attitudes to the Good News of Christ and guide our entire life by the faith we profess.

Secondly, an intensification of our *service* for others, under the impulse of the love and example of Christ, in Whom we are all brothers. This gift of ourselves means that we reject the spirit of selfishness and acquisitiveness (consumerism) that lies at the root of the evils of society.

Thirdly, implementing *human rights*, both individual and social, especially that first of all rights—the right to life. We want to join forces with those who fight in defence of the rights of the family, the victim of modern materialism and hedonism, and to do our share to eliminate the injustice and oppression that are the scourge of the world.

Fourthly, strengthening the apostolate of *education* in all its forms:—from literacy campaigns to the university and research.

Fifthly, the better and more extended use of *means of social communication*. For they are the means par excellence for proclaiming the Gospel, forming public opinion, and defending the human rights about which I was speaking.

In sixth place, the *continuing education and formation* of all of us, Jesuits included. We would like in a special way to help our former students to whose basic formation we contributed according to the norms of the times. We are all morally obliged to carry on our formation, building on foundations laid down in our school days, and thus responding to the orientations and spirit of the Second Vatican Council, in points that at times are of great importance. In this way we are able to respond personally, professionally, socially, and apostolically to the rightful expectations the Church has of us.

In seventh place, helping our alumni to become more and more *aware of the social and political issues* that we face, and in this way to reach ever larger sectors of society. . . It is you, graduates of our institutions working in concert with other members of the laity, who bear the responsibility of bringing Christian thought to grips with the issues of justice, peace and welfare which affect modern life. Should you not be at your post or remain indifferent, you may well be failing deplorably, and responsibility for that omission you cannot run away from. Neither the Church as such nor the Society of Jesus can directly enter the political arena by espousing a party line or a particular ideology. It is the laity who must make the concrete choices, and for that an adequate formation and awareness are indispensable.

5

Q: *So, let me see now what you are implying. You say that the Society of Jesus as such is organizing itself to decide with greater flexibility what it should be doing on a broader scale. And I think you are implying that, as former students, we should be aware of this change and ask ourselves how it affects our own organizations. Is that the point?*

A: Exactly. What is at stake here is a key concept of St. Ignatius; namely, *universality*. The day of compartmentalization is past.' Look, St. Ignatius used to say, 450 years ago, that "the more universal the good, the more divine it is." What was for him an intuition has today become a fact of life. Practically all of the great themes of our time—economic, cultural, social, structural—are planet-wide in scale. Interdependence is now a fact of life, a fact of almost unimaginable proportions and implications.

The Society of Jesus, which was aware of some of the meaning of interdependence from its origins, must therefore loosen up its structures with a view to universality. Its members must be completely available and ready to move in order to serve with effectiveness where the need is greater, more urgent, more universal, less attended to. Structures, therefore must be very flexible.

I think that this emphasis on availability and mobility has some implications for alumni associations. The World Union should develop into a united apostolic force, compact, strong. This vision of the World Union, I know, seems to have encountered difficulties which have not yet been overcome. I suppose I have to resign myself to that fact, despite my insistence for many years on this way of seeing the World Union. I fear, however, that alumni of the future will condemn us for our myopia and lack of efficiency if we fail to vitalize the World Union. Perhaps, despite what I have tried to do, I must accept part of the responsibility. But no matter; I will not give up. I will continue to insist on universality, confident that the facts will bear out its importance and that perhaps what now seems impossible can soon be a reality. I have not given up hope.

INDEX OF LETTER
on
INTELLECTUAL APOSTOLATE

II

THE INTELLECTUAL APOSTOLATE IN THE SOCIETY'S MISSION

A Letter of Father General Pedro Arrupe to the Whole Society

Rome
December 25, 1976

Referring to this letter on the Intellectual Apostolate, Father General said to the Delegates of the Provinces gathered with him in the Congregation of Procurators in his Report on the State of the Society (No. 24):

"I consider the Intellectual Apostolate one of the most privileged means for that defence and spreading of the faith mentioned in the first paragraph of the Formula of our Institute. Consequently I tried to dispel all doubts arising about the validity of this apostolate today by publishing a letter to the whole Society reaffirming its importance for the service of the Church and the readiness of the Society to undertake it"

*

Dear Brothers in Christ:

I write to you about the intellectual apostolate for two main reasons.

First, I want to stress its importance for our mission today. Some doubt this and ask whether the intellectual apostolate still has a place in the Society after the 32nd General Congregation. Certainly this uneasiness vanishes to a large extent when the documents of the General Congregation are carefully studied and really understood. Meanwhile, my duty to help the Society to carry out its mission ever more effectively moves me to insist on the need for a fresh approach to the intellectual apostolate in our day. The first part of my letter will deal with this topic.

The other reason that prompts me to write—perhaps the more important in fact—is that the 32nd General Congregation has posed certain questions about the intellectual apostolate and has given some guidelines to those engaged in it. I feel it is my duty to comment on and stress some of them. This will be the subject of the second part.

While addressing myself primarily to those directly involved in the intellectual apostolate, I write to all Jesuits because they all need a correct understanding of its place in the whole spectrum of our ministries and because, in the end, all our efforts in every field contribute to the one, integral mission of the Society.

Another preliminary remark: perhaps some may expect me to begin with a definition of the "intellectual apostolate". I'm afraid that there is none that would satisfy everyone or do justice to such a complex reality. I'll content myself, then, with stating very simply what I have in mind when using this expression.

I visualize at one and the same time an apostolate through intellectual activities and an apostolate among intellectuals. I have in mind involvement in science, research, reflection, literature, art; but I think also of many other tasks of training and teaching, of publication and also of popularization. And when I speak of "intellectuals", I mean not only scholars, research specialists, academicians and also artists, but no less, professional men whose activity is more specifically intellectual. Moreover, I think also of the young who are starting out on serious study. Intellectual pursuits begin even as early as the secondary school level. I will be dealing, however, more particularly with later stages.

FIRST PART

THE INTELLECTUAL APOSTOLATE
IN THE FRAMEWORK OF THE SOCIETY'S OPTIONS TODAY

What connection has the intellectual apostolate with the

mission of the Society today? And what place should this apostolate have in our work at present?

Intellectual and Cultural Crisis and Change

The answer is plain, it seems to me, when one looks at the needs of contemporary man. It is enough here to recall the judgment of the 32nd General Congregation about the state of the world at the present moment: there is widespread injustice but, equally, a profound crisis and change in the intellectual realm.

The General Congregation spelled out this latter aspect at the beginning of Decree 4 when it stressed the fact that "many of our contemporaries (are) dazzled and even dominated by the achievements of the human mind" (n. 5) and went on to describe the effects of progress in technology and the human sciences (n. 25).

Those cultural and structural changes are closely linked with "secularization" (n. 26).

Intellectual Dimension of the Key Options

Matters become clearer still when we move from a diagnosis of the situation to the priorities that the 32nd General Congregation derived from it: the service of faith and the promotion of justice. Both are described, in fact, as having important intellectual dimensions.

First, the service of faith. "We must find a new language", the Congregation says, "a new set of symbols" (D. 4, n. 26a) for the renewal and adaptation of "the structures of theological reflection, catechesis, liturgy and the pastoral ministry" (D. 4, n. 54), and for the study of "the main problems confronting humanity and the Church today" (D. 4, n. 60).

Likewise, the promotion of justice. It implies that we "are prepared to undertake the difficult and demanding labour of study" required for understanding and solving contemporary problems (D. 4, n. 35; cf. n. 44). At the same time, the General Congregation lays stress on the unjust structures of society (D. 4, nn. 31, 40). But how can we understand these structures and discover ways to modify them, without serious study?

An Objection

Despite all these requirements is there not a danger that the 32nd General Congregation is diverting us from intellectual matters and minimizing this apostolate by its stress on "the service of the poor" (D. 4, n. 60) or its desire that we become actively involved with "the voiceless and powerless" (D. 4, n. 42)?

An answer to this difficulty calls for certain distinctions. It is a fact that we can hardly serve the poor if we do not have real contact with them and enough actual experience of their life. Still, it is equally true that, for that very goal of promoting justice and serving the poor, we need to collaborate with other people besides the poor. We must have contact with those who exert influence on social structures (n. 43) or "who have the power to bring about social change" or are "persons who themselves will multiply the work of worldwide education" (D. 4, n. 60). The point is that intellectuals are in the ranks of those who wield influence on society. Moreover, it is partly, though not exclusively, from among young intellectuals that agents of social change continue to be drawn.

From the General Invitation to Serious Intellectual Work to the Need for an Intellectual Apostolate that is Detailed and Organized

It has to be noted, as well, that the General Congregation calls for the most profound intellectual effort in every Jesuit enterprise. Nonetheless, even though it is here most explicit, what it says cannot be boiled down to this single point. Speaking of the range of our actual works, for instance, the General Congregation mentions two that are closely linked with the intellectual apostolate: the education of youth ("continuing and more effective"); "theological research and reflection" (D. 4, n. 60). Moreover, it expressly confirms the decrees of the 31st General Congregation, many of which deal with the intellectual apostolate (DD. 28, 29, 30). And in the same way it backs up the 31st General Congregation's statement about the urgent need of having priests involved in "scientific research and teaching, especially in the sacred sciences"—"a genuine apostolate for the Society's priests" (GC. 31, n. 8).

But apart altogether from these references, it is clear that the Society as a "body" could not do justice to the intellectual dimension attaching to our key apostolic options unless a sufficient number of its members are committed with a special priority to research, to science, and, more broadly, to an apostolate that is explicitly intellectual. And further, what better means do we have, in many cases, for carrying out these tasks than well-organized centres, universities, colleges, research institutes, periodicals (cf. D. 4, n. 7)?

The Pope's Recommendations

To conclude this point let me remind you that after having listened to the General Congregation we ought to recall that our mission comes to us from an even higher source. For certain comments of the Pope, in whose light we ought to interpret the General Congregation itself, have an especially important bearing here. Think, for example, of his description of the Society (in his allocution of December 3, 1974) as "the Society of those 'sent' by the Church", to which he immediately added this further precision: "Hence there have come theological research and teaching...; the social apostolate and intellectual and cultural activity which extends from schools for the solid and complete education of youth to all the levels of advanced university studies and scholarly research."

A little further on, you will remember, the Pope singles out as a kind of hallmark of the Society, the fact that "even in the most difficult and extreme fields, in the crossroads of ideologies, in the front line of social conflict, where there has been and there is confrontation between the deepest desires of man and the perennial message of the Gospel, there also have been, and there are, Jesuits."

Obviously, he is not dealing only with the intellectual apostolate. Still, who can be blind to the fact that it occupies a special place in the Pope's view of things?

Moreover, Paul VI did not fail to remind us of the charge committed to us in 1965 on the subject of atheism: a mandate whose execution, at least in part, involves an intellectual apostolate. And on August 6, 1975, in the presence of the rectors and presidents of Jesuit universities, he reaffirmed the "serious mission" of the "Society within modern culture."

Going Beyond These Remarks ...

It is clearly impossible, without turning a simple letter into a treatise, to express in all their theological profundity the links between understanding or knowledge and faith or evangelization. Rather, I look to those of you who have reflected on these matters to produce this explanation. But this at least is clear: the mission that we have received and our options today call for a strong commitment to various types of intellectual apostolate.

SECOND PART

GUIDELINES OF THE 32ND GENERAL CONGREGATION FOR THE INTELLECTUAL APOSTOLATE

Does this mean simply the continuation of what we have traditionally done and, where necessary, the resumption of an activity that has been dropped here or there, or the initiation of new works and the modification in certain respects of existing ones?

The answer, I believe, must include both, with the need for wise discernment according to the circumstances. It is, to be sure, precisely for such discernment that the last General Congregation, and even more so the Constitutions, have furnished us with criteria.

The intellectual apostolate, just like other types of ministry we perform (D. 4, nn. 70ff), must be subjected to reappraisal and the Jesuits engaged in it ought in their own way to examine themselves on the questions put to all of us by the 32nd General Congregation (D. 4, n. 74). But, without being able to cover the whole ground, there are also certain particularly pertinent matters on which I wish to insist at this moment.

Choices of Areas and Subjects

In the first place, areas of the intellectual apostolate must be chosen in accordance with the key criteria designated by the General Congregation: the service of faith and the promotion of justice. It is especially necessary that these same criteria be used in guiding young Jesuits who have talents for these areas. Not every type of intellectual work or research is equally compatible with the aims of our mission. On the other hand, we are in fact far from being really involved in the intellectual field in all those areas to which we are summoned by the options of the last General Congregation.

When we come to the various disciplines, our criteria suggest that first place be given, as the 31st General Congregation had already asked (D. 29, n. 1B), to the sacred sciences, whether exegesis, theology, morals or spirituality. Our responsibility is here all the greater because the number of others working in this service of the Church is less.

On the same count, a priority must be given to philosophy, a field in which we need to improve our strength, and to the human sciences, including the social sciences (31st GC, D. 23, n. 8; 32nd GC, D. 4, nn. 35, 44).

It remains likewise useful, of course, to have some of our men engaged in the mathematical and natural sciences. The process of discernment must be more rigorous here, however, than with respect to the priorities given the theological and human sciences. Still, more than one factor is at work here. You will recall that the 31st General Congregation recognized the influence exercised by the mathematical and natural sciences, with the help of philosophers and popularizers, on the formation of the "contemporary mentality". How can we maintain suitable theological reflection however, without possessing a deep understanding of the well-springs of this mentality? Moreover, how otherwise can we guarantee the Church's presence and effective personal contacts in an important sector of the scientific and technological world? One should add that the achievements of the exact and natural sciences are often excellent means of helping men to overcome evils and sufferings of all kinds: here indeed is a summons of love.

Clearly we are not in a position to attempt to do everything. Our numbers would be too few and we would be scattering our forces. Still, it helps to keep an eye on the lengthy list of possibilities that are in principle open to our apostolic initiative or of areas that fit in with our vocation in terms of existing needs and our available resources. And I realize, too, that we ought to extend that list to include literature as well as the fine arts and the mass media, fields in which cooperation among Jesuits has lately experienced a welcome increase.

In order to make more exact choices, personal talents and callings must be taken into consideration and, with an eye to the future, a careful scrutiny made of what is relatively most urgent and most needed in different places.

I would be very grateful to those whose experience of the broad range of contemporary culture suggests further specifications for our choices if they would share their insights with me for the sake of the common good.

Research, Teaching, other Forms of Apostolic Involvement with Intellectuals

The same criteria should also determine the properly balanced distribution of our resources among research, teaching and other forms of apostolic involvement with intellectuals. Research looks in fact to the long range and on that account has always enjoyed a certain priority in the Society ("a more lasting good"). The education of youth has been understood by the 31st General Congregation as one of the sectors "where the destiny of the human person is at stake in a special way" (D. 23, n. 8); and the 32nd General Congregation has not contradicted that stand (cf. D. 4, n. 60). As to other types of apostolic involvement with intellectuals, they derive their significance from the communication they make possible with men and women who commonly exercise a considerable influence on their contemporaries, and even on society taken as a whole and on its structures.

Let me add, at this point, that every centre of higher studies under the direction of the Society—and in a very special way, every centre of theological and philosophical studies—has the responsibility of maintaining a high standard both for teaching and also for at least some carefully chosen branches of research. And such research programmes must undergo the same regular evaluation as the teaching programmes.

As to an apostolate on behalf of intellectuals that is neither scientific work on a full-time basis nor educational activity in the proper meaning, I would like to stress how important it is that those who are engaged in this way should be sufficiently open, at the scientific level, to the fields in which those they meet are working. They ought also keep in touch on a continuing basis with developments in these fields and at the same time in theology so as to keep pace with the problems that arise.

Continuing Formation of Men in Intellectual Work

Research men and teachers, to be sure, do not enjoy a special exemption from the rapid outdating of their first training. All, therefore, should ask themselves this question: who knows if we have not more or less abandoned serious study and our intellectual, as well as spiritual, renewal, the day we finished our doctorate or shortly after that?

The summons of the 32nd General Congregation to continuing formation (D. 6, nn. 18-20, 35) does not apply solely to apostolic men involved in pastoral ministries. Moreover, we ought to be well aware that the continuing formation of a Jesuit involved in intellectual pursuits implies, among other things, an attentive listening, not only to developments in theology, but also to the experience of companions who perhaps have more direct contact with men, or more frequent contacts with a far greater variety of people, including the most ordinary.

Collaboration, Interdisciplinary or Multidisciplinary Work

The last two General Congregations have stressed, moreover, the importance of collaboration among Jesuits in different disciplines and even of interdisciplinary research (31st GC, D. 3, n. 14; 32nd GC, D. 4, n. 60). We are well aware of the practical difficulties involved in multidisciplinary work if it is to be anything other than superficial. It cannot even begin unless each one perceives and grasps the questions that confront him from other disciplines as well as from his own. And mention should also be made of the fact that the Society needs at least some men who are researchers of a new type, men equipped with a gift for synthesis that inclines towards those global, deep and unified solutions demanded by the great human problems. But it is also necessary, as a general rule, to overcome our individualism and a tendency to self-centeredness that makes a man turn in on his own field.

We ought to be especially concerned about the concrete application of different disciplines to the study of questions posed by the local situation. In this connection, a realistic encounter ought to take place, not only among the several sciences, but also between those who have, for example, an existential acquaintance with the realities of poverty and those who investigate them rather from an intellectual point of view. When you take into consideration the variety of our intellectual activities, the geographical spread of the Society and the breadth of its contacts with different cultures and groups, it is easy to see that we have exceptional opportunities for interdisciplinary efforts. We thus have a great responsibility, and we are obliged to make an organized effort to cast light on these "great problems that the Church and mankind must face today" and that the 32nd General Congregation has called to our attention in a special way: problems that are almost always multidisciplianry. How often, in fact, do we touch them only in passing, on the surface, because we approach them only by starting out from the particular frame of reference that is familiar to each of us?

Care for Sensitivity and Simplicity

Another requirement for today's intellectual apostolate is a broad human sensitivity, one that embraces all categories of men, including the most marginalized.

I have also in mind the need to eliminate in ourselves, and to work for the elimination around us, of an arrogance or contempt with respect to the non-intellectual, an insensitivity born of a certain "objectivity" that the intellectual life sometimes produces.

There is an illusion involved in the wish to do away with all differences that exist among the different types of work men do, for example intellectual and manual, or the like. There is a genuine quest for justice, however, in the wish to eliminate the pride or contempt that is linked to these differences or the privileges that are sometimes derived from them. Don't we too often give in to the feelings of superiority? Has not each received almost everything from society? Don't we occasionally take advantage of such practical privileges? And all this when we ought to give a clear example.

Witness of Poverty in the Intellectual Apostolate

This entire matter is not divorced from our profession of poverty, another topic that the General Congregation asks us to review. Poverty is not limited to material dimensions; or, if you wish, poverty is also a thing of the spirit. This involves making available to everyone all that has been given us; it calls for modesty and collaboration; it calls for generosity in sharing our learning; it calls for acceptance of the little man.

On the other hand, as the 32nd General Congregation states, "solidarity with men who live a difficult life and suffer collective oppression cannot be the job of only some Jesuits." For our present purposes let us agree that this is demanded also of those who devote themselves to the intellectual apostolate. Perhaps they are not the ones who, to be sure, can most "partake of the lot of families of slender means", but still there are certain men who will be inspired to this sharing and at the same time to a life of intense intellectual work. I wish to encourage them with a view to discovering a new style of apostolic intellectual involvement. At least, all Jesuits involved in intellectual work are invited, as are the rest of the Society, to a conversion of their mode or style of life. Allowance being made for the legitimate needs that arise from the specific work of intellectuals, we are scarcely obliged to live in all respects like those with whom we work. Moreover, some intellectuals, of whatever persuasion, in this regard set a striking example that is far removed from prevailing middle-class standards. Could it be that we Jesuits are in arrears about desiring to be identified "with the poor Christ who himself is identified with the most defenceless" (D. 4, n. 48)? A witness of poverty, appropriate to the existing circumstances, is not only possible, but necessary, in the intellectual apostolate.

Fidelity to the Evangelical and Apostolic Motives of our Intellectual Commitment?

We are, in the end, religious apostles and very many of us are priests. It is, as I have said, under the very title of the apostolate and the priesthood that we commit ourselves to research, to scientific investigation, to teaching at the higher level, and to every sort of apostolic service in the intellectual world. But it is not enough to start off on the right foot. It still remains necessary, over the course of the years, to maintain a balance in such a life.

Those who dedicate themselves to the intellectual apostolate ought also, in accord once again with the advice of the 31st General Congregation, "to be on guard against the illusion that they could serve God in a more suitable fashion in other works that are apparently more pastoral" (D. 29, n. 2). They should not, then, allow themselves to become absorbed, after a few years of scientific work, by ministries that in certain respects are more attractive, to the detriment of their intellectual commitment.

But, while remaining faithful to this commitment, they ought to be equally alert to keep alive in their minds and hearts the explicitly evangelical and apostolic motives for which they undertook this work. Let us then put the question to ourselves again: have we not at times, caught up in the stream of life and in the absence of a frequently renewed awareness of our vocation, allowed our existence to be reduced to a type of research or intellectual exercise that no longer has a relationship to the service of the Gospel and has lost, for us as for other people, its apostolic meaning? If things stand that way, let us realize that unless we recapture the basic inspiration of our commitment, we place our vocation in danger, we risk in many cases becoming apostolically ineffective. This renewal ought to be regular, frequent, even constant, as one notices in the example, old and new, of Jesuit scholars and intellectuals who are recognised by all as apostles. It is particularly essential that each man should work out, and unceasingly renew, on his own and in a very personal fashion, the integration of his intellectual work and his priesthood. Free of inner divisions, the priesthood should vitalize our intellectual life even when the latter appears to be secular in certain respects.

Remaining "Sent on Mission"

As Jesuits, we are "men on a mission" (D. 2, n. 14). This essential characteristic holds true for the intellectual apostolate as for other types of mission. Yet here, the years that pass involve the risk, if we are not careful, of having an erosive impact. Thus, even though he enjoys scholarly prestige, or holds down important posts in the scientific and university world, a Jesuit should never stop practising the virtue of availability. Even if he is riveted to many aspects of a task that appears to demand his entire life, he must preserve this availability. Let us therefore accept with simplicity the summons that the 32nd General Congregation has made to us when it insists so strongly on mission.

Integrated into the Body of the Society

I wish further to stress what the General Congregation has given us in its vision of a mission "as a body". What is demanded here is integration of all tasks, including therefore all types of intellectual apostolate, in the apostolic plan of the Province, and in any case in that of the Society as a whole. This takes for granted that all enter into the spirit of that mutual support that different tasks should lend one another, and that all are open to common deliberation on various apostolic aims and their integration, under the responsibility of Superiors.

The Case of an Intellectual Apostolate of a more Individual Type

It is even more important that certain men should carry on an intellectual apostolate of a highly individual nature, outside the centres of the Society. Such an apostolate can fit perfectly within our vocation; it is at times the only way open to cultivate a given discipline; it can be essential for contact between the Church and certain milieux. Yet the motivations behind such commitments should be made the subject of a true spiritual discernment on the part of the men involved and of their superiors. The latter should attach great importance, in the matter of the choice of persons, to the heavy human and religious demands that will be asked of them. At the Province level it is certainly necessary before multiplying such commitments, that they be weighed carefully on the score of their apostolic values and in the concrete circumstances, against possibilities available through an apostolate that uses existing centres of the Society. Today as yesterday, many of the criteria for our choices that are set down in the Constitutions tend to favour, where the possibility exists, lasting centres, of extensive outreach, where activities are coordinated. Moreover, the Pope has recently reminded us, on his part, of the value of Catholic universities (*Address to the Presidents of Jesuit Universities*, August 6, 1975).

One way or other, men who receive a mission to engage in a more individualized intellectual apostolate must not become isolated in a Province, either through their own doing or that of the Province. The Provincial should exercise a special concern for these men, especially in their first years in such a ministry. Their work ought to emerge as an integral contribution to the corporate effort, thanks to frequent contacts, a deep mutual acquaintance, and participation in common discernment. Much less should these men be isolated in their own local communities.

Fidelity to the Church
because the Mission is from the Church

"Men on a mission", it is true, but it is always a mission from the Church that we have, even when our assignment comes from Jesuit superiors. I have quoted above the words of Paul VI on the Society as "sent by the Church", a description that he has applied to various works but in a very special way to undertakings of our intellectual apostolate. This means that, while making use of his legitimate freedom of research, every Jesuit intellectual, especially a theologian, ought to have an acute awareness of his duty in fidelity to the Church, and to act in fact with responsibility. This is also a point that the 32nd General Congregation has stressed for us.

Balance of Religious and Priestly Life

I return again, finally, to the balance of our religious and priestly life in which we should grow. Those who are priests, the 31st General Congregation tells us, should remain "united with all other priests in one total priestly ministry for the sake of men" (D. 23, n. 12). Since I am aware that the Brothers play their part in the intellectual apostolate, and that some scholastics have already had an introduction to it before they are ordained, I add that the same recommendation holds true for them; close union with all those who work in the Church's apostolate.

But I wish further to specify something that is taught us by experience: anyone who moves ahead in the intellectual life, whether it be in an area that is to all appearances secular or not, but who does not make progress at the same time in deepening his faith, exposes himself to danger (cf. 76/15). In the same way, without being able here to set down a general rule in view of the diversity of needs and circumstances, it can be said that the proper balance of the priestly life of a Jesuit intellectual often demands that he be involved to some extent in a ministry that is more directly pastoral, or among poorer people.

The Eucharist, finally, ought always to be plainly at the centre of his life: the sacrament of the consummation of all that transformation of the world which we strive to bring about by knowledge as well as by action (cf. 31st GC, D. 23, n. 12; 32nd GC, D. 11, n. 35).

CONCLUSION

In sum, today is no time to slacken the Society's commitment to the intellectual apostolate. This is certainly as true in the wake of the 32nd General Congregation as it was after the 31st General Congregation. It is the time, however, to search out new fields of involvement in this apostolate. It is the time to give a new style to this endeavour, in tune with the demands of faith and justice that the 32nd General Congregation stressed. It is the time to overcome factors that make for isolation, the time for interdisciplinary work and the apostolic integration of all our labours. It is, further, the time for a renewal of "mission" and of the spirit of mission.

In closing this letter I call on the Provincials to be concerned about the proper place of the intellectual apostolates in the planning of ministries for tomorrow.

I call on young Jesuits, who have the ability to prepare themselves for such works, to be open to them: this means facing up to long-term investments that yield deferred results, and a readiness to live patiently and, in a special way, in faith. Those who are in charge of formation should support and encourage such men in this effort.

All those, finally, who have already made this commitment and whose lives are being spent in this field—whether it be research, teaching or other forms of activity among intellectuals—I call on to return to the roots of their commitment if there is need, to rediscover its motives and to work to discover this new style of intellectual apostolate that the 32nd General Congregation demands.

If it should happen that they give in to bitterness in the face of a lack of understanding, let them seek strength in the Lord to overcome this sentiment through contact with the apostolic aspirations that animated the last General Congregation. Their renewal, based on their vocation, will enhance the effectiveness of the demanding life to which they are committed, often in an irrevocable manner. It will also provide a model and an encouragement to our young men that they need at the moment of their own entrance on a future whose austerity they perceive. By far one of the best examples will be always that of a fraternal union with the other Jesuits of the Province who are busy with other tasks and involved in other spheres.

As I am putting the last touches to this letter, all of mankind is about to celebrate Christmas. May the Word of God who broke into this earth of ours truly be the Light that illuminates our quests, the Wisdom presiding over our deliberations, and the Presence dwelling in our hearts.

Pedro Arrupe

Rome

On the Feast of the Nativity of

Our Lord

December 25, 1976.

Superior General

of the Society of Jesus.

12

JESUIT SCIENTISTS UNITE

A letter of Father General to the Group of Jesuit Scientists in India

Rome
April 28, 1980

An initial result of Father General's letter on the Intellectual Apostolate was that it inspired 16 Jesuit scientists in India to meet at Bangalore for a two-day seminar in April 1978 to reflect on the significance of the 'mission' they had received from the Society.

Official backing was not lacking. The local Archbishop and the Provincial of Karnataka were present. Fr Casimir Gnanadickam, a Doctor in Chemistry, and now Regional Assistant for India, gave the keynote address. The Provincial of India and that of Madurai also participated.

A Secretariate of the group of Jesuit Scientists was soon set up, with Fr Joe V. D'Souza as Secretary and editor of the quarterly INTERACT. The following letter of Father General is in reply to the official report of the objectives and activities of the group for 1979. The reflections and recommendations of Father General may be of general interest to other Jesuits.

*

Dear Father D'Souza,

I must first thank you for your excellent report of the Secretariat for the year ending 1979. I find it objective, deep, going into all the aspects of the scientific apostolate among Jesuits, pointing out the needs for the future and the tremendous opportunities that present themselves to Jesuit Scientists

from an apostolic point of view. Both Father Assistant and
the Provincial of India have kept me informed about the
progress of the Jesuit Scientists of the Indian Assistancy.
I think that it is one of the most successful efforts in the whole
Society to bring Jesuit Scientists together, and as such I
cannot but congratulate you and commend you for being
actively involved in the Secretariat and for editing regularly
the bulletin of communication INTERACT. Communication
is a very important part of this effort and I wish that you keep
it up as generously as you can and if there is any difficulty in
this that you let me know.

I think that you have touched upon every significant point
that concerns the Jesuit Scientists in India. I shall briefly
comment upon them more to emphasise them than to add
anything new.

You have rightly elaborated on the need for collaboration
among the Jesuits working in this area. You have only to
look at my letter on the Intellectual Apostolate and the relevant passages in the decree of the 31st and 32nd General
Congregations, referred to by Father Casimir during the first
meeting, to see how much this is in the best of the Society's
tradition. It is true, all cannot be engaged in this difficult
apostolate; but such apostolates should never be lacking in the
Society. Study in depth and working for long term objectives
should characterise this effort. Thus it needs men who are not
only willing to do hidden hard work, but men who will work
with a deep sense of faith, being content with sowing where
others will reap.

I see collaboration necessary so that Jesuits working in this
area will 'confirm' each other. In 2. 4. you speak about the need
of some to work in public sector undertakings. I have mentioned
this in my letter on the Intellectual Apostolate. However
I would add that this should be done in the spirit of GC 32,
d. 4 nn. 45, 65 with great care in the choice of persons and in
their continued relationship with the community.

Secondly I would emphasise the role of the Jesuit scientist
as one who could train young men in research to a sense
of objectivity, to a commitment to truth. How many of our
alumni prize not so much the content of knowledge that they

received, as the spirit, the method, the criteria they learnt from their Jesuit educators! Concerning the content of the subjects of research, we should be aware of our limitations and therefore develop criteria in the choice of the subjects, like what others are not doing, what will be of greater service to the poor and neglected, areas where we can do collaborative work etc.

What you say about the directly apostolic aspect of the Jesuit Scientist's work is very important, under its double aspect of theological - philosophical reflection, and the aspect of presence among men of science. Here I would emphasise the need for Indian Jesuits to reflect more on Indian problems, and make their just contribution to the work of the Society. An interdisciplinary formation in the same man, e.g. a scientist doing some advanced studies in theology or philosophy and vice versa is what seems to have given the best results so far. This of course does not exclude common meetings between scientists and theologians. This is all the more necessary in the context of the Pope's mandate to us to combat atheistic and secularist tendencies by reflecting on the roots of these trends and meet the challenges they pose to our Faith in certain values, and in Salvation History.

Well, dear Father D'Souza, I think I have written enough to tell you how much I am interested in this apostolate of our Jesuit Scientists of the Indian Assistancy, and how much I wish it to grow. I shall convey to the Superiors your desire for greater support and inspiration from them.

Rome   Devotedly yours in Christ our Lord,
28 April 1980   **Pedro Arrupe, S.J.**

13

SOCIAL COMMUNICATIONS: INVESTIGATION AND COLLABORATION

(A)

Apostolic Priority for Religious

Rome
April 24, 1973

The following introductory address was given by Father Pedro Arrupe—as President of the Union of Superiors General (USG)—during the Mass Media Information Day for Superiors General and Assistants, which was organized by the Secretariats of the UISG (International Union of Superiors General), the USG, and Multi-Media International. The original text was in Italian and the translation is by JESCOM International.

*

Just a few words to welcome you here. I do not think it is necessary to stress the importance of the means of social communications in today's world. Your presence here shows clearly your interest in this increasingly important sector of the Church's apostolate.

What is more important is to follow through from these premises, moving from an abstract knowledge of the extreme importance of these media of communication to the necessary measures to develop them as much as possible.

Let me emphasize very briefly two citeria which seem to me fundamental in this matter.

1. Apostolic priority

The first criterion refers to the need of apostolic priorities.
If we want to develop the apostolate of the mass media—
in which, up to now, we have used very inadequate means—
with our limited personnel and financial resources, we will
have to sacrifice other activities which traditionally we have
developed, but which today have lost their value, or at least
are less important in the scale of apostolic priorities of our
institutions. This sacrifice of activities which for many years
have been preferred, especially when the extinguishing or
slow death of them is necessary, will provoke a painful crisis.
But we have to be steadfast, and sometimes logic is cold and
pitiless.

We can't do everything; so we should ask ourselves in all
sincerity: Are we ready to sacrifice other forms of apostolate?
Are we ready to do so in spite of the protests and frustrations
of the people who have worked at such great sacrifice and so
meritoriously in those activities, because we are convinced
that today they are less important than the means of social
communication? There is no doubt that to do so we shall need
plenty of courage and energy. Otherwise our decisions will
remain mere words, which the wind will blow away!

2. Mutual cooperation necessary

The second criterion refers to indispensable mutual collaboration. We have to realize our weakness: we all know that each
institution separately cannot face an apostolate which needs
financial aid and trained personnel. Nobody is capable of
creating alone a programme adequate for the situation, or to
exert a strong influence in this field and on public opinion.
This realistic and humble admission of our helplessness must
lead us to opening a way towards collaboration and the unifica-
tion of our efforts in order to offer the Church a service so
necessary today. An individualistic and exclusive isolation
would be not only anachronistic and anti-strategic, but also
suicidal, for the fact is that nobody can survive in this activity
so necessary today, without the collaboration of others.

It is a fact that recently there have been more opportunities
and a great desire for collaboration. But this progress is more

evident in attitudes than in practical terms. Obviously the beginning will be something very modest, a small seed, like a pilot project, that will be able to grow rapidly, to dimensions beyond our present expectations.

God willing, in the spirit of the alleluia of this Easter liturgy, by the end of this meeting, when we look at the positive results that will be reached, you will say from the depths of your heart, with a feeling of joy "The assembly is fruitfully concluded; let us go in peace; alleluia, alleluia!"

(B)

International Collaboration and Investigation

Villa Cavalletti, Rome
April 26, 1973

Father Arrupe made the following observations during the Communication experts meeting, held in Villa Cavalletti (March 25-30, 1973), to study the feasibility of an International Communications Institute of the Society.

We are exploring something new. A communications research centre with two purposes: *basic research* into humanizing mass media (theory) and *applied research* (studies in the impact of mass media on man). Of course, much has already been done in this field. But I feel nothing of this special kind of operation we are looking for, exists in the western world — or (especially) the Church. If so, there is a need for such a centre, but this need is very complex. We have to see how to develop the idea and how to implement its many applications. Once the basic decision is made, we must realistically develop concrete ways for this new ministry.

I would like to clarify two basic points in the letter you received before this meeting. First, the *stress on local research* in one central place, and second, *work in mass media throughout the Society and the world.* Such an arrangement is necessary to be effective, and I endorse it one hundred per cent. One cannot function without the other. To be effective as a meaningful apostolate today, a mutual fraternal dependence, a co-operation and co-responsibility between centre and parts, head and members, is vitally important. Otherwise, I think we would lose that universality which is a tremendous value for the whole Church. Thus we are now experiencing a dialectic tension between local and universal. Today, unfortunately, we can be so parochial as to lose the universal vision. We are too busy with our own particular work, and consider the general — global — vision as utopic. We too often forget that it is precisely our speciality, our Jesuit vocation, to be universal — and a tremendous opportunity this affords us. That is not a utopic or paternalistic vision: that is reality.

As I reminded the Fathers at the Congregation of Procurators 5-10-'70, the Society has always adopted the cultural and technical means of the times: using all means for the purpose of gaining the world for Christ. What our founder and first Fathers did, we too ought to do. Today we cannot afford to be so weighed down by old practices as to lose the flexibility and adaptability of our original charism.

It is my judgment that we can accomplish much more for the service of souls if we learn how to use correctly these modern instruments of the apostolate; if we consider those mass media and all who toil in them as part of our present day apostolate; if, finally, we offer them our cooperation in preparing, aiding and directing them in their efforts in mass media.

There is a need to specialize, to have professionally trained people for a specific task, but we have to combine the two — the local needs and the immense importance of the universal centre. An analogous principle in our Jesuit work is the Church itself. The local Church and the universal Church. The bishop is working in a region, but the whole Church is there. So, while recognizing that we have to foster the local works, we also have to foster a co-ordination on the general level. Twenty years ago we had no means of universal communication. Today, in an instant, we can communicate universally.

The second point is, as I see it, that we should not have something exclusively Jesuit, limited to Jesuit institutions. Jesuits should work in other institutions too, be they in or outside the Church. We are not trying to compete with the big production companies, but we can cooperate with them, and certainly we should not work in isolation, jealously guarding our own little personal project. We should rather pool our ideas, talents and resources and work as a team of Jesuits, thereby multiplying our influence. Mutual collaboration is indispensable in this effort. It is our strength too, for we are united in a common philosophy, theology, Christian humanism, and vocation of service to men. Once this important research centre is established, Jesuits can go into other centres to integrate its values.

It is somewhat similar to the university situation today. It is fine for some Jesuits to teach at other universities other than ours. However, it seems to me that such a man has a very limited influence on too few people. He operates as a professor rather than a Jesuit priest. But if a team of Jesuits operate in one of our universities, they will be able to influence many people. So we need our own schools as well as Jesuits in other schools. One does not exclude the other: we need both. We must also collaborate with other religious and lay people who share our Jesuit vision.

I think it was important to comment on these two points, the *theory* and *practice* of our communications centre and Jesuit teams working in and out of our schools in communications. We cannot give up our institutions lest we miss much of our strength, especially our universality and our own proper Jesuit structure.

Sequel to this Address

A feasibility study and pilot project stage of the Jesuit Communications Research Unit was soon designed to investigate the need for and the possibilities of ongoing activities by the Society of Jesus in the communications field. A major development was an expert meeting in 1975 at Marquette University, Milwaukee. A later evaluation meeting involving Fr. Vincent O'Keefe (General Counsellor), Fr Stefan Bamberger (Jescom Director), Fr. Robert White (Subdirector, Institute of Socio-Economic Research, Honduras), and for a final exchange Father Pedro Arrupe was held, where the conclusion was reached that the information available allowed for a difinitive proposal.

In 1976, Father General approved the establishment of a 2-man Unit to engage in projects and to explore further directions of research for an initial period (1976-79). Father Bamberger was asked to assume the responsibility for the seetting up of the Unit.

Early in 1977, Fr. Bamberger left Rome for his new assignment as General Director of the Research Facilitator Unit for Social Communications in London. Brother William Biernatzki was appointed his assistant. The choice of London, with its numerous resources of communication work in the form of libraries, communication institutes, and general cultural infrastructures, proved a happy choice as the base of the Unit.

As a means of focusing the attention of researchers on problems of great significance to the Church, one of the Unit's primary tasks has been dedicated to the formulation of a list of questions about communication. The questions represent the concerns of some of the most knowledgeable Catholics active in religious communication, other persons informed in matters of communication, as well as the thinking of the Research Unit. This tentative list would be later refined and revised on suggestions from outside sources, and the new list would be circulated in the hope of providing a reservoir of topics for term papers, theses, and dissertations by graduate students in communications and other social and behavioural sciences, thereby yielding a harvest of research findings which can help meet some of the Church's needs for scientifically reliable information about communication.

Two years of building the foundations, planning, and establishing research contacts set the stage for broader activities. Early in 1979, the directors of the Secretariate presented their report directly to Father General in Rome and received great encouragement for their work. During the year a first international symposium on the theme "Symbolism in Cross-Cultural Communication" was co-sponsored with the Institute of Social Communications of Saint Paul University, Ottawa, Canada. Fr. Robert A. White has joined the London-based Jesuit Centre for the Study of Communications and Culture. This Centre seeks to set in motion research and action on the human and moral problems on modern communication. It encourages an interdisciplinary approach in applied research, and its services are international in scope. It brings out a quarterly survey of "Communication Research Trends".

(C)

Public Opinion and Evangelization

Vatican City
October 10, 1974

Father Arrupe presented this little study at the Episcopal Synod of 1974 on Evangelization. The original Spanish text was translated by the Jesuit Press and Information Office in Rome.

1. One of the Great World Powers

Public opinion is one of the great forces in today's world. It is evident in the attempts of politicians and businessmen to influence and mobilize it in order to attain their political objectives or commercial goals.

Pius XII defined public opinion as,

the natural echo, a more or less spontaneous communal repercussion of events and of the present situation in the spirit and judgment of men. (AAS 1950, p. 251)

In our time, the rapid increase and multiplication of means of communication, a higher standard of education, a greater social and democratic awareness, and a more active consciousness of the right to be informed have enormously developed the influence of public opinion.

The Church cannot ignore this phenomenon which constitutes a real "sign of the times". Formation of public opinion and its freedom from forces which would suppress or distort should constitute one of the prime objectives in the evangelization of the Church today.

A proper formation and expression of public opinion is necessary for the integral human development which evangelization seeks to promote. Therefore, as the Second Vatican Council put it:

Within the limits of morality and the general welfare, a man should be free to search for the truth, voice his mind and publicize it...and...have appropriate access to information about public affairs. (Gaudium et Spes, n. 59)

2. Two Factors in Social Communication

The two principal elements which in fact form and limit public opinion are: on the one hand, the information which is published concerning facts, ideas and the historic reality in which we live; on the other, the values, mental sets and attitudes which condition the reception of this reality and at times distort it.

To do the work of evangelization is to exert a force so that public opinion is not manipulated but formed in an objective and impartial manner, and so that this information can be received and interpreted in the light of a Christian vision of the world, man and society.

There is no doubt that means of social communication are among the most effective to inform and to shape public opinion. Frequently, these media are controlled by political or economic interests and the information they report, if not false is at least partial and incomplete, filtered, and contaminated at the very source.

Even when attempting to be objective, those responsible for means of social communication frequently find themselves subject (as is very well expressed) to a triple tyranny which constantly overpowers them: the tyranny of *time*, which forces them to present their contributions within very reduced time margins, hindering them from working with sufficient calm and tact, particularly in complex and delicate matters; the tyranny of *interest*, which demands that whatever is said be interesting, thus making the selection of topics people tend to choose preferably those that "shock", arouse interest, or cause surprise; the tyranny of *originality*, which forces them to have to say something that others have not said or in some way is different from what others have used or will use.

These circumstances and tensions explain in large part the inexactitude of information and the abundance of strange and scandalous cases and the sometimes deformed presentation of a fact or a point of information.

3. How the Church can help in Communications

The Church can help so that the mass-media of social communication can fulfil its task of forming healthy and objective public opinion if she collaborates with those in charge in a constructive plan: of sincerity and openness, of rapidity of information, of acceptance of criticism, and of greater use of the influential media.

Sincerity and openness, facilitating true and complete information, not only concerning facts and events of general interest, but concerning too the life and activity of the Church. Naturally, in some cases the Church may have particular reasons to maintain a certain reserve, given the nature of its mission and the sensitivity of the subjects that it treats. But in general, it is preferable to avoid secrecy, that is, to make secret what is not necessary to hide, the tendency to communicate the very least possible, as this forces the means of social communication to procure clandestine information — not always complete nor exact — or to speculate with the insufficient data that one has. The Church has made great strides in this field and it is to be hoped that it continues.

Rapidity of information. In the world of information time (sometimes minutes) is essential and has a decisive value. News as such has a very brief life. Delayed information is of no use, when news has already become subject to distortions or has lost its interest.

Acceptance of criticism. Credibility is quickly lost if we communicate only the good. The fear of criticism is always harmful; it leads to a public cover-up of possible errors or of limitations subject to criticism. An honest authenticity is the best foundation of credibility and is the best way to avoid recourse to a defensive attitude which induces us to overlook and even to defend our failings.

Greater use of the influential media, since these are the great agents and organs of information which can shape public opinion more efficiently. Ecclesiastic inversion and the almost exclusive use of ecclesiastical means of information must be avoided. Nevertheless, in cases in which advantages created by the political or economic order have reduced the normal means of communication to servitude, the Church should courageously create and operate its own veracious and reliable channels of information.

4. Dialogue between Church and Media

The need for dialogue between the Church and the media of social communication must be emphasized. They are not enemies, but collaborators in the building up of a well-informed and vigorous public opinion. They should therefore be open to a frank yet cordial exchange of views, leading to constructive self-criticism. It is true that the Church has suffered much from biases and distortions to which public opinion has been subjected. But it must also be asked whether certain limitations we have imposed on ourselves, and certain attitudes we have adopted with regard to the free flow of information have not provided the occasion, at least in part, for such biases and distortions.

But complete and impartial objective reporting is only one of the elements which constitutes public opinion: an indispensable requisite or condition for its evangelization.

The souls and minds of those who receive information must be free, not only individually but collectively, from prejudice, conditionings and emotions — products of our surroundings and our society which obstruct the perception of objective reality. But to be able to speak of evangelization it is also necessary for the minds and souls, once they are free, to be informed by evangelical values and criteria, by the ideals of truth, charity, and justice.

14

FRATERNAL COLLABORATION IN THE WORK OF EVANGELIZATION

Father General's Inaugural Address at the International Consultation on Evangelization

Rome
March 26-30, 1979

On Pentecost Sunday 1977, the Mission Secretariat of the Jesuit Generalate in Rome launched a consultation on Our Missionary Spirit Today. This was meant as a follow-up of the 32nd General Congregation, which stated that "This task of direct evangelization by proclaiming Jesus Christ remains essential today;" it also had in view the forthcoming Congregation of Procurators.

In fact, the question had been asked, how far this prime concern, "the defence and propagation of the faith and the progress of souls in Christian life and doctrine" of the Formula of the Institute, figured in the efforts of Jesuits all over the world for the implementation of the decree on "Our Mission Today".

The response to this consultation from all over the world was most satisfying, totalling 140 answers, some of them from groups. The material was under study for some months, and it was collected in a dossier, so that it might serve for inspiration and further reflection on the fundamental commitment of the Society to "the propagation of the faith". More in particular, it was used as a basis for the missionary meeting held in Rome.

Among the 24 participants, meeting with Father General, a missionary himself for many years, there were men from

*Mission Offices and Reviews in Europe and America,
and Conference Presidents or Provincials. A third category
belonged to the General Counsellors or Assistants from the
Curia. India was adequately represented by three Provincials and two Assistants.*

*Father General's key address, which we here publish,
opened up the broad vision of evangelization in the context
of the divine plan and the Jesuit vocation. He explored
several aspects of evangelization, among which was one
particular tension. On the one hand, each country has a lively
desire to be recognized in terms of that which is characteristic and proper to itself. On the other, the problems of
the contemporary world stretch beyond frontiers and
touch all men without distinction. Moreover, in countries
formerly called "missions", rapid changes and new experiences have cast new light on our reflections, while in those
countries which have been known as "traditionally christian",
evangelizers have come to question themselves about their
own manner of living the Gospel.*

*

A. INTRODUCTION

1. Why have this Consultation?

It is not only opportune but very necessary at this moment
in history, to reflect on the missionary activity of the Society,
which from the very beginning has been a privileged expression of our commitment to the service of the faith. We are all
aware of the tremendous changes that have taken place in
this area, as in others, of the life of the Church: among
Christians, there are new experiences and new theological
thinking; in the world at large, new socio-political situations;
within the Society, a new pattern of growth. We have adapted
ourselves in some measure, and almost inevitably, to the changed
circumstances. But there is need to examine more closely what
is happening and how we must respond to new challenges.

Some may judge that at present we are in a condition that
in ignatian terms could be called desolation. I do not quite

agree; and mush less can I accept that through discouragement some decide to withdraw — for it would be quite unignatian to make a change in time of desolation. We must indeed change, but precisely because we see new opportunities for service in the situation that faces us. The opportunities are all the greater because today the whole world is rightly regarded as "mission territory". And the work of evangelization is more and more one of fraternal collaboration. In these circumstances, how do we go about our task?

I have called you to reflect together on all aspects of this problem but with a definitely practical bias, so that we might arrive at an administrative policy in this area of apostolic service, a policy consistent with the Formula of our Institute.

Permit me, however, in this inaugural address, to put aside all pragmatic considerations for a while, and to climb into what may seem an ivory tower, in order to speak from a broader, panoramic point of view. You will need this point of view as background when you begin to reflect on concrete problems. Overwhelmed by everyday necessities, it is very easy to lose sight of the overview, to miss the forest for the trees.

2. What does evangelization mean?

Let us renew our basic understanding of this word, recalling some passages from *Evangelii Nuntiandi*:

"For the Church, evangelizing means bringing the Good News into all the strata of humanity, and through its influence transforming humanity from within and making it new... the Church evangelizes when she seeks to convert, solely through the divine power of the Message she proclaims, both the personal and collective consciences of people, the activities in which they engage, and the lives and concrete milieux which are theirs" (18).

"Strata of humanity which are transformed: for the Church it is a question not only of preaching the Gospel in ever wider geographic areas or to ever greater numbers of people, but also of affecting and as it were upsetting, through the power of the Gospel, mankind's criteria of judgment, determining values, points of interest, lines of thought, sources of inspiration and models of life, which are in contrast with the Word of God and the plan of salvation" (19).

". . . What matters is to evangelize man's culture and cultures (not in a purely decorative way as it were by applying a thin veneer, but in a vital way, in depth and right to their very roots), in the wide and rich sense which these terms have in *Gaudium et Spes*, always taking the person as one's starting-point. . ." (20).

"Above all the Gospel must be proclaimed by witness. . . this witness which involves presence, sharing, solidarity, and which is an essential elemment, and generally the first one, in evangelization" (21).

". . . even the finest witness will prove ineffective in the long run if it is not explained, justified. . . and made explicit by a clear and un-equivocal proclamation of the Lord Jesus" (22).

"Finally, the person who has been evangelized goes on to evangelize others. . . Evangelization, as we have said, is a complex process made up of varied elements: the renewal of humanity, witness, explicit proclamation, inner adherence, entry into the community, acceptance of signs, apostolic initiative. These elements may appear to be contradictory, indeed mutually exclusive. In fact they are complementary and mutually enriching. Each one must always be seen in relationship with the others" (24).

B. MISSION AND THE MISSIONS

In the light of *Evangelii Nuntiandi*, I would like to establish some aspects of evangelization with greater precision.

1. Respect for the particular

When we discuss large themes or problems that have worldwide relevance — such as evangelization — it is common practice to group diverse countries or cultures or situations in conventional blocks that have similar characteristics and distinguishing features. In this way we speak of "countries of the East" setting them off against the western block. We use the expression "the Third World".

This widely followed practice has its advantages. But it is a simplification which at times can be employed only by distorting reality, by violently reducing to uniformity the peculiar traits of the members of the group, and finally by damaging, even suppressing, their identity. Nowadays each country has a more lively desire than ever before to be recognized in terms of that which is proper to itself. It is impatient with ignorance about its specific character, since such ignorance supposes alienation, and a falsification of its true self. We have to be very careful in this area and not lightly take up such broad and misleading terms as "Latin America", "Africa", or the "Far East".

2. An ever-increasing interaction

On the other hand, in the areas of technology, science, economics, social development, politics and the like, civilization shows a strong unifying and concentrating force which reduces the world to a "global village" in which boundaries disappear and people feel closer to one another. On widely different levels — ideological, social, cultural, political, religious, etc. — that which differentiates is being overwhelmed by powerful collective movements. Sometimes, to be sure, it is not a question of mere interchange of ideas and mutual influence; what is involved is rather some sort of ideological colonialism, a domination in the cultural or other spheres. Whatever the case, the fact remains that the final result is a world in which differences are vanishing and every day sees more problems that are common to a greater number of people.

The same thing happens in the area of religion. The division of the world into "Christendom" and "lands of the infidels" in which we were brought up, is losing currency. The distinction between "Christian countries" and "mission territories" may have served some purpose of system and efficiency, and may even have fostered evangelical zeal; but nowadays it can be used only with delicate nuances.

Indeed, there has been a great change in the role played by the Christian religion in the different peoples of ancient Catholic tradition. On the one hand, secularism, materialism, the development in strength of various kinds of ideology —

having as their only common trait an incompatibility with the Faith — have put the Church in a *diaspora* situation and have drastically diminished the Christian stamp of society and culture.

On the other hand, in the countries conventionally labelled "pagan", confrontation of moral and religious issues has undergone extraordinary changes. And a wide range of new experiences, under Christian influence, cast a new light in which to study these problems.

In countries of Christian tradition one can sense puzzlement and frustration in the face of new kinds of problems and situations. One finds both intellectuals and the masses turning to ideologies that are exotic — be they philosophical or scientific, socio-economic or even religious — in which they think they will find answers which are more understandable to most people and more adapted to the secularized mentality of our times. It is as if contemporary problematic situations — in many ways quite new — had revealed the Christian Churches as devoid of resources to answer today's questions. Or it is as if the manner of interpreting and living out the gospel in practice — both individual and social — were incapable of standing up to a probing analysis as severe and honest as that to which today's problems are subjecting it. This challenge should force us to stop, think, and ask ourselves whether we should not put our conception and practice of the gospel through a searching re-examination in terms of the gospel itself. Our way of living the gospel has often become secularized and self centered. In other words, it is time for the evangelizers to be themselves evangelized.

3. The work of Evangelization

A country that is well established in the faith, and has a solidly based church, ought to feel obliged to pass on that faith to other countries where it is still lacking. "The person who has been evangelized goes on to evangelize others" (24). There are a number of points that have to be kept in mind for genuine evangelization: —

Christ, the one who reveals the Father through the Holy Spirit (26), the ideal man, the model, who in turn lifts up human values and through his grace confers on man the strength that he needs to achieve his supernatural purpose. This is the object of all evangelization.

Man, beneficiary of evangelization: despite his fallen nature man has a fundamental worth. In many cases doubtless this worth has almost disappeared or is so disfigured as to be hardly recognizable. But the value has to be rediscovered, purified and brought to perfection.

At present the interchange of ideas and values among individuals and groups at all levels can produce a certain standardization and bring about a kind of levelling. For this reason evangelization, of whatever kind it be and wherever it is being pursued, will have basically the same invariable objective: the human person, essentially the same wherever found. The value of each human being cannot be suppressed nor submitted to unjust oppression, whether by political power or economic interests, nor exploited and degraded as for example in pansexualism.

Nor can evangelization forget that the human person has a socio-cultural dimension which also demands attention. A human being shares with fellow-humans a culture which is at the same time common and exclusive; and every person is both an active and a passive subject of rights and obligations. The light of revelation must illumine those rights and obligations in order to make them stand out clearly.

Culture is the living framework in which man exists, i e., in which he thinks, expresses himself, acts and loves, in harmony with his ancestral tradition, which is full of meaning for him and for all others of his culture. Evangelization must never forget this reality. For each culture, like each individual, is different from all others and has to discover its true identity and self, and not just a mechanical duplicate of something from outside, whether freely accepted or not. Evangelization must be adapted to the individual, to his unique personality, in order to lead him to Christ, the inexhaustible Model and Compendium of all perfection. In this way it will vivify this personal and unrepeatable being that is a man, and a man inserted in the culture he has helped to fashion for himself.

Hence, evangelization has to keep in mind each people's special and distinctive context. We may at times legitimately speak of the great human groups, but when discussing evangelization we must deal with each people separately, prescinding from all others and taking it in its differentiated individuality.

An important consequence of this is that a recipient country has a right to decide the type and modality of the aid given and of the way it is to be given That is, the mission of the one sent must be determined by the needs of the country that receives him. Apart from extraordinary cases, his mission must be shaped in accordance with the request (direct or indirect) of the host country.

Let us not forget, though, that cultures have a social function too. They must be ready, therefore, in a reciprocal giving and taking, to share their own values with other cultures, as well as to take from them. This supposes that every culture is willing to set aside any attitude of self-sufficiency, and to receive — and assimilate — contributions from other cultures, even if these latter seem, in some sense, less developed.

Naturally, the problem is complex: What criteria are to determine which are the "superior" values that one culture should offer to another? How is the transfer to be made? And what is the proper pedagogy for the culture that gives; what is the right manner of accepting and assimilating for the one that receives?

C. THE DIVINE PLAN

Gazing at this wondrous variety of men and cultures, I feel drawn like our Father St. Ignatius, whose thoughts while contemplating the Incarnation soared to the Trinity. If I may say so, I too want to penetrate the mind and heart of God, adoring and humbling myself before the immensity of his plan of salvation. The God who saves is the God who created.

What must be summed up in Christ is more than this present world to which we direct our apostolic effort, more than this generation of which we form a part, and even more than all preceding and succeeding generations; it is every organic and inorganic creature, everything that falls between Alpha and Omega, everything that has passed from nothing to being.

1. Expanding vision of the universe

Humanity is situated in the universe and the whole universe rests in the hands of God. This year a Nobel Prize has been given to those who have uncovered the tracks of the first great explosion, the "big-bang" of 20,000 million years ago (before anything was, according to scientists; which marks the beginning of creation, and of time and space). Expanding at the rate of two million miles per hour, the universe has already a diameter of more than 20,000 million light years. There are approximately 10,000 million galaxies. One of them — certainly not the biggest — is the Milky Way, composed of millions of stars. And our sun is only one of these stars, not the largest, but the nearest to our earth. The earth rotates around one star and is really only a speck of cosmic dust in so vast a universe. And on this speck of dust is something smaller still — man. This is where God chose to take on flesh. "The heavens proclaim the glory of God" (Ps 18:2).

If the macrocosm overwhelms us with its immensity, the marvels of the microcosm surprise us even more. Descending from molecules we arrive at atoms; we think we have reached the smallest. But the atom is still a giant: its radius is 100,000 times greater than its nucleus, and the nucleus, in its turn, is a world breeding the forces of matter and antimatter, a world in which some particles and anti-particles last less than one hundred trillionth of a second.

Creation has been expanding for 20,000 million years and man can only be traced back to three and a half million of these years. "What is man that you should be mindful of him?" (Ps 8:5). What is man in the whole of creation and what is Redemption in the history of man? If we let a line of 20 kilometres represent the 20,000 million years since the origin of the universe, every thousand years would equal one millimetre. The history of mankind would be represented by the last 3 and a half metres of these 20 kilometres; the Redemption by Christ would be less than two millimetres with hardly a millimetre more for the Old Testament.

2. Consequences for our apostolic vision

The mind boggles at this. God "is seated over the world, whose inhabitants are like locusts. He stretches the heavens like a veil" (Is. 40,22). God, judging by our measure of time, does not seem to have been in a hurry to create intelligent beings, who presumbaly give sense to creation, nor once he had created them, to initiate the process of Redemption. Thousands of generations were born and died without ever knowing that God, in addition to being Father and Creator, is Redeemer, and that they were destined to participate in everlasting life.

These facts are not merely a pastime for lovers of science fiction, because when they are coupled with fundamental tenets of our theology (Christ is the only Saviour, the salvific will of God is universal) they rouse us to a humble acceptance of the mystery of God's Providence and give us an idea of the measure of time in God's plan.

These facts are important for those concerned with evangelization. Do they not suggest that the three and a half million years since the appearance of man on the earth and the two thousand since the Incarnation are only a prologue to a story just unfolding? Science tells us that the sun, with its 5,000 million years of life, is but halfway through its life-span.

There is nothing that excludes the possibility that the Church may be still at the beginning of its history. This consideration makes us take fresh stock of our perspective, our concern and our possible despair. Here are some reflections from this standpoint:

What is the time and what are the means held in reserve by Providence for countries and cultures that have not yet been reached by the Good News so as to come finally to "the knowledge of the Truth?" For it is certain that God desires to save all men and bring them to recognize this truth (1 Tim 2:4). To what extent does God make this salvation and this knowledge depend on the truth of our apostolic initiative?

Because — and this is a second consideration — it is certain that ever since Christ said to his Twelve: "Go into the whole world to spread the Good News and to baptize all people"

(Mk 16:15), the Church has been in a situation of "being sent", of permanent mission, which is a constitutive element that the Church cannot renounce. The whole Church is "mission" unto itself, renewing ceaselessly the joyous proclamation of the Paschal Mystery among its children. But the Church is also specifically "missionary", "sent" by Christ, who is Himself "sent forth from the Father", who is not only the bearer, but also the object, of the Good News. By his blood we have become "a new creation", for He came that we might have life — all of us — and might have it more abundantly (Jn 10:10). We in our turn, must be heralds of that life.

D. THE JESUIT VOCATION

The Jesuit is a missionary; what is more, he is so by deliberate choice. The Society has always seen its vow to the Supreme Pontiff in all that concerns "missions" as its "wellspring and principal foundation" (MI, ser. 3a, I, 162). To be sure, in the *Formula Instituti* and the *Constitutions* the word "missions" has a content and sense broader than evangelization "among unbelievers". But it is also certain that this evangelization "among unbelievers" is the first and most important element contained in the expression. To enter into the Society is to make choice of a life of service of Christ in which "the missions" take the highest priority.

1. Ignatian Perspective in the Exercises

The Spiritual Exercises provide us with several insights into the perfect cohesion between that which could be called "Ignatian cosmogony and anthropology" and God's plan for the whole of creation and for the human race, to which I referred earlier.

— "Man was created" (23). Ignatius could not have sunk a deeper foundation for his entire spiritual building and for his concept of the human being. He went right to the starting point from which the whole range of human possibility rises and apart from which none is conceivable. The human person comes into being with an existential tension between his littleness in the face of his Creator and his greatness as God's creature, God's image, God's son — destined for God.

— The meditation on the Three Sins picks up the same tension from the viewpoint of one redeemed by Christ: "What have I done for Christ?" (53). St. Ignatius opens up the retreatant to every possibility by urging the question: "What am I doing now, what ought I to do for Christ?" It amounts to a blank cheque to be drawn on limitless generosity: "to reflect on what shall present itself to my mind". In this way the ground is prepared for a response which, in the more radical cases such as those of Xavier and the first companions, takes on the form of a commitment that is distinctly missionary.

— In the second exercise Ignatius situates the retreatant more explicitly in a cosmic context. "Abasing myself by examples" in order to appreciate how insignificant and small I am, a sinner, in the midst of a creation which, incomprehensibly, tolerates my sinful disorder: "...the heavens, the sun, the moon, the stars, and the elements, the fruits of the earth, the birds, the fishes, and the animals..." (60).

The second week of the Exercises jumps abruptly *"in medias res"* with a perspective that is explicitly proselytizing and pluralistic. The temporal King wants to conquer all the land of the unbelievers (93). Then we see Christ, "and before Him the whole world, all of whom and each in particular He calls, and says: My will is to conquer the whole world... and thus to enter into the glory of My Father" (95).

What is presented to the retreatant is nothing more nor less than a call to arms. In the confirmatory colloquy Saint Ignatius is not content with letting the retreatant "reflect on what comes to mind". Rather, with explicit reference to generosity, he makes him choose between two categories: if he is a person "of judgement and reason," he will offer his whole self for labour. But if, beyond that, he wishes to signalize himself "in every kind of service of the Eternal King and Universal Lord", he will make offers of "greater worth and moment" (97). Ignatius goes to the unusual length of dictating the formula of offering. Instead of simply being received in this life and state, the retreatant "wishes and desires and it is his deliberate determination" to imitate and follow Christ in this call to conquer the whole world.

2. Universal Mission of the Society

The body of the Society, therefore, is made up of men who, in their individual spiritual life, have desired "to show greater affection and to signalize themselves." They have joined together under the Roman Pontiff for "the defence and propagation of the faith" (Form. Inst. I).

The Society becomes aware of this "global mission" as the final consequence of our vision of the Blessed Trinity. Ours is an awesome responsibility which demands the marshalling of all our energies and talents. This mission, given by God the Creator of the world, crucified for love of the world, is characterized by "universality". This is what we express by our fourth vow, which explicitly rules out any limitation or condition. It is in function of this universality that we understand our "apostolic availability" to be similarly without limit. The organic elasticity of the Society permits us to adopt any form of life which we consider necessary to reach any area of the world whatever, in whatever model of community structure or of personal accommodation, and to establish contact with any culture. We exclude no area of scientific specialization nor any social group. Any kind of particularization or restriction of our apostolic policy would damage one of the vital centres of the Society's life.

It becomes apparent that by reason of the origin and finality of our mission, as well as of the means we take to carry it out, the principal agent — or even, in a sense, the only one — is the *Holy Spirit,* who is promised and sent by Christ in order to make known the truth and to instruct us in it. If in the biblical account we are given a vision of the Spirit hovering over the world being born (Gen 1,2), now we can perceive — and it is not mere symbolism — the Spirit labouring in the whole of history through all human generations for thousands of years. In the souls of men and women He leaves a trace of His action and He sows the "seeds" of truth and of grace in all human cultures, pregnant with the mystery of His purpose. Above all, He enlivens the Church like the soul in the body, and works within hearts in a hidden, interior, personal way, preparing the *"Anakephalaiosis",* the final achievement of the unity of all creation in Christ as head. Our evangelizing activity, carried on under the guidance of the Spirit and with His power, is marked by an eschatological purposefulness in the building up of the Kingdom. Only to the extent to which we work in this way — rooted in, led by, and identified with the Spirit — can our activity make sense and bear fruit.

3. Consequences for our Activity

This approach to understanding the missionary activity of the Society and of each Jesuit has its consequences:

We should follow God's way: able to do big things and small, just as God creates the macrocosm and the microcosm, with a perfect harmony between the whole and its parts. He ". . . before whom the whole universe is like a dew-drop that falls on the earth at morn" (Wis 11:22), who is "great in big things, but greatest in the small", He should have from us that "cooperation which the Lord asks of his creatures" (Const. 134), that a tiny piece of mosaic be fitted into the divine plan. The Lord has used small things to manifest his mighty deeds: a poor Hebrew to liberate His people, five pebbles in a sling to fell a giant, five loaves and two fishes to feed a multitude, a few jars of water for his first miracle in Cana.

We should keep to God's pace. What I have said above about space and time would seem to tell us that God is not in a hurry: "With the Lord a day is like a thousand years, and a thousand years like a day" (2 Pet 3:8). We should rethink our own impatience, our eagerness to get results. Our impatience can be an obstacle to a long term as well as more profound evangelization. Take, for example, the case of Ricci. His life could appear to some as having little significance as an evangelizer. And yet, in the larger view it had an enormous influence.

In the same way, we can ask ourselves if there are not circumstances when, rather than seeking quick conversions and other works that bear immediately visible results, we should better use a slower, even indirect, approach which ultimately would produce much greater fruit. For example: evangelize a culture, help a new social condition to evolve, direct public opinion towards the Gospel with the intelligent use of the mass media. These tasks take time, but they are the ones that affect the course of history.

In Japan, for example, in a population of 115 million, only 700,000 (0.6%) are baptized. And yet 14 million (14%) say that they are well disposed towards Christianity. This is undoubtedly a long term result of patient inculturation exercised through the indirect apostolate of education.

So we have to abandon our activism and our semi-Pelagian self-reliance and let our enterprise be one based primarily on the grace of God, one that can succeed only if it respects God's way and God's timing.

Spiritualism, as a radical attitude, is a temptation that threatens us from the opposite direction: leaving everything to the action of the Spirit, and regarding our own contribution as of no efficacy at all. It is the attitude of those who, disheartened by the disproportion between their efforts and the results obtained, and seeing the immense and ever growing number of those who either do not yet belong to the Church or live in it with a pagan heart, conclude that the battle is lost and take the pessimistic attitude of helpless resignation. The Church is for only a few, we hear these people say; Christianity, of its very nature, is meant for a charismatic minority of chosen souls able to live according to the Gospel demands in all their purity and rigour. If Paul and the Apostles had thought that way, Christianity would never have got beyond the frontiers of Judaism. But they had heard the Lord say: "Go out to the whole world; proclaim the Good News to all creation" (Mk 16:16). How firmly Paul was convinced of that mandate, we can tell from his words, that God "wants all men to be saved and to come to the full knowledge of the truth" (1 Tim 2:4). And so he turned towards the gentiles and the Hellenistic world.

"I am perfectly willing to spend what I have, and to be expended, in the interests of your souls" (2 Cor 12:15); such was Paul's attitude. "The love of Christ spurs me on"; such should be our disposition, as necessary envoys in God's present plan. We must evangelize with no less energy than Paul, and yet with a great serenity that can say: 'We are merely servants: we have done no more than our duty" (Lk 17:10).

That was the balance that St. Ignatius struck in his famous rule: "We should strive as if the outcome depended entirely on God, but put our trust in God as if it depended entirely on us". We will act that way regarding those whom we are sent to, "like guardian angels, in two ways: helping them as much as we can for their salvation and yet not worrying or losing our peace if, when we have done all we could, they do not listen to us" (FN III, 635, n. 11).

This attitude is nothing new. For St. Paul wrote: "Christ did not send me to baptize, but to preach the Good News" (1 Cor 1:17), because the results did not depend on him: "Neither he who plants nor he who waters is of any importance, but only God" (1 Cor 3:7). This did not make him any less conscious of his obligation of faithfully living up to his apostolic calling: "Preaching the Gospel is a duty laid on me. And woe to me if I do not preach it'." (1 Cor 9:16). Every member of the Society can apply these words to himself in their most literal sense.

Explicitation of the faith. I quoted earlier the words of *Evangelii Nuntiandi* that identify the value of our witness with our explicitation of the faith. This should make us appreciate deeply the sacrifice of those who must be satisfied with only an implicit proclamation of the Gospel, because they work in areas where there is religious intolerance or other similar obstacle. The witness of their lives, the disinterestedness of their service, will sometimes be all they can contribute, together with their hope that although no real evangelizing is possible "as long as the name, the teachings, the life, the promises, the kingdom and the mystery of Jesus of Nazareth, the Son of God, are not proclaimed" (EN 22), yet this may yet be possible at some unforeseen future date. Sowers who must labour under this limitation can only think of the evangelizers who will come after them and who may then harvest the crop. "The time is close... Very soon now, I shall be with you again, bringing the reward to be given to every man according to what he deserves... I shall indeed be with you soon. Amen; come, Lord Jesus" (Rev 22:10-20). The evangelizer has to have this eschatological perspective.

E. THE TASK BEFORE US

Of special pertinence to the Society's missionary activity—

since we are dealing with a fundamental point of our Institute — are my remarks in the final address to the Congregation of Procurators last October. I referred to the challenge facing our Society today, and specifically to the meaning for us today of the Ignatian criteria for our ministries. When St. Ignatius wrote these norms, he was thinking quite explicitly of "missions" in the broad sense of that expression in our Institute. But the norms do have a privileged application in the area of missionary activity traditionally so called. Please reread what I said with regard to deepening St. Ignatius' original criteria under the headings of the greater need, the wider effects, and priorities. These notions are the parameters for the present and future missionary activity of the Society. When properly understood, they contain all the impetus and caution needed to bring about the best possible evangelization.

1. Universality in practice

I appeal to you as Jesuits especially involved or expert in this primary sector of the Society's apostolate, to reflect on and share your experience, to point out possible lines of action, and to advise and help me in this important area of my responsibility to the Church and the Society. This is the precise reason for having your meeting here. Very concretely, it would help to concentrate your reflections on some of the following points:

The concept of "universal" applied to the missionary activity of the Society. I did not mention this before when treating the Ignatian criteria, precisely because I wanted to treat of it in particular. When we are dealing with missionary activity, it has to be taken into account. Actually, the Constitutions think in terms of the universal and conceive the Society as one body in which the division into Provinces or Vice-Provinces is merely a help towards better universal government. The Constitutions speak less, much less, of Provinces than of Provincials; and this is enjoined on Provincials as a duty: "First of all, the provincial superiors...should be obliged... to consider and to do what they ought to do for the universal good of the Society..." (778). This is why, in the final address to the Procurators, I voiced my concern that administrative structures could be harmful to apostolic works that require a basis of cooperation that goes beyond province boundaries. "The broad vision of the Constitutions and a hierarchical structure of government giving all authority to the General *ad aedificationem* is not matched by the stability which in fact characterizes so much of our apostolate".

This is why I indicated that we must begin first of all *by planning on a universal scale and according to priorities.* Provinces and particular regions would then have to adapt their contribution to the overall strategy. "By calling the whole Society to a basic option, GC 32 follows this path. We are slowly beginning to see the results. But when the central government launches a specific project requiring cooperation between Provinces, it is still considered by some an intrusion, an unwelcome interference with local plans". You can easily see how much all this applies to the apostolate of young Provinces in former mission territories. Almost by definition, many such Provinces are the ones most in need of a strong helping hand from the other Provinces of the Society. "I repeat", to continue my remarks to the Procurators, "the future calls us to think differently: options which are *'universaliores'* and therefore *'diviniores'* must determine the direction of the Society's apostolate according to the manner and guidelines of the Constitutions (206, 662, 668, 971, 821). (Cf. Final Address to the Congregation of Procurators, 1978, n. 15 et al).

And therefore I come back again to what I said: "What I am trying to say with all the emphasis I can is this: While being fully committed to a local apostolate or particular ministry, we must always be ready to offer ourselves for more universal or important work if the Society asks us. And we should show this by anticipating the desires of Superiors".

The tension between universality and inculturation is connected with this. Please take it into account during your discussions so that you will not fall into contradictions in your conclusions or run the risk of a "double message" that could cause confusion.

Of course a universal vision does entail a corresponding universal planning that moves down by a kind of capillary action to concrete and complementary action in successive steps. Commissions for the planning of ministries should be aware of this, and one of the purposes of the evaluation process is precisely to see the relationship of needs and available forces for their application where they can be productive apostolically.

2. Our spiritual resources

My next point is the need of a "robust spirituality". I referred to this also in the address to the Procurators, and I feel that I should repeat it here. It is what is asked of a Jesuit committed to evangelization in an outpost, quite alone, in an atmosphere at times hostile, living in the midst of so many material or spiritual needs. If there is no ongoing spiritual nourishment in which prayer can help him to assimilate what he experiences in the life about him, he runs the risk of emptying himself in a meaningless activism. If prayer is the lifeblood of every apostolate, this is all the more true of the missionary apostolate. The support of a very solid spiritual life is much more necessary for an apostolate in the world of unbelief than it is for one in a Christian context or with Christian communities.

That was the reason why I mentioned "fervour", a word that St. Ignatius used to describe the spiritual stance of the Jesuit and of the Society itself: "Fervour is the Society" (Nadal, *Schol.* 584, note 382). The aim of the Society is "to advance with fervour in the salvation and perfection of one's neighbour" (cf. Ms. Arch. SI, Roma. *Vitae* 15, fol 18 rv). St. Ignatius, reflecting on the spiritual needs of his time, new needs resulting from the geographical discoveries and the breach in the Catholic unity of Christianity, remained nevertheless cool-headed in his control of the missionary and apostolic zeal of Jesuits. For "fervour is the Society, but not an unbalanced fervour, rather a fervour that is enlightened as well as being courageous" (Mon. Nadal 5, 310).

In our day too such balance is needed, in this age in which the challenge has assumed gigantic proportions. The younger generation, because they are perhaps more sensitive to the needs of all sectors and specifically in the social, human sphere, particularly need to be helped in controlling their impulsiveness even though it springs from a most praiseworthy generosity. They ought to have a formation which will help them in their acceptance of reality, and what I already said about God's "way" and the divine "timing" is relevant to this point. There is need too for witness in ordinary life: with regard to this, what steps have to be taken in the area of inculturation, so that witness to faith can be understood by those to whom our evangelical action is directed?

3. A series of questions

I would like you to consider this question also: has the 'missionary' spirit in the Society declined? Or is there perhaps a search for a new understanding of the word 'mission' and for a more meaningful motivation in proclaiming the Good News than that there is no salvation without conversion to the faith? There seems to be a call for a new presentation of the theology of evangelization.

Then, reflection on the slow movement of divine action can lead us to an effort to influence dominant ideologies, as a step towards conversion. How is the tension to be resolved between the option of a long term, indeed ultimate, evangelization and the demands of individual conversion? Given that everything cannot be done all at once, what are the criteria that will in practice determine priority options and their achievement?

In the collaboration between donor and recipient countries, how can we rid ourselves of any vestige of colonialism or cultural paternalism which could understandably be hurtful to the sensitivity of young developing churches and so damage the work of evangelization?

How resolve the problem in regions of 'primary evangelization', when trying to keep in proper balance our faith-justice option? In other words: What policy and what criteria adapted to varying countries need to be followed so as to emphasise in one case conversion, in another social development, or again the institutional apostolate like education?

What is the best and most desirable relationship between mission offices and the territories they serve? And what is the status of these offices in relation to the Provinces in which they are based? How are we to look after some of those Provinces or Vice-Provinces in countries of 'primary evangelization' who lack the support of a 'Mother Province' or a 'Mission Office' to help with fraternal aid?

Finally, what kind of help do you yourselves think that the Society expects the General to give in this whole area of missionary activity? And more specifically, how do you look on the work of the Curia, in particular that of the Mission Secretariat, as a co-ordinating centre of the global resources of the Society to meet universal needs?

These questions, as you see, demand a good deal of reflection and bring us face to face with a vista of enormous problems and possibilities. But we should meet them with stout hearts because, although we know our own weakness, we are encouraged by the promise of the Lord when he sent his disciples to convert the whole world. He told them, — and we take the words as addressed to ourselves too, — "Go and teach. And know that I am with you always; yes, to the end of time" (Mt 28:19,20). We feel ourselves strengthened by that promise of "Christ, *Redeemer of man,* centre of the universe and of history" (RH. 1).

CATECHIZING
THE WIDE WORLD

Father Arrupe's Interventions in the
Synod of Bishops on Catechesis, October, 1977:

(A) Catechesis and Inculturation
(B) The Possibilities of Catechesis

(A)
CATECHESIS and INCULTURATION

The first intervention by Father General Arrupe during the 1977 Synod of Bishops was on a topic of special interest to Jesuits in view of the document of the 32nd General Congregation on the theme of Inculturation. Here is the text of that intervention, echoes of which were easily discovered in one of the 34 "Propositions" later approved by the Synod for transmission to Pope Paul.

*

One of the important problems which the Church and catechesis in particular have to face is the real influence of faith on the living conditions of man, on his culture. One element which can lead to a solution of this vital problem is "inculturation." The absence of inculturation is one of the main obstacles to evangelization.

Catechesis presupposes the inculturation of the faith; catechesis comes after this inculturation; and likewise catechesis continues to be a very powerful and dynamic means of inculturation.

What Inculturation in Catechesis Is Not

Inculturation in catechesis

— is not merely an adaptation of older forms of catechetical instruction, rejuvenated by the introduction of new terminology and by the use of modern pedagogical techniques.

— nor is it just an effort to bridge the generation gap by making a few concessions to the demands of youth;

— nor is it a strategy adopted to make Christian doctrine more attractive;

— nor is it a subtle means of destroying the preponderance of the West;

— nor is it a simplistic acceptance of the past to the detriment of the future,

— nor such an accommodation of faith to culture as would damage the substance of Revelation;

— nor is it a kind of benevolent, almost folkloristic approach which the West substitutes for the criticism of other cultures;

— nor is it finally some sort of 'ethnocentrism' (Levi Strauss): a false theory which tries to construct a Western model as the type towards which other cultures ought to evolve.

What Inculturation in Catechesis Really Is

Inculturation in catechesis is the practical corollary of that theological principle which asserts that Christ is the one and only Saviour and saves only what he assumes to himself. Hence Christ must assume in his Body (which is the Church) all cultures, purifying them and removing everything which is contrary to his Spirit, thus saving them without destroying them.

It means faith reaching man in his most profound experience of life, even to the extent of influencing his way of thinking, feeling and acting under the inspiration of the Spirit of God.

It makes possible the widespread contribution of all cultural values in the service of the Gospel.

Inculturation means a continued sharing between the Word of God and the rich varieties of human expression.

Hence it enables us to speak *with* (not just *to*) the men and women of our times about their problems, needs, hopes and desires.

Difficulties in the Area of Inculturation and Guiding Principles

1) *Difficulties:*

The first is an *instinctive fear* when confronted by new ideas and the people who propose them. Our fear of change makes us feel unhappy and threatened as it were; it leads us to think that the new expressions of the faith can contradict what we have expressed and practised up till now.

Secondly, *pluralism* is thought to be a danger for the Church, whereas true pluralism introduces us to a much deeper unity. In fact the crisis of unity often results from an insufficient pluralism that makes it difficult for some to express and live their faith within their own culture.

Thirdly, *a flight from reality* — due to fear of unavoidable dangers; this can lead us to separate faith from real life.

Fourthly, *immobilism,* that is, the fear of unavoidable dangers. This gradually transforms the faith into something abstract which has no influence over life.

Finally, the lack of a *fair and sober assessment* of modern culture, however materialistic, irreligious and atheistic it may seem, can result in the teaching and practice of a faith that is conceptual, divorced from culture, not incarnated.

2) *Principles:*

Faith does not exist unless it is incarnate because it is a way of life. It has always been incarnate in a culture, or rather it has always been incarnate in human beings as they really are and these human beings are part of a given culture.

While faith and culture are distinct, in reality they are inseparable in the human condition. If the whole man is to be saved (and only Christ can achieve this), Christ must assume the various cultures.

No culture is perfect, nor are cultural values absolute. A culture which remains enclosed within itself becomes impoverished and rigid and finally dies. If the faith allows itself to be imprisoned in a particular culture, it suffers from the limitations of that culture.

There has to be a continuing dialogue between the faith and all cultures, including the contemporary cultures that are developing. Between the faith and culture a mutual emulation should exist. Faith purifies and enriches culture and vice versa inasmuch as this continuing dialogue frees the faith and enables it to express itself more completely and to transcend the limitatons which a particular culture might impose. Faith sheds on ordinary everyday life a light which is supernatural.

A balanced pluralism in the expression of the faith must not be considered just as a necessary evil, but rather as something good for which we should be striving in proportion as it helps the manifestation and growth of God's gifts, whether natural or supernatural. Moreover unity is preserved thanks to the oneness of human nature and the unity of the Spirit who animates all life and supports every effort.

The Holy Spirit can fulfil that deepest human aspiration which mankind finds it impossible to achieve, namely, genuine unity within the most widespread diversity.

Catechesis then should be the focal point of the meeting between faith and the culture of each individual man — especially the culture of the rising generations who are even now preparing for lives that will be integral and with real meaning.

Attitudes Towards Inculturation

Clearly, successful inculturation calls for a combination of apparently contradictory qualities: audacity and prudence, initiative and docility, creative imagination and practical good judgement, a strong will and unending patience, esteem for one's own culture and the humility to be open to other cultures. "Why should anyone wish to impose the colours of the sunset on the dawn?

Visible catholicity is the normal expression of the Church's interior richness, of its beauty which shines in its variety:

'circumdata varietate'. The Church is catholic, neither Latin nor Greek; it is universal" (cf. Henri de Lubac, *Catholicism. The social aspects of dogma*).

To sum up briefly, we need to have the mind and heart of Christ, *"sensus Christi"*. Genuine inculturation rooted in a profound unity, whose richness depends on the variety which is the reflection of the whole human race in its eschatological fulfilment, will be the living sign of Christ's victory, the apotheosis of the Lamb (Rev. 19, 1-8).

(B)
THE POSSIBILITIES OF CATECHESIS

> *Father Arrupe tells us here that he was struck by "the range and breadth of our Ministry", and by "the cosmic horizons" of the Church's catechesis as proposed by Pope Paul VI to the members of the Synod in his homily at its inauguration in the Sistine Chapel.*
>
> *In this short exposition he points out some fields and agents of catechetical activity besides the traditional ones of home, parish and school.*

*

After listening to the reports from the *Circuli Minores*, I experienced a deep feeling of complacency in the face of this abundant wealth of insights and proposals. Here was a clear witness to the action of the Spirit in God's Church.

And yet, later on — perhaps because of an Ignatian tendency to discern the spirits — I discovered that this reaction was noticeably different from that produced in me by the Holy Father's homily in the Mass opening the Synod in the Sistine Chapel, in which he spoke to us of the "range and breadth of our Ministry". He defined our ministry as "universal and catholic, even, with the native force of the Greek word, cosmic" (*Oss. Rom. 1 Oct, 1977*).

In this way, the Holy Father opened up for us wide, "cosmic" horizons. And we were breathing the air of *"go into the whole world and preach the Gospel to every creature"* (*Mk 16, 15*), a text which he himself cited.

Instead of this, some of the concerns of the Synod seem to me to reflect a worried, narrowing or restrictive tendency, as if that wide open, limitless horizon were shrinking and narrowing because of a preponderant absorption in a select group of people which the Church is *de facto* reaching today — a group very small in comparison with the world-wide Catholic population.

Perhaps the understandable concern for planning a Catechesis in the strict sense of the term, complete and orthodox, could give the impression of fostering a policy of elitism, giving rise to a process of inbreeding.

To achieve a balance between this position, more *"ad intra"*, and another complementary position *"ad extra"*, centrifugal, extra-mural, we should put the questions: Where are the catechumens of today? Who are they? and with no less urgency and concern: Where are those who could — or should — be catechumens? Who are they?

Locus of Catechesis

The *loci* of catechesis have been listed: family, parish, catechetical groups, the school.

Family

How many families are today in reality a valid vehicle of catechesis? Has not the de-Christianization of the family become axiomatic in wide sectors of the population? And, even if they were able to catechize their small children, are parents with their older mentality the right ones to reach their children of 15 years and older? Where are the large majority of teenagers going to receive their catechism?

Parish

How many does the parish in fact reach? Amid the diversity of rural, urban and suburban parishes, in so-called Catholic countries as well as on the missioin in, every kind of culture, according to statistical data in many countries it is only 10% of the faithful who have the opportunity — when they come to Sunday Mass — to receive a brief instruction by way of the Homily. What happens to the other 90%?

Catholic School

In many countries, the school reaches less than 15% of

the Catholic school-age population. What will happen to the 85% who are educated in other schools?

Catechetical Groups

What percentage of genuine practising Catholics are organized in this systematic catechesis for seven years? 10%? Still less?

I do not intend these questions as merely rhetorical — still less am I suggesting a critical or pessimistic position. Rather, I urge realistic reflection so that we can work with hard data.

Catechumens, Catechists, Catechism

For these reasons, I would like to draw your attention to other fields of activity which offer great possibilities, in which, if we go about it correctly, we will be able to find effective co-workers who can be trained as agents of a catechesis adapted to their cultural milieu.

Who are the people we have to reach in catechesis?

They are either totally, or to a great degree, cut off from the Church and her catechetical activity. They would be well disposed for instruction if anyone would seek them out where they live and would speak to them in a language they understand. Who are they? They are the professionals (doctors, engineers, etc.), artists, politicians, young athletes, mountain climbers, hippies, workers in their unions or in their factories or in their neighbourhoods or in their co-operatives. They are all the natural groupings in which people are drawn together for various reasons, people who have the same problems, personal or professional.

Where are they?

Every one in his own milieu, in his own group. That is where we have to go to find them and carry on our catechesis. Sharing in the same milieu, and the same group, participating in their professional meetings or recreational activities, instructing on their ground, catechizing on a trip to the mountains, surrounded by the beauties of nature, or getting our word in between the light music and the Beatles' records.

Sometimes the undertaking of getting people to come to church can only be accomplished after a preliminary stage in which the church has to come to them. For their part, they have not come yet, and they are not going to come. Perhaps the thought of coming has occurred to them, but given the conditioning of their cultural situation, they are not able to come. And yet, many would like to come and they would listen to us if we could find the way to talk to them where they are, in a way they understand.

Who will be the catechists?

Of necessity, it will be members of the groups we are trying to reach, a true multiplication effect of ecclesial action. Once such people are formed, they will carry on a specialised catechesis, with new forms, channelling their experience and their life of faith through stream-beds as yet unknown. They too are the ones to answer the question: How catechize?

What will be their catechism?

It will not be the same for all. They will need one that, keeping intact the deposit of faith, will know how to present it in a form, with a tone, adapted to the mentality and the needs and milieu of the group. The catechism of artists will be very different from that of workmen, of judges or drug addicts.

It is an enormous field. Such a large segment of humanity, in comparison with which those who find their way to our churches show up as a very small remnant. In my opinion, the Synod should be attentive to this problem and avoid an almost exclusive preoccupation with a perfectionist catechesis of traditional methods — reaching numbers necessarily small — relegating to a secondary position a catechesis (can we keep on calling it that?) of penetration in the multitude (I avoid the word "mass"). A multitude powerful and dynamic in other respects, which has proved impervious to the methods we have used up till now. And they are souls who are looking for a special effort from the Church.

I close with a reference to the catechesis of the first days of the Church. I think of Paul who did not limit his catechesis to the synagogues but went out to slaves and masters, to followers of the Old Law and, with preference, to Gentiles. He wrote to this Church of Rome, which he had dreamed of visiting, "*How shall they believe in Him of whom they have not heard? How shall they hear unless someone preach to them? And how shall they preach if they are not sent?*" (*Rom 10, 14*). God grant that we will be able to respond with Paul: *Your Word has gone forth to the ends of the earth.*

16

ON INCULTURATION

Two Letters of Father Arrupe on Inculturation:

(A) To the whole Society
Rome: May 14, 1978
(AR, XVII, 1979, pp. 256-263)

(B) To the Members of the Indian Assistancy
Rome: June 27, 1978

(A)

ON INCULTURATION TO THE WHOLE SOCIETY

The Decree on Inculturation — Fr Parmananda Divarkar wrote once — is one of the shortest and most pedestrian pruducts of the 32nd General Congregation, but the interest it soon aroused is an indication of the importance of the issues it raises and of the urgency of the task it imposes on the Society and the individual Jesuit.

Inculturation — at least the term — was born in the Congregation. It was the experience of a deep-rooted one-ness at the heart of a wide-ranging variety: never had there been such diversity in a Jesuit assembly before, never such a problem of language — and yet there was real communication, seemingly effortless because of the overwhelm-ing consciousness of belonging together, of having very much to share. It was even said that the tensions that some members reported as existing in various quarters seemed so trifling, and paradoxically so serious, in the light of their own felt unity. Old timers who had attended previous Congregations could not help remarking that though this

> *was the first time that they had no common tongue —
> for Latin was in general use even at the 31st — yet there
> was greater mutual acceptance and understanding than
> before, in spite of a greater variety of background — with,
> of course, differences of opinions.*
>
> *It was only three years after GC 32, after much study,
> consultations and experience, that Father Arrupe addressed
> the Society on this complex subject. He also wrote a special
> letter on the subject to the Jesuits in India and Sri Lanka.*

*

Dear Brothers in Christ:

The Thirty-second General Congregation in its decree on Inculturation entrusted Father General with the task of "further development and promotion of this work throughout the Society" (decr. 5, n. 2).

I accepted this mandate of the Congregation with all the greater interest because my experience both before and after my election as General has profoundly convinced me of the importance of this problem.

Taking "culture" in the same sense in which it is understood by the Pastoral Constitution *Gaudium et Spes* (53), and subsequently by the Apostolic Exhortation *Evangelii Nuntiandi* (20), and by the recent Synod of 1977 in its final message (n. 5), the problem of inculturation presents itself on such a large scale, in situations of such wide diversity and with such profound and varied implications, that it is not at all easy to settle on concrete lines of approach that are universally valid.

For this reason, I have decided to limit myself in this letter to a few considerations that may serve as a stimulus for you not only to promote this process of inculturation but to be actively involved in it. I want to tell you how I see this problem as it touches the Society.

In a separate document, attached to this letter, some reflections are offered, and various issues raised; questions are formulated that are intended to focus our efforts to find solutions. For, in spite of the progress we have made, this is a subject that still requires much study, consultation, and discernment.

1. The notion of inculturation and its universal relevance today

Inculturation can be looked at from many viewpoints and seen at different levels, which must be distinguished but cannot be separated. Yet, amid the multiple formulations of the problem which we have to reckon with, the fundamental and constantly valid principle is that inculturation is the incarnation of christian life and of the christian message in a particular cultural context, in such a way that this experience not only finds expression through elements proper to the culture in question (this alone would be no more than a superficial adaptation), but becomes a principle that animates, directs and unifies the culture, transforming and remaking it so as to bring about "a new creation".

In every case, this christian experience is that of the People of God, that lives in a definite cultural space and has assimilated the traditional values of its own culture, but is open to other cultures. In other words, it is the experience of a local Church which, accepting the past with discernment, constructs the future with its present resources.

I believe that we are much more conscious nowadays than we were before of the urgent importance and the deep implications of this process.

It is clear that the need for inculturation is universal. Until a few years ago one might have thought that it was a concern only of countries or continents that were different from those in which the Gospel was assumed to have been inculturated for centuries. But the galloping pace of change in these latter areas—and change has already become a permanent situation—persuades us that today there is need of a new and continuous inculturation of the faith everywhere if we want the gospel message to reach modern man and the new "sub-cultural" groups. It would be a dangerous error to deny that these areas need a re-inculturation of the faith.

So you should not think that this document which I am sending you has reference only to what have been called "Mission Countries" until now. It finds application everywhere, perhaps all the more so where people think they do not have this need. The concepts, "Missions", "Third World",

"East/West", etc., are relative and we should get beyond them, considering the whole world as one single family, whose members are beset by the same varied problems.

The christian experience in a given culture has an influence that transforms and renews and, perhaps after a crisis of confrontation, leads to a fresh wholeness in that culture. Further, christian experience helps a culture to assimilate universal values which no one culture can exhaustively realize. Christian experience invites us to enter into a new and profound communion with other cultures, inasmuch as all the nations are called to form, with mutual enrichment and complementarity, the "robe of many colours" of the cultural reality of the one pilgrim People of God. In today's world, a large contact between cultures is inevitable, and this provides a providential opportunity for inculturation. The problem lies in a wise channelling of this intercultural influence. It is here that christianity can play a most important role: its mission is that of searching the depths of the past with lucid discernment, whilst it opens a culture both to values that are universal and common to all human beings, and to the particular values of other cultures; it must ease tensions and conflicts, and create genuine communion.

Surely this is one of the great contributions that we should be making.

2. Inculturation and the Society of Jesus

As Jesuits we should feel especially challenged by this problem. It is one we have confronted throughout the history of the Society; and unless we solve it, great obstacles to our work of evangelization will block our path.

Ignatian spirituality, with its unifying vision of Salvation History, and its ideal of service to the whole human race ("with such diversity...of dress and behaviour;...some white, others black..." Sp.Ex., 106), was a stroke of genius which, according to some experts, channelled the sensibilities and the cultural characteristics of the 16th century into the steady stream of christian spirituality; nevertheless, it did not confine itself to its own age, but in the course of history has been able to promote both the dynamism of the Spirit and human creativity, in a never ending process of adaptation to all peoples and times.

Quite obviously, St. Ignatius never used the word "inculturation". But the theological content of this term is present in his writings, including the Constitutions.

The *Presupposition* of the Exercises demands a basic disposition at the outset of the retreat which is of immense value in inculturation: to be ready to "save the proposition of the neighbour" (22). This is where authentic dialogue begins.

The Exercises ask us to reflect on the one beginning and end for all human beings (23), their solidarity in sin (51, 71), the call of the King addressed to the whole world (102). Furthermore, they recall that everything comes to us as a token of God's love, as gifts that descend from above (234,235,257).

The personal experience of Christ and his message which we live in the Exercises, the interior knowledge of the Lord (104), helps us to discern correctly what is inalienable in christian faith and what might be merely its cultural wrappings.

Concern for the concrete situation is a constant in the thought of St. Ignatius and in his government. It appears in more than 20 passages of the Constitutions. He keeps insisting that attention be paid to the circumstances of country, place, language, different mentalities, and personal temperaments (Cfr. Constitutions, 301, 508, 581, 747, 395, 458, 462, 671, 64, 66, 71, 136, 211, 238, 449, etc.).

Along the same line are the words of advice he gives in various instructions: "They should make themselves approachable by humility and love, becoming all things for the sake of all (I Cor 9,22); let them clearly adopt, as far as the Institute of the Society allows, the customs of those peoples" (to the Fathers and Brothers sent on ministries: Rome, 24 September, 1549; MI Epp XII, 239-242). He orders that penances be given to those who do not learn the local language (to the Superiors of the Society: Rome, 1 January, 1556).

The tradition of the Society has always been faithful to this principle of adaptation. This is the way our great missionaries acted—Xavier, Ricci, de Nobili and so many others, each according to the mentality of his time—when they launched bravely and creatively on an effort at pastoral adjustment to a given situation.

The task of evangelization of cultures, which is one aspect of the total problem, cannot be ignored in our days, and it calls for Jesuits who make a similar creative effort. Paul VI invites us to take up this responsibility, so much in keeping with the tradition of the Society, when he encourages messengers of the Gospel to make every effort and give serious attention to the evangelization of cultures (Cf. *Evangelii Nuntiandi*, 20).

This is surely one of those difficult and yet very important areas mentioned by the Pope, in which there has been or now is a tension between pressing human needs and the christian message, and where Jesuits have always been ready to work (Cf. Allocution to the members of GC 32, 3.xii.74).

The ignatian spirit was once summed up in this sentence: "*Non cohiberi a maximo, contineri tamen a minimo, divinum est.*" In our context, this maxim challenges us to hold on to the concrete and the particular, even to the last cultural detail, but without renouncing the breadth and universality of those human values which no culture, nor the totality of them all, can assimilate and incarnate in perfect and exhaustive way.

3. Necessary attitudes

Many factors contribute to achieve a successful inculturation, and these demand from whoever is involved in the process a fine sensibility and some definite attitudes.

Beyond the fundamental attitude already mentioned, that is, of the *unifying vision* of Salvation History, one needs in the first place *docility to the Spirit*, who is the real "*causa agens*" of all new inculturation of the faith. This docility demands a continuous and attentive listening in prayer, so that the action of the Spirit is effective in the midst of all our studies and projects. This docility guards against preconceived conclusions. Putting it in ignatian language, it presupposes *indifference*, adopting a stance that is open both to receive and to give.

Genuine inculturation also supposes an attitude of ignatian *discernment*, which is ruled by evangelical principles that give to human values a transcendental dimension, so that we neither overestimate the elements of our own culture nor underestimate elements that can be found in other cultures. Discernment leads to readiness to learn from others and makes one cautious in the face of misleading appearances or superficial judgments; otherwise one might accept indiscriminately values of secondary importance while sacrificing fundamentals —for example, one might overstress technical development at the cost of destroying basic values of the person such as freedom and justice. This kind of "discretion" is vital today when all around us we see a tendency towards extremes.

Objective authenticity, which is fostered by this discretion, leads to an *interior humility* which makes us recognize our own errors and helps us to be understanding towards those of others. The countries with a long christian tradition have certainly made mistakes in their work of evangelization, but today these are openly admitted and should be forgiven and forgotten. Likewise, the new nations who have received the Gospel from others, have made mistakes which they recognize; and these too should be forgiven and forgotten. Thus the way is open for a collaboration in which there is mutual acceptance in the creation of a present and a future, without prejudice or reservations, without limits set on the power of the Spirit.

Inculturation also requires a *persevering patience*, which is indispensable for studies in depth (psychological, anthropological, sociological, etc.) and for the unhurried experimental projects which will surely have to be undertaken. We must also steer clear of sterile polemics and, still more, of easy bargains with error.

On the contrary, it is necessary patiently to search for the *"semina Verbi"*, those *"pierres d'attente"* predestined by Providence for the building up of truth.

Caritas discreta is another requirement for inculturation, so that prophetic boldness and the fearlessness of apostolic zeal are blended with the prudence of the Spirit. Thus we can avoid extreme positions and counterproductive imprudence without restricting the impulses of a sound prophetic sense that can inspire us to take calculated risks.

Above all, we need the ignatian *sensus Ecclesiae*. In a process that is so important and full of implications, one cannot remain on the fringe of the Church—and we understand the Church as does Vatican II, that is, in its twofold aspect of People of God and of Hierarchy. Neither of these elements can be overlooked. It is evident that final responsibility rests with the Hierarchy. But we have to avoid two extremes: the excess *"non secundum scientiam"* (Rom 10:2) which would have us proceed regardless of the Hierarchy, and the small-mindedness which would keep us timid and passive, inhibited in our creativity. As in all else, so too in this process of incultu-ration, the love which we profess for the "Spouse of Christ" must lead us to think "with the Church" and "in the Church", submitting our activities and experiments in this delicate matter to the Church's direction.

These dispositions should awaken in the members of the Society that *universal charity* which urges them to outstanding efforts as creators of communion, not only at the level of the local Church, but with concern for the communion of the entire pilgrim People of God.

4. Internal consequences

The effect this process would have on the inner life of the Society should be obvious. The changes which have taken place and which will keep on taking place in the future, as we try to adapt ourselves to contemporary cultural changes, have their origin in the criteria of Vatican II and in the priorities and directives of the Thirty-first and Thirty-second General Congregations. But these changes will have no practical effect if we do not allow the transforming power of the Spirit to modify our personal life from within. We might call this "the personal interior inculturation", which must necessarily precede, or at least accompany, the external task of incultura-tion. All changes arising from Vatican II and from our last two General Congregations have precisely this objective: to make us effective agents of a genuine inculturation of the Gospel.

In order to understand our charism in contemporary terms and to discern in apostolic spirit our service to the Church today, we have to rethink our way of applying ignatian criteria to the concrete situations that face us. This is a kind of inculturation which is personal and *"intra Societatem"* and it is not easy. Although we admit in theory the necessity of inculturation, when it comes to practice and touches us personally, demanding of us profound changes in our attitudes and scale of values, often there is insensibility and resistance. This shows up our lack of inner disposition for "personal inculturation".

If we want to let ourselves be caught up in the process of inculturation, theory and study are not enough. We need the "shock" of a deep personal experience. For those called to live in another culture, it will mean being integrated in a new country, a new language, a whole new life. For those who remain in their own country, it will mean experiencing the new styles of our changing contemporary world—not the mere theoretical knowledge of the new mentalities, but the experiential assimilation of the way of life of the groups with which we must work, the outcasts, Chicanos, slum dwellers, intellectuals, students, artists, etc.

Take, for example, the wide world of the young people whom we serve in our schools, parishes, Chrisian Life Communities, Centres of Spirituality, etc. They belong to a culture that is quite different from that of many Jesuits, with mental structures, scales of value and language (especially religious language) not always easily intelligible. Communication is difficult. In a certain sense, we are "foreigners" in their world. I think that many Jesuits, especially in the developed countries, have no idea of the abyss which separates faith and culture; and for that very reason they are less well equipped servants of the Word.

The experience of what is called insertion into another culture should free us from so much that keeps us shackled: class prejudice and narrow loyalties, cultural and racial discrimination, etc.

The total inculturation required of a Jesuit should never turn him into a hidebound nationalist or regionalist. Our universalism, the sense of belonging to the "universal body" of the Society, must be kept inviolate, "lest diversity damage the bond of charity", as St. Ignatius notes in the Constitutions

(672). So too, we have to maintain in full vigour the disposition of availability, a fundamental attitude of every Jesuit, which makes him ready to go wherever there is hope of greater service of the Church, if he is sent on mission by obedience.

It is in keeping alive this availability that we feel more personally and intimately the tension between the particular and the universal, between the sense of being identified with the culture of a particular people and, at the same time, keeping ourselves free and ready to be sent to any part of the world where our apostolic service is required.

Authentic inculturation, with the above-mentioned characteristics of particularity and universality, has an obvious importance in the *formation of our young men*. They are called to become agents of inculturation and must, therefore, be formed in its spirit and in its concrete expression.

In line with the desire of the Thirty-second General Congregation that we "continue with even greater intensity today" the work of inculturation, I would like that a persevering effort in this area become the object of "ever growing concern on the part of the Society" (Decree 5, n. 1). I want us to be vitally aware of the capital importance of inculturation for our mission of defence and propagation of the faith, conscious that we belong at one and the same time to the local Church and to the Universal Church.

But this will not come about without personal and profound convictions—so whoever does not have these should strive for them—and without the well-ordered collaboration of all, in study, in reflection and in concrete experiences. Only in that way will we discover those living channels of communication and expression that will enable the christian message to reach the individuals and the peoples with whom we work, opening them up at the same time to the riches of other cultures.

A delicate task this, to be sure; but indispensable. It is one of the best services which the Society of today can render in the cause of evangelization. All of us, sons of the Society, should be conscious of being sent as heralds and agents of a communion that not only gathers together people of our own countries, but brings to unity, whilst respecting distinct identity, "all God's children scattered far and wide" (John 11:52).

I am sending you this letter on the Solemnity of Pentecost, and I invoke upon all of you the light and grace of God's Spirit.

Feast of Pentecost,
Rome, 14 May, 1978

Pedro Arrupe,
Superior General
of the Society of Jesus

(B)
ON INCULTURATION
TO THE MEMBERS OF THE INDIAN ASSISTANCY

In this Indian edition of some documents of Father Arrupe it was thought proper and useful to add here the special letter he wrote to Jesuits in India and Sri Lanka on Inculturation after the Final Report of the Commission on Inculturation and the Conclusions published by the Jesuit Conference of India.

*

Dear Fathers and Brothers in Christ: P. C.

I was indeed very happy to receive the 'Conclusions of the Jesuit Conference of India on the Report of the Commission on Inculturation'. It is the fruit of hard and sustained work undertaken for over two years by the Inculturation Commission set up by the Major Superiors of India and Sri Lanka after the first meeting of the Formatores in October 1975. The meeting of the Jesuit Conference of India held in March this year was the culmination of a process that involved the whole Assistancy. The several meetings which the members of the Inculturation Commission had with you individually and in groups helped clarify issues, suggest new solutions and chalk out a whole programme of action, as reflected in the interim report and in the final recommendations of the Commission. The members of the Commission deserve our gratitude and congratulations for having brought this difficult task to successful completion. This is the biggest effort made in any Assistancy in the Society to implement decree 5 of the 32nd GC "on Promoting the Work of Inculturation of Faih and Christian Life". The Whole Society, therefore, will look towards you for the next few years to see the working and fruits of your programme. Remember the great influence of India in antiquity. May your example and achievements be an inspiration and guide for all of us!

Your Major Superiors have selected some key areas which, being more fundamental, would need greater attention. I wish, that all the Jesuits of the Assistancy and more especially those engaged in Formation cooperate with the Major Superiors in the implementation of the tasks outlined in the Conclusions. The fact that they have identified not only areas, but also the persons responsible for the programmes in those areas, is an indication of their determination to see them through. You are ready to accept the challenge; you are aware of the difficulties and risks involved; you are refreshingly lucid and realistic about your undertaking.

The very concreteness of the recommendations could turn into a mirage if it is not kept in mind that they deal mostly with externals, and may not necessarily produce the fruits desired unless you have the spirit and the attitudes which should animate their implementation. All of you Fathers and Brothers — not only the Formators and those in formation — need to develop these attitudes, and accept in the right spirit the recommendations made concerning lifestyle and other points pertaining to the apostolate. This will mean for many a great sacrifice, but the service of the Church and of the great people of India and Sri Lanka demands this of you. Our young men in formation need to find in the formed houses a suitable and congenial atmosphere to grow into the Jesuit of tomorrow that we desire. I have elaborated on these attitudes in my letter on 'Inculturation', and I would ask you to reflect on them. Here I shall point out some of them which seem to me of particular importance in the context of India and Sri Lanka.

Inculturation represents for us the dynamic aspect of the Incarnation and hence is intimately bound up with evangelisation. It is a process by which our experience of Christ so liberates us to be truly ourselves that in our lives there is no "split between Culture and Gospel" and that as a 'new creation' we can perform the duty which the Holy Father proposes to us "of proclaiming the liberation of human beings, and of assisting the birth of this liberation, of giving witness to it, of ensuring that it is complete" (*Evangelii Nuntiandi*, nn. 20, 30). That will be the foundation of the real "Indian incarnation" of the charism of St. Ignatius.

You can now understand why I insist in my letter on docility to the Spirit of God in prayer, Ignatian indifference and discernment, and interior openness, persevering patience, '*discreta caritas*' which combines daring and prudence, and above all an ecclesial sense. Among these I would recommend in a special way interior openness, apostolic daring and a keen ecclesial sense. Your countries are characterised by a variety of cultures even in the same country, whose multicoloured beauty has at times been enhanced, but often marred, by a history of cultural dominations. A whole new generation of youth is rising, avid for progress and eager to take their due place in life, in company with the youth of the world. That is why the task you have undertaken is not only challenging but also delicate. There is need for mutual respect, 'collaboration in reconciliation' towards the building up of the present and the future, with no prejudices, no suspicions, no limits to the power and action of the Spirit. This interior openness will also help you to integrate into the body of the Society ever more deeply, because you will bring to the apostolic effort of the Society a new inspiration, a fresh manifestation of the Spirit.

I have referred also to the need of a keen sense of the Church. You have some Christian communities dating from the beginning of the Christian era, others just a few years old, some in urban and industrial areas, others in rural and tribal territories, dispersed among different religious and social groups. The Christian experience of all these communities are at different levels, and so their apostolic needs too. While we avoid the two extremes of an unenlightened zeal and pride on the one hand, and paralysing pusillanimity on the other, we shall always remember that the ultimate responsibility for directing the work of inculturation rests with the Hierarchy and so shall carry out our programmes in a sentiment of genuine love for the Church, the 'Spouse of Christ', submitting our activities to the directives of the Hierarchy.

I would like to insist on the need of combining deepest insertion and identification with your culture in order to enlighten it with the wisdom of Christ, with the openness to the rest of the world with a true catholic, universal spirit which knows to assimilate genuine values of other cultures, and is ready to communicate your own to them. India can contribute much to the world of today, but to carry out this rule she has to be open. Please take care lest the fervour for local inculturation degenerates into a pernicious regionalism which together with isolationism thwarts the growth-process necessary in the world of today.

The Society in India and Sri Lanka can truly be said to be in an exciting era of its growth. As you start implementing the recommendations contained in your document, you will meet with new problems. You will experience tensions to which I referred in my letter to you after Goregaon I. You will need the 'apostolic discernment' which will help you to be daring without being imprudent, looking not so much to the past as to the future, to the more lasting than to the immediate good. Others will reap where you have sown. I can only encourage you to go forward with confidence, recalling the words of the Apostle Paul: "I did the planting, Apollo did the watering, but God made things grow". (1 Cor 3:6). I assure you all of my prayers.

Rome   Yours devotedly in Christ,
June 27, 1978   **Pedro Arrupe, S.J.**

17

WHY INTERPROVINCIAL AND INTERNATIONAL COLLABORATION ?

A Conference to the Participants of a Meeting on the Society's Interprovincial and International Apostolate

Rome
September 25, 1975

The present General has by now made it a practice to call an annual meeting for autumn of representatives from Conferences of Provincials or other organizations to discuss matters of general interest to Jesuits. In 1975, after the 32nd General Congregation, he summoned 26 representatives to Rome. The general theme was ' Interprovincial and International Collaboration in the Society of Jesus in the light of the Decree on 'Our Mission Today'."

Father Arrupe's talk to the delegates concentrated on the existing structures for our universal ministry and our failure thus far to make adequate use of what is already ours, as we turn to face the world with new demands and perspectives.

*

I. PRINCIPLES OF UNIVERSALITY

1. Cutting across Provincial and National Boundaries

Often there has been talk in the Society about interprovincial and international collaboration and about the international dimensions of our life and apostolate. During these last years many factors have contributed to develop the international awareness of Jesuits and have led to greater communication

and collaboration among our different provinces, particularly
at the national and regional level, but also at the level of the
universal Society. Communication and cooperation have also
increased among Jesuits working in different sectors of apostolic
activity across provincial and national boundaries. Many
concrete examples could be mentioned to illustrate this. The
setting up of new channels and structures of government,
communication and collaboration at the national or assistancy
level, or specialized secretariats for the whole Society in Rome,
have also contributed to accelerate this trend. Many of those
present here in this meeting have been and are actively
engaged in these developments.

The increased interprovincial and international cooperation
in the Society reflects one of the salient features of the modern
world. It has been made possible thanks largely to modern
technical advances in the fields of communication and
transportation. Today we can do at the international level
what a few decades ago we could not even dream of.

The reason for this meeting, therefore, is not to discuss
something entirely new, but to develop further that communication and cooperation in the Society by learning from our
past experience, from our achievements and from our failures,
and in the light of present apostolic needs and trends. We
are still very far from having fully exploited our international
potential and all the possibilities offered to us by the development of the modern means of communication.

It might be good right from the start to dispel any doubts
or misunderstandings that could arise about the need for
this interprovincial and international collaboration. There
are still some who, while granting the need for a few common
works and services, are rather skeptical about that collaboration, particularly at the international level. They seem to believe only in the international cooperation which might help
them to carry on better the task that they are already doing
at the local, provincial and sometimes national level. And
even then, given the great variety of situations in the different
regions and cultures, the advantages of such cooperation
appear to them necessarily very limited. It is at the local level,
they say, that people with concrete needs and problems are

met and that our apostolic presence and action are really required. Besides, needs are numerous and urgent and the resources available to answer them are not only limited, but in many regions rapidly decreasing. They do not see, therefore, why their time, attention and energy, already so heavily taxed, should be diverted to consider other problems which, if not less real, have apparently little bearing on the reality in which they work, and remain out of their reach and influence. In this context, to talk about greater communication and collaboration at the interprovincial and international level, may appear to them as something utopic, as a kind of escapism from the demands that concrete situations place on us.

2. Steady Drudgery Work not against Jesuit Mobility

No doubt that there is some danger of running away from concrete local realities and taking refuge in a vaguely defined international apostolate; of avoiding the often hard and monotonous labour of a pastor, professor, administrator, writer or scientist, for less exacting and more pleasant tasks, in the exercise of which we enjoy sometimes greater freedom and we experience less the demands of our religious and community life.

As I shall point out later, the opposite danger is also very real. It is true, however, that most Jesuits will be called to work at a definite task, in a particular city or province and with or for a limited number of people. They will spend most of their lives in those places and occupations and among those people. Their primary obligation will be to exercise as best they can those concrete tasks. But even then we cannot forget the international nature of the Jesuit vocation: international not only in the sense of being ready to be sent wherever there is hope of God's greater glory and the service of men (*Jesuits Today*, § 13). All of us wherever we are and whatever we do, have to express somehow the international character of our vocation.

3. Jesuit Charism of Universality

As I already stated on another occasion: "Religious have a special responsibility for developing in themselves and in the Christian communities in which they work an international concern and a world-wide view of today's problems. Religious institutes 'may be removed from the jurisdiction of the local ordinaries by the Supreme Pontiff and subjected to himself alone. This is done in virtue of his primacy over the entire church in order to provide more fully for the necessities of the entire flock of the Lord and in consideration of the common good' (*L.G.* § 45). This concern that religious should have for the good of the universal church should be reflected in their dedication to meet one of the most urgent pastoral and missionary needs of our time: to instill in all a true love and respect for neighbour which will go beyond the narrow limits of one's own country or culture and embrace the whole of mankind" (*Witnessing to Justice,* p. 58).

If this is true of all religious, how much more of Jesuits. When we enter into the Society of Jesus, strictly speaking, we do not join a particular province or assistancy, but the *corpus universale Societatis.* We are directly called to serve the apostolic needs not so much of a particular country or region, but of the whole world and of the universal Church.

We can say, therefore, that a Jesuit fails in his apostolic duty if he does not try to develop in himself and in those among whom he works a concern for the universal good of the Church and of mankind. In a way, then, we need always to keep in touch with the needs and problems which the Church and the Society face in regions and cultures different from our own, if we are to fulfill adequately our own task, here and now.

Interprovincial and international collaboration should help us to give an international dimension to the concrete task that we are called to perform. Interprovincial and international collaboration should lead us to a closer solidarity and to a more generous sharing of our material and human resources to satisfy apostolic needs, wherever these needs are greater and more urgent. These aspects are extremely important and we are still far from the ideal, in spite of the progress achieved in their regard. But, as you are well aware, when we speak about the international apostolate, we mean more than this. Interprovincial and international cooperation is also and mainly necessary to meet needs and problems which are not local in nature, but common to several provinces, nations or regions: problems which are of a truly international and universal nature. Because of this, these problems are not less real or less grave and urgent. On the contrary, their international or universal nature should place them among our apostolic priorities. Whatever we do for their understanding and solution is bound to have a world-wide impact: "The more universal and good, the more is it divine" (*Const.* p. VII, ch. 2, § 622d). This principle of the Constitutions is taken up again in the *Epitome*: "In seligendis ministeriis hanc regulam sequitur Societas, ut quaerat semper maius divinum obsequium et utilitatem magis universalem" (*Epit.* n. 602, § 1).

In the Constitutions we are continually reminded by St. Ignatius that we should "keep always in view the greater service of God and the universal good" (e.g. *Const.* p. VII, ch. 2, § 623a; ch. 4, § 650). In the time of St. Ignatius this universal good was conceived more in terms of persons or places "which, through their own improvement, become a cause which can spread the good accomplished to many others who are under their influence or take guidance from them" (*Const.* p. VII, ch. 2, § 622d). Today, without denying the universal impact that particular persons and places can have, we would rather emphasize the universal and global importance of spiritual well-being of large segments of the human race. The principle of St. Ignatius, about the priority to be given to the more universal good, keeps all its validity today.

Are we convinced of this? Are we convinced in such a way that we are ready to make the necessary sacrifices which this implies? St. Ignatius, after enumerating certain criteria that should guide Superiors in the choice of the missions or ministries entursted to Jesuits, adds: "When everything mentioned above is equal and when there are some occupations which are of more universal good and extend to the aid of more of our fellowmen...and others which are concerned more with individuals.. and when further it is impossible to accomplish both sets of occupations simultaneously, preference should be given to the first set, unless there should be some circumstances through which it would be judged that to take up the second set would be more expedient" (*Const.* p. VII, ch. 2, § 623f).

II. VATICAN II AND GGCC 31 & 32

4. Local Culture and World-wide Interest in GC 32

The last General Congregation was very aware of the great diversity of situations that we encounter in our apostolate, in the different regions where we work, and which require from us great flexibility and adaptability. It emphasized the need for a more resolute insertion into the concrete human and social reality, for a deeper knowledge and awareness, not only conceptual but experienced and lived, of the concrete conditions in which men live and work today and of the concrete problems and needs that they experience. But at the same time, it also stressed that today the challenges we face are not simply of a local nature. It recognized that some of the major problems of our time have a universal and global extent and hence require a universal and global approach: think, e.g., of the root-causes of contemporary unbelief, atheism and injustice; think of the impact of secularization on our religious life and apostolic works all over the world.

Speaking of inculturation, the Congregation remarked that we "must take into account not only the cultural values proper to each nation but also the new, more universal values emerging from the closer and more continuous interchange between nations in our time. Here, too, our Society is called upon to serve the Church; take part in her task of *aggiornamento*, of "bringing up-to-date": that is, of incarnating the Gospel in these values as well, these new values that are becoming increasingly planetary in scope" (*Our Mission Today*, § 56).

The universal nature of many of today's problems, and the need for closer cooperation and coordination of our resources and of our efforts to meet them, became even more apparent when the Congregation looked at the world from the point of view of our mission today in the service of faith and for the promotion of justice: "The extent to which our contemporaries depend on one another in their outlook and even in their religious aspirations, to say nothing of the structural connections that span our planet, makes this overall coordination of our efforts indispensable if we are to remain faithful to our apostolic mission" (*Idem*, § 69).

As you know, the 32nd General Congregation concluded its decree on *Our Mission Today* with an appeal for a greater international collaboration in the Society, as required by our service of faith and the promotion of justice. The Congregation was well aware that this collaboration cannot be achieved without sacrifices and without "a real availability and openness to change" (*Idem*, § 81), because it will "shake us up in our settled habits or trouble our horizons, which may be less than all-embracing" (*Idem*, § 69).

Though the international apostolate may be seen by some as an escape from concrete needs and responsibilities, today the dangers of exaggerated provincialisms, nationalisms or regionalisms are in a way greater. We have certainly apostolic responsibilities towards our own province, country or culture and towards our own local churches, but this should not make us forget our Jesuit commitment to the more universal good of mankind and of the Church.

Nor should we get so involved in local tasks that we are unable to think of any other need which does not directly fall under our concrete responsibility here and now. Sometimes the comfortable feeling of being "at home" among people who know and understand us, the sense of security that a permanent job or working contract provide, greatly diminish our apostolic freedom and mobility, and our interest and concern for broader issues and problems.

While recognizing the specific cultural character of our own country or region, we should not over-emphasize that specificity to the extent of denying our common cultural heritage and the many common factors that today, more than in the past, bind all of us together in one human family and in one Church of God.

Some, Jesuits not excluded, seem to believe that their local problems and needs are so specific that nobody else can understand them or help in solving them. Others are so convinced of the value and importance of their own culture that they feel there is little or nothing to learn from others.

The fact that today foreigners find it difficult to get admittance into some countries and also the present stress being laid on the need for each local church and each country to free themselves from foreign dependence and to develop with their own means and resources, have sometimes contributed to lower the esteem for international solidarity. Whatever is foreign tends to be seen as an obstacle to a healthy development.

We have to recognize and accept the positive values of modern trends, but we cannot be blind to some of their ambiguities and dangers. A greater interprovincial and international cooperation is demanded from us by the apostolic needs of the times and also in virtue of our own Jesuit vocation: "The apostolic body of the Society to which we belong should not be thought of just in terms of the local community. We belong to a province, which should itself constitute an apostolic community in which discernment and coordination of the apostolate on a larger scale than at the local level can and should take place. Moreover, the province is part of the whole Society, which also forms one single apostolic body and community. It is at this level that the overall apostolic choices and guidelines must be decided and worked out: choices and guidelines for which we should all feel jointly responsible" (*Idem, § 68*).

5. Trend of Vatican II

The General Congregation, therefore, was not simply "innovating," but merely applying to present conditions and trends, the principles that have always been characteristic of our apostolic life and activity. It was part of the *renovatio accommodata* requested from us by the Church through the Second Vatican Council and already initiated by the previous Congregation. If we read again the documents of that Council, we will realize that what the 32nd General Congregation is asking from us in the field of interprovincial and international cooperation, is, after all, only to implement faithfully and in an eminent way, in the context of our own particular vocation, what the Church expects from all Christians in the present circumstances.

The international dimension of the Church's mission, the need for international cooperation and for organized forms of apostolate at the international level to meet present needs are repeatedly stressed in several of the Council documents (e.g.: *Lumen Gentium*, § § 13, 23; *Apostolicam Actuositatem*, § 19; *Ad Gentes*, § 41; *Inter Mirifica*, § 22), but particularly and with greater insistence, as it was to be expected, in the Pastoral Constitution on the Church in the Modern World (*Gaudium et Spes*, §§ 23, 83-84, 85-87, 89-90). In the light of that Constitution and of more recent documents of the magisterium (*cf.* Episcopal Synod of 1971, "Justice in the World"), the directives of the General Congregation concerning our role in the international field appear rather modest and make us realize the smallness of our contribution so far: smallness that makes us feel as belonging to "this least Society of Jesus" (*Preamble to the Const.*, § 1), not only because our resources and possibilities are necessarily limited, but because, in spite of repeated appeals, we are still very far from having achieved in the field of interprovincial and international collaboration what we should achieve and the Church and the men of today expect from us.

6. Earlier Congregations

I say "repeated appeals," because before the 32nd General Congregation, other Congregations had already insisted on the importance of the international apostolate and on the need for interprovincial cooperation. Already in 1938, when the interdependence of men one on the other and the key role of the mass-media of social communication in shaping public opinion were much less evident than today, the 28th General Congregation urged us, while continuing to carry on the traditional apostolic ministries, to get more and more involved in activities designed to influence that opinion at all levels: "ut..tota societas humana doctrina Evangelii penetretur atque intime reformetur" (*Collect. Decret.* § 125).

Almost twenty years later, the 30th General Congregation, convinced of the need to foster a "universal spirit" and mentality in the Society, not only promulgated a decree on this question (d. 49), but also requested Fr. General to issue norms to foster the establishment and development of inter-provincial and international works. Among these, special attention was given to the apostolate with international orga-nizations and with the people working in them (*Collect. Decr.* § 339g).

Finally, the 31st General Congregation stressed once again the importance of international organizations (d. 21, § 11d) and issued a decree on interprovincial cooperation "which is more and more a requisite for our apostolic action today" (d. 47, § 1). Among other things, that Congregation requested that each meeting of all the Provincials, when it is assembled under the presidency of Fr. General, should treat explicitly of this interprovincial cooperation (d. 47, § 4). This decree, as well as the decree of the 30th General Congregation request-ing us to foster a "supraprovincial and supranational spirit," keep all their meaning and relevance today. I invite you to read them again and meditate on them during these days.

7. Our Limitations and Possibilities

We cannot do everything. We should be realistic and humble. We should realize that we are only a small group within God's Church: smaller still if we consider all the men and organizations outside the Church that, with a relative abundance of personnel and material resources, strive to solve some of the very problems that concern us. It is true. We should not simply raise hopes and expectations that we cannot possibly in any way fulfill. On the other hand, it is also true that the Society still counts with a considerable number of highly qualified men and institutions and with a world-wide organization which under some respects is unique in the Church.

In spite of our shortcomings and limitations, we are better equipped than other religious groups to meet the international challenges of today's world. I cannot forget the words that the Holy Father addressed to us, at the beginning of the 32nd General Congregation: "Wherever in the Church, even in the most difficult and extreme fields, in the crossroads of ideologies, in the front line of social conflict, there has been and there is confrontation between the deepest desires of man and the perennial message of the Gospel, here also there have been, and there are Jesuits" (Address of Pope Paul VI to the 32nd General Congregation, December 3, 1974).

While these words reveal the high esteem in which the Holy Father holds the Society, they also place on us great demands and a tremendous responsibility. We should be there where the universal Church needs us today; there where the big battles are fought and the future of man is being shaped. Are we really there and in the way the Church wants us to be?

We are not alone on the battle field, and in certain areas like, e.g., the promotion of justice, powerful international organizations and many men of good will are also deeply involved. But the contribution that the Church expects from us does not always coincide with their contribution. Our specific concern, as apostles, priests and religious, are not always exactly theirs. In any case, it is a fact that we are often approached by the Church and our cooperation is requested to provide light and guidance regarding some of the major problems of our age having international dimensions. At times we have to give a negative reply: sometimes because we do not seem to have the needed resources, at least in the number or of the quality required; but sometimes also because we lack the means or the will to mobilize effectively for the good of the universal Church, the limited resources that we do have.

8. Universal Aspect of Decree 4 to be Implemented

The decree of the 32nd General Congregation on *Our Mission Today* offers us an excellent opportunity to reflect once again on our international responsibilities towards the Church and the men of today: to reflect and to think realistically, but also radically and creatively, of concrete means to strengthen the international dimensions of our apostolate and to mobilize our resources on a world-wide basis, at the service of faith and for the promotion of justice.

The main thrust and impact of this decree, once it has been

translated in terms of concrete objectives and programmes, will be naturally felt at the provincial and national level. However, in countries where we have several provinces, some interprovincial cooperation and coordination will be necessary to insure its successful implementation at the national level: e.g., in U.S.A., India, Spain, and other countries of Western Europe. There are aspects of this decree that will need the collaboration of all our provinces in regions comprising several nations and facing similar cultural, religious and social problems: think, e.g., of Latin America. Other points in the decree might require cooperation on an even larger scale. Some of these touch problems which may assume different forms in different regions, but which contain enough common elements to justify being studied at the international level, without excluding more specific studies at lower levels. I am thinking — to mention a concrete example in the field of reflection and study — of the need to clarify and further develop what constitutes today our specific contribution, as priests and religious, to social change and to the promotion of justice, particularly regarding the political dimensions of that promotion: a problem which we encounter today in many of the regions where we work. The same could be said of problems regarding the service of faith in today's secularized world: a question on which an exchange of ideas and experiences is already being fostered throughout the whole Society. Finally, some other aspects, by their very nature, seem to demand a concerted approach at the international level, both in the field of study and action: examples of this are the present search for a new international economic order and also for a new humanism that, while meeting the needs of our technological society, will also answer man's deepest religious and human aspirations.

In any hypothesis, the implementation of this decree, even at the local and provincial level, would greatly benefit by a frequent exchange of information, reflection and experiences on a world-wide basis. Out of this exchange common problems might emerge which at present we do not even suspect and which might provide the basis for concrete cooperation programmes among the Provinces of one or several assistancies or even of the whole Society.

Cooperation at the international level has also other advantages that, though of secondary importance, cannot be entirely overlooked. Often, for example, it is much easier to get from foundations or aid-giving agencies the necessary resources to finance projects of local or national interest, if these projects can be presented as part of an over-all and well coordinated international approach to solve common problems.

The purpose of this meeting is to study the problem of interprovincial and international cooperation in the light of the decree on *Our Mission Today* and, if possible, to come out with some concrete proposals, at least of a pilot nature, to set this collaboration in motion, in a few well-defined areas and regions. To this effect, it will help to reflect on past attempts in the field of interprovincial cooperation, so that we learn from our experience and do not commit again the same mistakes. We have also to see how existing structures of government and the channels of communication can be strengthened and better utilized to foster that cooperation, and whether new structures or channels are necessary.

You are not going to answer all the questions and solve all the problems simply in one meeting. But you can certainly make a very valuable contribution in a field which is of vital importance for our apostolic mission today and even for the future of the Society as an international body at the service of the universal Church.

ASPECTS OF THE MINISTRY
OF RECONCILIATION

**Homily preached by Father General at
Farm Street Church, London, in the presence
of Cardinal Heenan and the Apostolic Delegate**

London
January 23, 1970

*Father Arrupe paid his first official visit to the Jesuits in
England and Scotland on January 20-24, 1970. He met
most of his men at Heythrop, Edinburgh, Glasgow,
Stonyhurst, Preston, Manchester, Liverpool and London.
He gave two Press Conferences, two Radio interviews and
took part in a Television discussion with Malcolm Muggeridge
(included in this book, p. 9).*

*On January 23, he concelebrated the Eucharist at the
Jesuit parish church of Farm Street, London, with Cardinal
Heenan, the Apostolic Delegate to Great Britain, and
Archbishop Roberts, then a member of that Jesuit community
and formerly Archbishop of Bombay. The Congregation
of about six hundred was made up mostly of close relatives
of Jesuits and friends and benefactors of the Society.*

*At this Mass, Father Arrupe gave the homily proposing
"some thoughts about being a Jesuit in the contemporary
world." These thoughts revolved around the ministry of
reconciliation under several aspects, as the declared aim of
the founding of the Society. This appears in the Formula of
the Institute approved by Julius III, and was to be soon
echoed in various documents of the 32nd General Congregation.
(As a sequel to the homily, we may here mention that at the*

*end of the Mass, His Eminence Cardinal Heenan addressed
Father General and the congregation and spoke in a most
complimentary way of his friendship and association with
the Society and with the English Jesuits in particular.
He recalled that he himself, like many others present, had
been educated by the Society. He told Father General that
the members of the Province were collaborating most
harmoniously with the diocesan clergy in the country and
assured him that he need have no anxieties about his English
Jesuits).*

*

Your Eminence, my dear brothers and sisters in Christ

This is not the first time a Jesuit General has been to
England. Saint Ignatius himself, in his student days, came
to London and was deeply moved by the generosity of the
people. In 1848 Fr. Roothaan came here, fleeing revolution,
and Fr. Martin came towards the end of the last century.
Unlike Saint Ignatius I have not come to beg, and unlike
Fr. Roothaan I am not fleeing revolution. I have come simply
to visit and encourage my brethren of the English Province.
This visit has been a great joy to me and I want to share
with you, on this occasion, some thoughts about being a
Jesuit in the contemporary world.

These thoughts will be very simple — and they spring out
of the readings we have just heard. Every religious order —
and the Society of Jesus is no exception — represents an
original attempt, inspired by a charismatic personality, to
rediscover the spirit of the Gospels and live out that spirit
in its own time. When the first companions of Saint Ignatius
were trying to work out how best to serve the Lord, they
came upon this text of Saint Paul: "All this is from God, who
through Christ reconciled us to himself and gave us the
ministry of reconciliation" (2 Cor 5:18). This text summed up
what they wanted to do in the world, and why. Christ, "our
peace" (Ephes 2:14), first reconciles us to the Father, wins us
access to the Father. Those who wish to serve Christ become
his "ambassadors" (2 Cor 5:20), handing on his message,
following in his footsteps, using his methods, and striving,
through prayer, to catch something of his spirit.

So their ministry is appropriately described as "the ministry of reconciliation". There are so many levels of reconciliation. In practice, reconciliation means *breaking down the barriers that separate men from God and from each other.* In an increasingly secularized world, the reality of God is more difficult to realize: Jesuits, having learned to pray themselves, would hope to help others to lift up their hearts to the Lord and speak to him in familiar conversation of prayer. That is the condition of a fruitful apostolic work. It is a necessary condition.

But then the ministry of reconciliation extends into many other spheres. It is found, first of all, in the Church, since charity is in the Church, not as in a container, but as its constitutive element. The peace and unity of the Church are best served by *working with the bishops of the Church.* Four years ago, this Church of Farm Street, after 120 years, became a parish church. Cardinal Heenan said on that occasion: "This event mirrors . . the spirit of the recent Council, but it also symbolizes the entirely changed relationship within the Church between the religious orders and the hierarchy and the diocesan clergy" (*The Month*, April 1966, p. 238). We Jesuits are not individualists. We are at the service of the Church today, and at the service of the local Church. The move of Heythrop College from the country to London is another step in that direction.

There is another aspect of the "ministry of reconciliation" which we cannot overlook especially during this Octave of Prayer for Church Unity: *reconciliation with our separated brothers in Christ.* In history the Jesuits have been associated with the implementation of the Council of Trent. Today, following the mandate of Pope Paul, the Jesuits are concerned with the implementation of Vatican II, and that includes, not as optional extra, the work of ecumenism. Happily the English Province counts among its members some of the pioneers of the ecumenical movement. At the heart of this movement, which is the work of the Holy Spirit in our day, is the desire to seek together the Christ into whom we have all been baptized. Dr. Michael Ramsey, Archbishop of Canterbury, expressed the ecumenical task memorably when he said: "Our quest is not just the right doctrine or the right institution, but *through them* the sanctification of human lives in Christ in the adoration of the mystery of God" (*Minutes of the Faith and Order Commission*, Saint Andrews, August 3-8, 1960, p. 17).

But the unity of the Church is for the service of the world, and there are other, higher barriers which "the ministry of reconciliation" impels us to break down: *the barriers of prejudice between classes and peoples and races*. The new pattern of Jesuit education in this country will keep these aims in view. From our diversified schools, we would hope to see emerging mature Christians who are not afraid to commit themselves to the transformation of society as a whole. And what is true of educational work in England, is even more urgently true of education in the mission territories entrusted to the English Province in Guyana and Rhodesia.

The ministry of reconciliation excludes nothing from its scope, *neither science nor art nor any truly human enterprise*. Saint Ignatius has a "Meditation to grow in love" and the grace of this meditation is that we may "seek God in all things and find all things in him". The last General Congregation spoke of the way prayer "is a precious chance to see the unity of creation and to refer creation to the Father" (14:3). Here we see echoed the great theme of Saint Paul: "For in Christ the fulness of God was pleased to dwell, and through him to reconcile to himself all things, whether on earth or in heaven, making peace by the blood of his cross" (Col 1:19). This is the vision that has sustained so many humble, hidden apostolic lives. This is the vision which was shared by your English Jesuit poet, Gerard Manley Hopkins, who saw the glory and grandeur of God flashing out from the created world.

Reconciliation means, finally, *renewal*. "Therefore", says Saint Paul, "if anyone is in Christ, he is a new creation; the old has passed away, behold, the new has come" (2 Cor 5:17). We need to innovate with fidelity, to make courageous decisions for the future while respecting the past but not being imprisoned by it. The English Province — everyone knows — has a glorious past, with its martyrs to provide inspiration: but now it moves towards its future in "joyous hope". We all recognize the difficulties. But the words spoken by Edmund Campion, as the Jesuits came to England, are still relevant and still ring in our ears: "The enterprise is begun: it is God: it cannot fail".

JESUIT FORMATION FOR ECUMENISM ACTION AND UNITED WITNESS

Address of Father General Pedro Arrupe to the 4th International Congress of Jesuit Ecumenists

Dublin, Ireland
August 16-20, 1971

During the Second Vatican Council, a small Jesuit group of Council 'periti', particularly interested in the ecumenical movement, decided to pursue and deepen their personal and theological contacts by meeting regularly. The result was the first international Congress of Jesuit Ecumenists, held at Bad Schombrum, Switzerland in 1966. A second meeting was held in Rome, where some themes for the Bishops' Synod were prepared (1967). Others followed in Chicago, Dublin, Beirut, Frankfurt, Yaunde and (in 1979) Barcelona. The next (in 1981) is to be held in Toronto.

The Dublin Congress on "Ecumenical Ecclesiology", attended by some 120 Jesuit participants, was of particular importance. Father General Arrupe was present and gave the following address.

*

I. CONCERN AND FORMATION FOR ALL

This is a very happy occasion for all of us, for me as well as for you. We meet as fellow-Jesuits who are deeply concerned about the common cause of Christian unity and who are trying to express this concern in the different ways appropriate to our different ministries.

1. The Irish Scene and Jesuit Involvement

We are particularly happy to be in Ireland. Wherever we have come from, we have already met Irish people. They are to be found all over the world engaged everywhere in the work of evangelization. We are happy to visit their homeland, the source of their great missionary zeal, and we would hope to help forward, by our presence and our prayers, the valiant efforts in the cause of Christian reconciliation now being made on all sides throughout the whole of Ireland.

And we owe a special gratitude to the community of Milltown Park and more particularly to the Irish School of Ecumenics for the successful organization of this meeting. I would like to use this occasion to congratulate this institute for its successful first year and for the hopeful prospects it offers for the future.

One might well ask at the outset of this conference why Jesuits from many parts of the world should choose to meet together to discuss their common involvement in the ecumenical movement. What could be less ecumenical than a meeting composed only of Jesuits? The Church has made it clear that prayer and work for Christian unity is a call of Christ to all in his Church without exception: so, though one is glad to see individual Jesuits involved with other Christians both in the official dialogues of the Church and on their local scene, can there be a special role for the Society of Jesus in the ecumenical movement? Ecumenism, moreover, demands so much local commitment, local development and progress, which necessarily varies greatly with local circumstances: so, how can Jesuits serve the Church, or serve the world, or help each other, by an international meeting like this?

2. An All-pervading Dimension

In considering these questions I have been led first of all to reflect (as indeed I have had occasion to remark to various groups of Superiors of our order) that ecumenism is not a separate field of apostolate but is a dimension of all the Church's mission and therefore of all our apostolates. Our Society has the opportunity of making a considerable contribution to the one ecumenical movement, precisely because it is involved all over the world in such a variety of work. Hence there is always some ecumenical value in any international meeting of this kind, in so far as any of us is thereby enabled to see the wider context and implication of his own more specialized activity. It is of great profit to those of us in Europe to share the ecumenical experience of North America and Australia, where the barriers arising from language, culture and history have largely been broken down. And it is of particular value to this conference that it includes some whose service of Christ in his Church lies in other areas, especially in countries struggling for development. So, we can share with each other a wide variety of ecumenical experience and help each other with the brotherly encouragement and support which you need and which I need in order to sustain our common dedication to the cause of Christian unity.

Again, it is worth noting that any religious order has its own contribution to make in the Christian dialogue. That contribution should follow the lines of its own unique charism and characteristic spirituality. And the Society, which draws its existence and character from the Spiritual Exercises of St Ignatius Loyola, should be reflecting on how its distinctive spirituality can acquire a fully ecumenical dimension.

3. Formation for Ecumenism

We should not be satisfied with the idea of having some groups of Jesuits (however active they may be) working in this field of ecumenism: there should be a spirit in all of us, priests and brothers, which permeates all our prayer and all our ministries and work. But if it is true that there are signs that Jesuits everywhere are becoming increasingly aware of their ecumenical obligations, it is also true that past and present achievements have depended chiefly on individual initiative and in relatively few cases on a corporate effort of the Society of Jesus. We have relevant documents from the Church and the Society. The mind of the Church and specifically of Pope Paul VI is well known to all of us; it is not knowledge which seems to be lacking but decision and conviction, the realization that Christian disunity does indeed "block the way to the faith for many" (*Vat. II, Decree on Missionary Activity of the Church*, n. 6). We have to know, but today we have to act, following the spirit and the directives of the Church. But we are still very far from this ideal. In this regard I would recommend very seriously to those in charge of the formation of our young fellow-Jesuits that they incorporate this spirit in their formation programmes and activities, because "An education in ecumenism is not a matter of the intellect alone, but must be part of one's spiritual formation as well, since a truly ecumenical spirit cannot be had without a change of heart" (General Congregation XXXI, decree 26, n. 5; cf. Vat. II Decree on Ecumenism, n. 7). I would recommend first of all that those in charge of formation be imbued with such a spirit, because nobody can give what he does not have.

In regard to the Brothers, we may recall the recommendation of the same General Congregation: "Due consideration being had for their religious formation and the offices they hold, Brothers are to be informed in the matter of ecumenism so that by prayer, suitable understanding, and such personal contacts as fall to them, they too may participate in this activity of the Society" (ibid. n. 7).

And in general I would recommend that every one of us reread the Decree on Ecumenism of the Thirty-first General Congregation and reflect upon it, asking ourselves: "What have I done to put it into practice? What should I do?"

Through this renewal of our formation, we will become more ecumenically-minded in our whole life and work and give our own contribution to the important task of the instruction and formation of the faithful in the ecumenical spirit.

4. Let the Movement Keep Moving

Then too, the ecumenical movement is meant to move. And I hope it would not be in any way inappropriate to suggest, with the ecumenical movement particularly in view, that it is the nature of our Jesuit vocation not to be too closely bound to accepted patterns of ministry, to be as sensitive as we can to the newly emerging needs of the Church, and to do some of the pioneering and exploratory work to which God is calling his People. So we in the Society have always understood the need to be, here and now, sensitive and responsive to the greater glory of God. A constant openness to the Spirit of Christ, with a great docility and discernment is characteristic of our spirituality. We must be ever alert to the voice and inspirations of the Spirit because He has His own ways to guide us to real unity. Who knows the how and when of the realization of Christian unity? "Who knows the mind of the Lord? Who has been his counsellor?" (*Rom* 11:34). "The Spirit blows where it wills" (*John* 3:8), and we have to be very humble and open to receive these inspirations. This will give us the right ecumenical attitude. If work for Christian unity is to go forward with energy and enthusiasm and attract the younger generation, then the ecumenical movement must become bolder, more representative and more binding on the life of the Church. We should consider this appeal as addressed in a special way to our Society, in order to break out of the apathy for things ecumenical and the lack of conviction about the urgency of the problem that afflict some of our fellow-Jesuits.

II. SCOPE FOR JESUIT ACTION

5. Fields of Ecumenical Activity

Let us consider now some of the fields in which ecumenical development is of most urgent importance. One large area of our apostolate is spiritual direction and especially through the giving of retreats and missions, and the maintenance of retreat houses. Some ideas do come immediately to mind: can we not now use some of our Jesuit houses for ecumenical activities where Christians of different communities, in separate groups as well as in common, can receive spiritual guidance? Can we not help the development of the religious life of poverty, chastity and obedience in other Christian communions?

The general field of education is certainly one in which our Society is involved at every level and in so many countries. we therefore bear a particular responsibility for an integral ecumenical education of the young and of the young adult. They can often relate more easily on a personal level with other Christians than those of an older generation. And so in this apostolate we have the double task of building bridges within our own Catholic Church, and at the same time of creating the conditions for an ecumenical formation that is in every sense fully catholic. There is surely here an immense field for exploration and discovery. Moreover, I would earnestly appeal to all those engaged in the important Jesuit apostolate of secondary education not only to see to it that their students acquire the ecumenical spirit but also to address themselves, in collaboration with their counterparts in other Churches, to the more fundamental, difficult and urgent problem of discovering what the true nature of Christian education is and what its appropriate forms are in this world of the late twentieth century.

6. Theological Reflection

In considering the questions raised by the holding of this conference, I have so far touched more generally on the part that I see the Society is called upon to play in the ecumenical movement. But, if I were asked to select one role above all others for the Society in this field, various considerations would lead me to concentrate on theological reflection. In choosing the phrase "theological *reflection*", I am not, of course, forgetting the responsibilities of the Society for the teaching of theology and the training of priests in many parts of the world: here we need to give a clear and bold response to Part II of the Ecumenical Directory, which gives such warm and wide encouragement to Christian cooperation in higher studies and pastoral training, opening new possibilities which have not yet been fully exploited.

I say "theological reflection", as I said a year ago at the Procurators' Congregation in Rome because of the request made by many people in positions of leadership in the Church for scholarly and concerted theological reflection on the new problems that face the Church in her relation to the modern world as well as on the problems this world itself is facing which are our own problems. The Society seems particularly well equipped in some ways to meet this urgent need. This calls for a thorough, scholarly study of these problems which will provide profound doctrinal guidance for practical action and common witness. It will also show common positive points, which will be a great encouragement to go all the way to the unity desired by Christ. And we cannot forget in this regard "to examine the possibilities of a common Christian approach to the phenomenon of unbelief", as Pope Paul VI suggested in his speech at the headquarters of the World Council of Churches in Geneva (June 10, 1969).

This deep theological reflection will give us the right orientation and attitude of mind. I have been told that in many areas there are no longer significant differences between scholars from various Christian communities. If that means that they have been able to deepen their Chrisian communion and their common witness to the gospel of Christ in rigorous fidelity to God revealing Himself in His divine Son, I can only rejoice that Christian scholars are sensitive and faithful to what the Spirit is saying to the Churches. I would be saddened however if it were to mean a tendency to make light of different traditions long held by the various Christian communities and an impatience w'th these differences leading to neglect of them for the sake of some general unity. For this would be a sign of a certain impoverishment taking place precisely at the moment when we are deeply interested in searching out ways to preserve legitimate diversity joined to deep unity. Profound theological reflection assures that our ecumenical efforts will not be impoverished, but really enriched.

A combination of factors has in our day at once broadened the scope for theological reflection and increased our need for it. The pace and trend of renewal in all the Churches, the progress of dialogue on matteis of faith and order between Christians of all traditions, the development of the natural and human sciences and the advances of technology have raised new questions and re-opened questions which we thought answered. And these are not just academic, esoteric questions. They are practical and they concern everyone. On the answers to these questions depends to a great extent the future of the Church, the world and mankind. In God's saving plan what is the meaning, the role, the reality of the non-Christian religions, of the Christian traditions not in full communion with the Roman Catholic Church, of the various secular agencies promoting social reform, progress and peace? Everyone every day is giving an implicit answer to these questions. The grave danger is that the answer may not be a response to the question as now posed or that it may be superficial and unsound, or that it may even block further sound development.

7. Our Resources and Obligations

To face these questions our Society has, in God's Providence, considerable resources and corresponding obligations. All over the world there are Jesuits and Jesuit institutions working in close contact with non-Christians. They can come to realize the spiritual value and true role of the non-Christian religions. Their experience is vital in developing and adopting a new theology of mission. There are also many Jesuits and Jesuit institutions involved in the development of the natural and human sciences and of technology. Because they are not outsiders, they can approach and help us all to approach the questions being raised in this area with the required sympathy and understanding. Again there are Jesuits and Jesuit institutions involved in theological teaching and research and already in many places working together with their Protestant counterparts.

We are experiencing in this regard something very consoling. Seeing the way in which our professors and young students of theology deal in so many places with their colleagues of other denominations brings to my mind the words of Paul VI: "To come together, to meet others, to greet them, and to speak with them — what is easier, more natural and more human? Yes, but there is something further: to listen to each other, to pray for each other, and after such long years of separation, and such painful quarrels, to begin anew to love one another" (*Paul VI*: Address to the Delegates and Observers to the Second Vatican Council, *October 17, 1963*). This dialogue and this understanding is the best way to prepare for fruitful theological discussion. Charity is an irresistible force which brings us first to a union of hearts which inspires the union of minds. It is a wonderful step forward that today we can smile together at some of the less amicable moments in our histories without any feelings of superiority towards our forefathers, but with gratitude to God. It is interesting to see how our younger Jesuits speak so casually about ecumenism, and I would say almost unconsciously are practising it.

Because of their situation and competence our Jesuit professors and institutions are able, among other things, to appreciate, and help us to appreciate, how important theological pluralism can be for the successful outcome of the ecumenical dialogue and of the dialogue between Church and world. There are finally Jesuits with a special insight into the traditions of the East and Jesuit institutions devoted to sharing and deepening this insight. They are in a position not only to help the dialogue between East and West and assist the approach to full communion between the Catholic and the Orthodox Churches, but also to enrich the dialogue between the various Western traditions, ensuring that it is not only Western Catholicism that other Churches encounter in their many dialogues with the Roman Catholic Church, but the full range of catholic theological tradition.

8. Need for United Witness

Someone may say: today, when men are weary of the great number of spoken or written declarations and are looking for 'deeds', what is really important is common witness. As a rather recent study document, prepared by a mixed theological committee and accepted by the Joint Working Group of the Roman Catholic Church and the World Council of Churches, says: "Christians cannot remain divided in their witness. Any situations where contact and cooperation between Churches are refused must be regarded as abnormal". But here again theological reflection not only can provide a form of common witness in the specific field of scholarly research, but is required to give a clear basis and guidance to the whole range of this common witness in order to avoid "procedures that are superficial, rash and counter-productive... in this sudden enthusiasm for reconciliation... so that the many good desires and the many 'promising possibilities may not perish in misunderstanding, indifference and in a false irenicism" (*Paul VI: January 22,* 1969).

To cite an example, the Society is in a variety of ways involved in the social apostolate of the Church, and here too it must learn to exercise its mission in full cooperation with other Christians. Again, it is precisely this ecumenical social apostolate that has given rise to so many new theological problems. And there is great need for serious theological study of these questions, in order to support and to guide the social involvement of Christians.

9. Postconciliar Ecclesiology

But it is the most basic of all these theological problems that you are here to discuss. The Church does not exist to preserve itself in a kind of splendid isolation, but to preach the Gospel to the world. Christians are not seeking to unite for their own comfort, but in order to carry out more fully the Church's mission according to the will of Christ. And if we are to understand that mission better today, we have to ask not only, 'What is the world?' but also, 'What is the Church?' And, to use the term of St Ignatius Loyola, what is our holy mother the Hierarchical Church, and how is she speaking to us? Hence I can think of few more relevant exercises today than this discussion of postconciliar ecclesiology. I hope that its fruits can in some way be of benefit to others besides yourselves, and prove of wider service in the Church.

To whom much is given, of him much will be required. A deep conversion of our hearts to ecumenism is required of us so that the ecumenical movement may become more binding on the life of the whole Society of Jesus. We are being asked to renew ourselves radically in this spirit, to practise what we preach to others: reform, cooperation and dialogue so that Christians may come closer together that the world may believe. Let us pray for each other that our faith may not fail and let us strengthen each other by word and example for this task of ecumenizing all our formation, prayer life, institutions and all our ministries for the ever greater glory of God. In the true Ignatian spirit, "I must be convinced that in Christ our Lord... only one Spirit holds sway, which governs and rules for the salvation of souls. For it is by the same Spirit and Lord who gave the Ten Commandments that our holy

Mother Church is ruled and governed" (Spiritual Exercises, n. 365).

Now we prefer to look not to the past, but to the future, and to what ought to be. We look to something new which has yet to be born, a dream which has yet to be realized. We say with St. Paul, "forgetting what is behind me and reaching out for that which lies ahead, I press towards the goal to win the prize which is God's call to the life above in Christ Jesus" (*Phil* 3, 13-14; cf. *Paul VI: October 17, 1963*).

20

ECUMENICAL DIALOGUE WITH OTHER CHRISTIAN CHURCHES

Address of Father Pedro Arrupe to Representatives of Christian Churches at Cardinal Bea Institute

**Loyola Heights, Manila
September 20, 1971**

The 31st General Congregation, that elected Father Pedro Arrupe as General of the Society in 1965, produced a decree (the 26th) on Ecumenism so complete that the 32nd General Congregation did not consider necessary to issue a new one but only to confirm and apply the existing legislation.

This 26th decree, issued soon after the closing of Vatican II, offered directives for a suitable training of Jesuits in the matter of ecumenism. The value of personal contact with the separated brethren was stressed. Where considered fruitful, professors and ministers of other confessions are, on appropriate occasions, to be invited to give lectures in our scholasticates, and Jesuits are to accept their invitations willingly in return. All should be on their guard against prejudices and eliminate offensive expressions in this matter.

That decree recommended to the new General that there be established a council on ecumenical affairs, composed of experts from various nations, and at the same time he appoint one of the Assistants or expert advisers as delegate for fostering the ecumenical movement. (The present incumbent is Fr Parmananda Divarkar). The recommendation is also made that there be established, either by Jesuits alone or in collaboration with others, institutes or houses of study

*for experts and students, and this in centres renowned for
ecumenical studies. Echoes of these directives and recommendations can be discerned in the following address of Father
Arrupe.*

*

1. Jesuits trying to understand non-Catholics

I don't think it is necessary to explain how very happy I
am to have this occasion to meet with some of the representatives of the Christian Churches here in the Philippines. As
you know, we, in the Society of Jesus, are trying to foster in
our communities, particularly among our theologians, this
sense of unity and ecumenism based on the charity of Christ
and mutual personal understanding.

In this regard, the reputation of the Jesuits is not so good.
We are supposed to have been founded to fight Protestantism.
But that is not true; not even at the beginning. It is not
true now.

Since Vatican II, we Catholics have been trying to promote
this spirit of mutual understanding and cooperation. We
have so many things in common, especially if you think of the
possibilities of working for the poor in the developing countries,
bringing to the people a sense of justice and charity. We could
pool our efforts, our ideas, our resources — personal or financial — in order to accomplish much in a broad sense. Also,
this would avoid, especially in the mission countries, the
scandal of "division among Christians". I think this negative
aspect should be taken seriously. If the people see that, inspite
of some differences, we can work together in charity and mutual
understanding, this would be a way of evangelization. That
is why in the Society of Jesus we are trying to develop this
spirit.

2. Cardinal Bea and Ecumenism

One of the personalities, I should say, who contributed
enormously to the spirit of ecumenism during the Second
Vatican Council was our dear Cardinal Bea, after whom this
Institute is named. He was a Jesuit. He was Rector of the
Pontifical Biblical Institute in Rome. When he was 76 years

old, he was made a Cardinal. Everyone thought that it was time for him to retire and that his days were numbered. He was very well but this rejuvenated him. He became a young man, full of life and spirit, and he lived for another ten fruitful years.

He was a leading Scripture scholar, but today few remember him as such. Everyone remembers him as the pioneer of ecumenism. Many think of him as the architect of the Decree on Ecumenism of Vatican II.

3.   Jesuits gradually turn to Ecumenism

In our general chapter in 1965 — this is a meeting of representatives of Jesuits in the whole world — in which I was elected General, we came out with a Decree on Ecumenism. In this decree the Society of Jesus took a positive stand in developing the ecumenical spirit through the Society of Jesus and the people who work with us.

Unfortunately, as in everything else that requires a change of mental attitudes, we have to admit with all humility, that the application of this decree was not as fast and as effective as it should have been. But this does not mean opposition. It's rather some kind of inertia. You see, some people have set mental attitudes, and it is very difficult, especially for older persons, to change. But this is not a conscious opposition. The change will come in time.

4.   Ecumenical Social Action

You might like to know what the Society of Jesus is doing in particular in this field. We are not only trying to foster the spirit, but to be genuinely involved in ecumenical activities. A very significant example for me would be SODEPAX. As you know, SODEPAX is a collaboration between the World Council of Churches and the Catholics in development work.

I was having lunch with Carson Blake, the Secretary General of the World Council of Churches. We were talking about getting involved in common ecumenical action. We do have points that separate us, but we have many more

things in common. I suggested social work. We have such
tremendous problems of injustice in the world

We became very enthusiastic about the whole idea and
we decided to start something along this line. The first thing
we did was to have Father George Dunne, a Jesuit from
California, take care of the preparations for the Beirut Conference on World Cooperation for Development. It was a success!
That gave a tremendous boost to the work of SODEPAX.

5. Ecumenical Theology

In the United States we are trying to build up ecumenism
in the "centre of concern". I was there last May visiting our
different scholasticates. That is what we call our seminaries,
where our theologians are in training. It was a brand new
experience for me.

Until recently, we had our seminaries far out in the country.
But we thought today, forming our young men in the modern
way, we had better put them in contact with the reality of
life. And so we put our theologates where they could see the
challenge of the modern world, in the middle of the cities
which would be their theatre of activities.

In the United States, these theologates or seminaries are in
the middle of the great secular universities. We have Weston
College at Harvard University; Woodstock College, at Colum-
bia University; Bellarmine College, at Chicago University;
Alma College at Berkeley; and St Mary's at St Louis University.

I was greatly surprised at the development of this ecumenical spirit. In the beginning we were rather hesitant about
putting our young men in the secular universities or in the
cities. We were also worried about how we would develop our
relations with the other Christian Churches. But my experiences
have been very inspiring. I was received by the Protestant
faculties and communities with such warmth! Really, I
was astonished!

There is real collaboration between the Catholics and the
Christian Churches. For example, at Chicago University there
is a library of 70,000 volumes for the Jesuits. On the other

wing of the building is another library of 60,000 volumes for Protestants. All use both without any difficulty.

The same thing in teaching. In the Hebrew courses, Exegesis and so forth, there is complete collaboration among the professors. Strangely enough, in Berkeley, the students for the Protestant ministry are coming to our Exegesis lectures. Therefore, now the Jesuits are contributing to the training of Protestant pastors. That would have been incredible two years ago. But now, wonderful to say, there is a real cordial collaboration. There is also collaboration with the Orthodox Church. I have just spent three days in Moscow and two days in Leningrad. Again, such warm hospitality! Incredible. Really incredible.

6. The Moving Spirit

So you see, there is something moving the world. It must be the Holy Spirit. We simply have to let the Holy Spirit move us and put no obstacles. Where are we going? Probably nobody knows. But we are going; and as long as we go under the guidance of the Holy Spirit we shall be all right. Therefore, I think we have to be objectively optimistic in this regard, and sincerely try to foster the ecumenical spirit. You know better than I; I'm not trying to teach you something new. The world is Christ's, today more than ever before. And we have to put our efforts together in order spread the knowledge and love of Christ.

We can do this together in social action, works of charity, and even in education — in our institutions of learning, research... so many things! And therefore, I think you will understand the joy we have today in having this personal contact with you, and also to thank you for your collaboration. I have heard from Father Achutegui and the other Jesuits about the cordial relations we have here in the Philippines. And I would like to promise you that we are always ready to collaborate with you as far as we can. And we could be of help in any way, please don't hesitate to ask the Fathers here. Perhaps you have specific questions you may want to ask. I myself would like to ask you some questions.

21

ECCLESIAL SERVICE OF THE CHRISTIAN LIFE COMMUNITIES

POOR WITH CHRIST FOR A BETTER SERVICE

Message of Father Arrupe to the General Assembly of the World Federation of the CLC

Manila
August, 1976

The main source of the spirituality of groups of Christian Life Communities, as expressed in the General Principles approved by the Holy See in 1968, is the person of Christ and the participation in the paschal mystery, through the Sacred Scriptures, the Liturgy, the doctrinal development of the Church, and the revelation of the divine will through the events and needs of our time. The groups consider the Spiritual Exercises of Saint Ignatius as one of their specific sources of inspiration and strength and the characteristic instrument of their spirituality. (AR XV, 1968, pp. 195, 322).

The Executive Council of the World Federation usually invites Father Arrupe to their annual meeting. They find him appreciative and grateful for the good the CLC is doing to Jesuits themselves.

In 1976, he was unable to attend their Manila meeting, but sent a message of guidance and encouragement to the "world community of lay people committed to the full living of the Spiritual Exercises in the world." The theme of the General Assembly was one dear to Father Arrupe's heart — the vocation of the CLC in the Church as serving Christ in the poor of the world.

Dear Friends,

As you gather in the Philippines for your General Assembly, a world community of lay people committed to the full living of the Spiritual Exercises in the world, you are all much in my thoughts and prayers. Your theme — *Poor with Christ for a Better Service: The Vocation of CLC in the Mission of the Church* — is one I find both apt and stirring. I know you intend to pursue it in a climate of true discernment. And with the long and thorough preparation you have been making, I am sure you will do so effectively.

I find especially courageous and inspiring your decision to accompany your Assembly with three different formation courses, all deeply rooted in the Spiritual Exercises, so that, in coming together from the four corners of the planet, you can make the fullest use of the occasion to enter more deeply into the way of life you have chosen. I am happy too that your World Federation, while insistent on the lay responsibility which is its special characteristic, reflects too a close and mutually fruitful collaboration between laity, clergy and religious in the ensemble of your activities.

Your theme, I said, finds a special place in my heart. May I say a word more to tell you why? Your stress on solidarity with the poor is surely what is needed in a world where the cry of the oppressed grows ever louder, and where we Christians are called by the leaders of our Church, as never before, to witness to justice, whatever the cost to us might be. But I am especially pleased with your clear grasp of the fact that, for a Christian, solidarity with the poor begins with identification with Jesus, the Man-for-others, who emptied himself totally and, becoming poor for our sakes, lived and died in poverty and in solidarity with the poor.

Above all is this true for us whose following of Christ is inspired by the Spiritual Exercises. The Christ we have met in the great meditations on the Kingdom, the Two Standards, the Third Mode of Humility, is a Christ who is poor, powerless and rejected and if we want to be with Him, to be where He is, we too will need to "choose poverty with Christ poor rather than riches" (*Spir. Exercises*, 167). So our identification with the poor must, it seems to me, spring from this faith-experience of Christ's emptying of himself.

But this is not enough. We need also, in some way, to become poor ourselves. The language in which such poverty is expressed today is simplicity of living: opting for a simple life, one that excludes ostentation and vanity and a preoccupation with creature comforts. It means saying no both to our built-in egoism and to the consumer society that incessantly prods us to want to acquire more and to possess more.

We need something else as well: to know what the poverty of poor people is in actuality. We need a lived experience of being really poor. I notice that one of your formation courses aims at affording such an experience, in ways that are compatible with the family and occupational obligations that many of you have. Let me congratulate you on this initiative. It will surely, by giving you an experimental knowledge of the places and ways in which Christ poor lives and labours in our world of 1976, fit you for "a better service" in that world.

And this identification with Christ poor you see as what it is: an expression of your own participation in mission. Participation in the mission of Christ, who said of himself: "He sent me to bring the good news to the poor" (Luke 4:18). Participation in the mission of the Church, to whose leaders Jesus passed on his mission: "As the Father sent me, so I also send you" (*John* 20:21). Our witness to justice, our solidarity with the poor, our simplicity of living is, then, part of our mission, the mission to which we have been called. It is a mission whose concrete implementation requires much discernment and takes many forms: from relieving immediate needs to transforming the structures of whatever kind and on whatever level — and not least the international level — that are barriers, sometimes stubborn and unyielding barriers, to the building of God's kingdom of justice and love.

So your theme and orientations of "Manila '76" find a strong echo in my own heart. And indeed, in the whole Society of Jesus. Enough to say that the key decree of our recent Jesuit General Congregation was that on "*Our Mission Today: the Service of Faith and the Promotion of Justice*".

I hope that all this vast effort and wonderful goodwill will express itself in works. We can well apply here, I think, what Pope Paul VI wrote in his Apostolic Letter, "*Octogesima Adveniens*": "Let each one examine himself, to see what he has done up to now, and what he ought to do. It is not enough to recall principles, state intentions, point to crying injustices and utter prophetic denunciations; these words will lack real weight unless they are accompanied for each individual by a livelier awareness of personal responsibility and by effective action. It is too easy to throw back at others responsibility for injustices, if at the same time one does not realize how each one shares in it personally, and how personal conversion is needed first" (no. 48).

May this be, then, a gathering from which issues the true conversion of each one, a conversion that then goes on to show itself in works and in effective and intelligent action, that is, in what you express in your theme: "poor for a better service: the vocation of CLC in the mission of the Church".

We must be convinced that the undertaking the Lord asks of us today is difficult and that there is need to count of course on the help of God, but also on persons who are determined and generous. Otherwise, we may hear the words that God said to Gedeon: "There are too many people with you... proclaim this now in the ears of the people: Let anyone who is frightened or fearful go home!" (*Judges* 7:2-3).

My warm good wishes, then, as your Assembly begins its deliberations. May the Spirit of God, who was upon Jesus as he began his mission at Nazareth, and who is "Father of the poor, Giver of gifts, Light of hearts", be with you in your labours. And may St Ignatius Loyola, from whom, in different ways, you as we draw our inspiration, win for you from Christ Poor the grace to "know Him more intimately, love Him more ardently, follow Him more closely".

In warmest friendship,

Pedro Arrupe, S.J.
General of the Society of Jesus

22

A WORLD COMMUNITY
AT THE SERVICE OF ONE WORLD

Address to the General Assembly
of the World Federation of the
Christian Life Communities

Villa Cavalletti, Grottaferrata
September 13, 1979

*From September 8th to 19th, 1979 representatives of
42 National Federations of the Christian Life Communities
held their General Assembly at Villa Cavalletti, the
Retreat House on the Alban Hill near Rome. The theme of
this important meeting was "Towards a World Community at the Service of One World."*

*Roma '79, as the meeting was called, was attended by
87 representatives of 36 affiliated national federations
(from Argentina to Zambia) and another 6 of countries
where the CLC is in the process of development.*

*Three stages of work were covered by the assembly during
the congress: (a) a deepening of the CLC charism; (b) a
look at the CLC reality today; (c) a discernment of future
orientations. The three major preoccupations that came up
for deliberation were: (a) lay spirituality: the service of
faith (formation in the CLC charism); (b) the role of the
lay person in the world: the promotion of justice (mission
and service); (c) in the context of community: the Church
as the People of God (towards a World Community).*

*Father Arrupe's address to the Assembly was reproduced
in Documentation no. 44 of the SJ Press and Information
Office in Rome. This exposition of the theme of the Congress*

offers a deep insight into the ignatian ideal of service as applicable to the Christian Life Community along the lines of Vatican II and according to the CLC General Principles. The address was followed by a lively Open Forum with Father Arrupe. (see here on page 245)

*

At this Assembly, I understand you are discussing whether or not you are being called to form a world community at the service of one world. This is a theme that has an immediate appeal to me — it is an area of concern that I, too, share.

I am most heartened by such a world vision, which is characteristic of large hearted people, who have well understood the universality of to-day's problems, and the need to reach solutions which are truly universal. For this reason you are aspiring towards a world community.

I am also heartened to see that it is through *service* that you want to be present among all the peoples of the world. Such an attitude is truly consistent with the essence of the CLC, and so I find it most appropriate that you have focused on this theme.

As a matter of fact, it is "service" — more precisely, "the greater service" which is the basic, underlying concept of the CLC's. When in 1967, the Holy See was asked to approve the transformation of the Marian Congregations into the Christian Life Communities, and approval was also sought for the General Principles which replaced the Common Rules of 1910, the very reasons behind these requests were "the better service" of the Church, and renewal according to the spirit and norms of Vatican II. The changes asked for would also allow members of the new Communities "to consecrate themselves with greater simplicity and efficacy to the service of God and of men in the world of to-day." (Letter of Confirmation of Cardinal Cicognani, March 25th, 1968). The Church judged that this aspiration was sincere and realistic; she gave her approval.

Both the spirit and the letter of your General Principles confirm this very point — that the CLC's are the institutionalization of a vocation of service. As is stated in the Preamble, the General Principles are meant to help (the members of the CLC's) "to give themselves always more generously to God in loving and serving all mankind in the world of today." (G.P., no. 1)

The generosity of this self-giving and the constant pull of the *"magis"* are clearly two features of Ignatian origin. There is nothing strange in this, for you expressly recognise the Exercises of St. Ignatius "as a specific source and the characteristic instrument of our spirituality." (G.P., no. 4)

All of this encourages me to share with you some reflections on service according to the mind of St. Ignatius, together with some comments of my own.

I. SERVICE — CONSTANT IGNATIAN IDEAL

1. The Man of Honour

From his earliest years, the idea of service came as naturally to Ignatius as the air we breathe. Everything he saw in the ancestral home of *Casa-Torre* spoke to him of service — the pursuits of his brothers, his family traditions, the service of "serfdom" given by the peasants as they worked and tilled the fields, the service of "loyal servants" rendered by members of his own family to their far-away Lord, whom one helped in time of war and who rewarded this faithful service in time of peace.

When he was barely 15, Ignatius entered the service of an important member of the court, the royal treasurer, and followed him for 10 years. At his death, Ignatius passed into the service of the Duke of Najera, Viceroy of Navarre, and from there he moved into the royal service, until, 4 years later, he fell wounded on the walls of Pamplona.

As a result of his own experiences, Ignatius' concept of service was a knightly one that included honour, fidelity, courage and the desire for glory. The books of knight-errantry which he enjoyed reading were the embodiment of such ideals.

In the course of his convalescence, when he thought of a certain lady, "who had taken such a hold on his heart" (Autobiography, 6), his love still expresses itself in terms of service: "...he imagined what he would do in the service of a certain lady...the verses, the words he would say to her, the deeds of arms he would do in her service". (Autobiography, 6) For Ignatius, to love was to serve.

2. Ignatius' Conversion

Ignatius' conversion led him, not to give up the ideal of service, but to find a new "Lord". During the first phase of his conversion, he had in mind to serve the Lord in a way that was still rather worldly — not to say belligerent and competitive! — "St. Francis did this, therefore I have to do it." (Autobiography, 7) It is only later, through a graced masterpiece of introspection and discernment, that he takes apart and analyses all the different elements that have combined to form his ideal. Ignatius purifies his idea of serivce and then proceeds to build his whole spirituality on the foundation of this purified concept — which becomes the first principle and foundation of the Exercises: "Man is created to praise, reverence and serve God our Lord." (S.E., no. 23)

For Ignatius, service of the Creator is axiomatic — there is simply no call to justify or prove it. It is the natural condition of "the creature": he is created "for", that is to say, for a purpose which binds him to the One who gives him his very existence.

Two elements of service progressively develop in the dynamic of the Exercises: service in love (the final contemplation in the Exercises is precisely aimed at seeking this love), and the person one serves out of love: God, the Divine Majesty, the Three Divine Persons, Christ in His Incarnation, in His life, His Passion, and in the glory of His Resurrection.

All the Exercises will be based on the concept of service — in one way or another, the words "service", or "to serve" will appear 50 times. Even Christ's relationship to the Father is seen as one of service. (S.E., no. 135)

For Ignatius, the service of God is the criterion for discernment in the ordering of one's life: "...the reason he (the retreatant) wants or retains anything will be solely the service, honour and glory of the Divine Majesty." (S.E., no. 16)

Service is an unconditional attitude: "(the retreatant should) enter upon the Exercises with magnanimity and generosity towards his Creator and Lord, and offer Him his entire will and liberty, that his Divine Majesty may dispose of him and all he possesses according to His most holy will." (S.E., no. 5). This service of God disposes the retreatant "for the way in which he can better serve God in the future." (S.E. no. 15).

However, the ideal of service is most fully and clearly expressed in the centre point of the Exercises — the Call of the Earthly King, the introduction to the consideration of different states of life, the Two Standards. Ignatius' best memories of his knightly ideas are recalled here: "If anyone would refuse the invitation of such a king, how justly he would deserve to be condemned by the whole world and looked upon as an ignoble knight." (S.E., no. 94). And he continues: "those who wish to give greater proof of their love, and to distinguish themselves in whatever concerns the service of the Eternal King and Lord of All" will want to imitate Christ humble and poor, for his "greater service and praise." (S.E., no. 97).

The last part of the Exercises closes with the idea of service, but with a certain tone that is quite different from the First Principle and Foundation, where the word "love" is not mentioned: "The zealous service of God our Lord out of pure love should be esteemed above all." (S.E., no. 370).

3. Ignatius — the Founder

St. Ignatius is not only the author of the Exercises — he is, first and foremost, *the* exercitant. He left Manresa, having decided "to distinguish himself in whatever concerns the service of the Eternal King and Lord of all." (S.E., no. 97). The ideal of the service of God — the greater service — will be the star that guides his steps for the rest of his life, as pilgrim, student, Founder and General of the Society of Jesus. The one-time man of honour, whose ideal was to serve in chivalrous enterprises of love and war, had learnt that God had to be served in another way: through imitating the life and works of the apostoles, in preaching the Kingdom in poverty and humility. Because apostolic service requires a knowledge of doctrine, he becomes a student. Because the apostolic service of one's neighbour only reaches its fullness in bringing to him the grace of the Sacraments, he becomes a priest. (FN III/816).

He lived his ideal with so much purity and intensity that it could not fail to become contagious. One after another, follow-wers begin to join Ignatius. On the 15th of August, 1534, at Montmartre, Ignatius and his companions, in what could be called a foreshadowing of the founding of the Society of Jesus, take a vow that contains a double clause of service: To go to Jerusalem "to spend their lives there in the service of souls," or, if this could not be accomplished in the course of a year, to "present themselves to the Vicar of Christ, so that he could make use of them wherever he thought it would be to the greater glory of God and the service of souls." (Auto-biography, 85).

The very words and ideas expressed here could not be more Ignatian. Since, in the course of that year, there was no ship leaving Venice for the Holy Land, and since the "papal clause" in the vows at Montmartre offered an alternative, we can see Providence opening up a way for Ignatius to follow, which leads to the birth of the Society. The essential elements of this "papal clause" are: to spend one's life in what is for the greater glory of God and for the good of souls, under the Vicar of Christ. In a word — service.

In 1537 Ignatius goes to Rome with Favre and Lainez to fulfill their promise. There a crucial event takes place. Igna-tius has a vision in the little chapel of La Storta — located some 16 kilometers from Rome, in the Via Cassia, the only road, at that time, which led to Rome from the north.

Ignatius had been ordained three months previously, but he had not yet celebrated the Eucharist, as he wished to pre-pare himself thoroughly for his first Mass. And by way of preparing himself — in the depths of his own heart — he had prayed to the Virgin Mary that she would "place him with her Son." In this extraordinary mystical event at La Storta, Igna-tius "experienced such a change in his soul, and he saw so clearly that God the Father had placed him with His Son Christ that his mind could not doubt (it)." The Father turns to the Son who stands at his side with the cross over his shoulder, and tells him, pointing to Ignatius: "I want you to take this man as your servant." Jesus then turns to Ignatius and says: "I want you to serve us."

For Ignatius, this moment marks a turning point in his spiritual odyssey; it permeates the rest of his life, when later he becomes the founder of the Society of Jesus. For this experience underlines *service* as a determining factor in Ignatius' relationship with the Divine Persons: the Father assigns him to be the servant of His Son; the Son accepts him into his own service, and into the service of the Father. This is the climax of a process which had begun 31 years before, in 1506, when the 15 years old Iñigo had entered into the service of his earthly lord. And so no wonder that Ignatius now considers himself as a man of divine service, or, more precisely, of "greater divine service."

Henceforth, Ignatius institutionalises his charism and shares it with the group he has gathered around himself, so that the group becomes even more united. Inspired by the vision at La Storta, he calls himself and his companions "the Company of Jesus", which carries clear overtones of militant service. The Formula for the Society of Jesus (in the Bull *"Exposcit debitum"* of Julius III) begins in such a way as to make the mind of Ignatius and companions abundantly clear: "Whoever desires to serve as a soldier of God beneath the banner of the cross in our Society, which we desire to be designated by the name of Jesus, and to serve the Lord alone and the Church, His Spouse, under the Roman Pontiff, the vicar of Christ on earth..."

The Constitutions of the Society of Jesus are filled with references and specific exhortations to the divine service; I shall not pause here to quote the relevant passages. What I have already said should sufficiently clarify how central the idea of service — the theme chosen for this Assembly — is in Ignatian spirituality, the very spirituality which inspires you, according to your General Principles.

II. CHRISTIAN LIFE COMMUNITY—

ONE COMMUNITY FOR SERVICE

We might say that the basic connection between the CLC and the Society of Jesus is found here — in the common inspiration that derives from the Spiritual Exercises, and in the communion of a shared spirituality. All other considerations run along divergent lines. Along one line, this Ignatian spirituality, with its own proper character, gives birth to the Society of Jesus as a religious, apostolic and priestly order, closely linked with the Vicar of Christ, by special bonds.

Along another line, this same Ignatian spirituality has inspired your own movement, which is not any less valuable than, but simply different from a religious order — because you have a different concrete apostolic orientation. The CLC is essentially a spiritual movement for lay people — with its limitations, certainly, but also with its unique apostolic opportunities.

Furthermore, only a fraction of the CLC's are established in Jesuit centres, or assisted by Jesuits. Theoretically, the CLC's allow for (and indeed do admit) the creation of groups totally free from direct contact with the Society of Jesus. Of course, such groups will hold the Spiritual Exercises of St. Ignatius as a specific source and characteristic instrument of their spirituality. (G.P. 4) Consequently, your spirituality and your apostolic life shoud make full use of all the opportunities offered by your situation as lay people — given that such possibilities would be less fitting, or clearly inappropriate, for religious. Likewise, you should be careful not to adopt lines of action that are more properly clerical, or religious — for this would surely limit your own range of apostolic initiatives.

In mentioning this danger to you, I have in mind the kind of service which, according to your own General Principles, you should render to the Church and to all peoples to-day. This, certainly, is a grave responsibility you undertake — to "form committed men and women, adults and youth, for service to the Church and the world in every area of life: family, professional, civic, ecclesial..." (G.P. 3) Those last

4 words were chosen, I am sure, with great care; they cover the 4 fundamental areas of human life.

Your work is to bring to birth, within the framework of your daily environment, "human life in all its dimensions with the fullness of Christian faith, especially among those concerned with temporal affairs." (G.P. 3) For in this way you are responding to "the call of Christ from within the world in which we live" (G.P. 3) And in this way, too, you are with Christ seeking "constantly the answers to the needs of our times and to work together with the people of God for progress and peace, justice and charity, liberty and the dignity of all men." (G.P. 2) These words entail a specific programme: "We are aware we must consecrate ourselves first of all, to the renewal and sanctification of the temporal order." (G.P. 7) This, then, is your service to the world — a thorough, intelligent, unremitting lay apostolate, which most surely presupposes an interior life no less intense, intelligent and constant. But the theme you have chosen for your General Assembly leads me specifically to focus on the apostolic orientation of your groups — at the service of al peoples, in the world of to-day.

1. A Contemporary Service

Your lay apostolate should be of a kind I dare call new. In 1967 when the Marian Congregations decided to 'take the leap' introducing changes, "some of which were fundamental," (Letter of Cardinal Cicognani, 25 March, 1968) to become the CLC's, they did so because they were conscious of the fact that a world with new needs should be approached also with new lines of action. The Second Vatican Council recently ended, itself offered a most brilliant example of the need and the possibility of such transformations.

And so the apostolic activity which formerly had been auxiliary to the priestly ministry (teaching catechism, formation activities, etc.) was directed — as provided for in the General Principles — towards a new service, the "renewal and sanctification of the temporal order...to work for the reform of the structures of society, participating in efforts to liberate the victims of all forms of discrimination and especially to abolish differences between rich and poor within the Church."

(G.P. 7) Your purpose, according to your General Principles, is to work "in a spirit of service to establish justice and peace among all men." (G.P. 7).

Reading these lines, I almost get the impression of citing you the fourth decree of our 32nd General Congregation, written four years later, and which states that — "the mission of the Society of Jesus to-day is the service of faith, of which the promotion of justice is an abolsute requirement. For reconciliation with God demands the reconciliation of people with one another." (G.C. 32; Decree 4, no. 2).

2. Along the Lines of the Council

The qualitative change in your apostolic orientation is no mere passing phase, much less the fruit of some particular individual's private intuition. On the contrary, it is exactly according to the mind of the Council.

Permit me to clarify this point somewhat. One of the principal graces the Lord gave to the Church, through the Second Vatican Council, was to highlight, in a new way, the importance of the lay person, and his or her role in the Church. The entire fourth chapter of the Constitution on the Church (*Lumen Gentium*) is dedicated to the laity, and their participation in the saving mystery of the Church, in Christ's priestly and prophetic functions, and in his royal character. This section is entirely given over to a theology of the laity; through studying it at depth, you will gain even clearer insights into your own importance — and responsibilities — in the Church.

But that is not all. One year later, in 1965, the Council prepared a decree dedicated exclusively to the apostolic activity of the laity, *Apostolicam Actuositatem* — a decree based on the theology of the laity. Both these documents I have referred to have inspired some of the most striking and courageous phrases in your General Principles. This is why your ongoing formation should be centred round these texts, and why you should reflect on them over and over again, trusting that you will find there the most authentic expression of the hopes that the Church places in you. These documents will serve you as reference — points for the "revision of life" that you all practise, (G.P. 7) and also as a source of light for your future decisions.

Well then, the qualitative leap in your apostolic mission that I have already mentioned corresponds to one of the Council's directives, namely: "An apostolate of this kind does not consist only in the witness of one's way of life." (A.A.6) "The laity must take on the renewal of the temporal order as their own special obligation. Led by the light of the gospel and the mind of the Church, and motivated by Christian love, let them act directly and definitively in the temporal sphere. As citizens they must cooperate with other citizens, using their own particular skills and acting on their own responsibility. Everywhere and in all things they must seek the justice characteristic of God's kingdom. The temporal order must be renewed in such a way that, without the slightest detriment to its own proper laws, it can be brought into conformity with the higher principles of the Christian life and adapted to the shifting circumstances of time, place, and person. Outstanding among the works of this type of apostolate is that of Christian social action. This sacred Synod desires to see it extended now to the whole temporal sphere, including culture." (A.A. 7).

Your General Principles, elaborated two years later in 1967, include this directive of the Council: "We are aware we must consecrate ourselves first of all to the renewal and sanctification of the temporal order." (G.P. 7).

3. A Temptation

Perhaps some of you have an opposite temptation, and that would be very understandable. Tired of grappling with your daily professional and family life, haunted by a social environment which each day becomes more materialistic, selfish, sexually-oriented and corrupt, you may be tempted to consider the CLC's — of which you are a part — as an oasis of peace: a spiritual haven in which a person can rest, recover himself or herself, and become closer to God through the encouragement that flows from the community ideals of members of the group. This certainly is *one* aspect of the situation, but it is by no means the full picture — and there is no greater deceit than the deceit of a half-truth. (As the famous English author, G.K. Chesterton, once said: "A half-truth, like a half-brick, travels twice the distance.") Such a limited view is alien to your General Principles; it parts from the vision the Council proposes about the role of the laity in the Church; and to diminish the Council's vision of the laity, in this way, would be to mutilate, or cripple, the Body of Christ. Why? Because there are things to be done which you alone — as laity — are able to accomplish. As I have mentioned previously, the lay person — through the very fact of being a lay person — has apostolic opportunities and possibilities that are lacking in the case of many other categories of persons in the Church, for instance, the hierarchy, priests and religious. Let us take an example — political action, on the party level. Some priests and religious who have great apostolic zeal and a clear insight into the problems of to-day could fall into the temptation of using their civic rights to intervene in politics, for they believe, and not without reason, that the establishing of peace and justice depends in a large part on political action. It is painful for the superiors of such religious to impose, for good reasons, limitations on their apostolic service. One of the reasons for imposing these restrictions is that it is your duty, as lay people and members of the secular city, to exercise fully your civil rights and carry out this kind of apostolic service. In this area, concrete action should be exclusively yours. The Church can, and must give — and in fact, it is providing — the doctrinal orientations and clarifications, as well as the kind of support that is compatible with its supernatural mission. But only that part of the Church to which you belong is able to assume this serious responsibility, within the very wide context of possible concrete options.

At this point I would like to stop to make special note of the four "areas of life" that are expressly mentioned in your General Principles: family, professional, civic, ecclesial. (G.P. 3).

4. The Family

The family is, so to speak, "the domestic Church", as the Council calls it (L.G. 11), and, by nature, it is the first area for your apostolic service. One should begin naturally with one's own family. When I say "family", I include all those issues that impinge on a family — marital life, abortion, divorce, education, freedom of education, premarital relations, the feminist movement, morality, drugs, housing, and so on. "Where Christianity pervades a whole way of (family) life and ever increasingly transforms it, there will exist both the practice and an excellent school for the lay apostolate." (L.G. 35).

Each member of a Christian Life Community has under his or her own roof the first and most immediate area for his or her apostolic service. The group to which a person belongs should be of assistance to him, just as he in turn should offer his help to the group. There are a thousand ways to offer one's help that only concrete circumstances can dictate.

But this is not enough. One must declare and promote Christian values outside of the family circle as well, by always avoiding ambivalence in announcing one's values, by refusing one's vote to those who pursue policies that are contrary to the family values proclaimed by the Church. Even more so, according to the possibilities of the individual, one should participate actively in movements that defend and promote such values.

This brings to mind a story from the rector of one of our schools, who told me that private education in his country was going through considerable difficulties — for example, in maintaining the explicit confessionality of the school. Throughout these difficulties, his principal support came from CLC members and from the teams of Our Lady for married couples — a movement similar to yours. Members of these groups stood for elections to the board of directors of the parents' association, and as a result of the elections, they occupied the most important seats of the board. This is a good example of one of the numerous possibilities available to you.

5. Professional Life

On 3 different occasions during the last 2 months, Pope John Paul II has spoken about the apostolate of the lay person, placing special emphasis on his or her profession. It is through our profession that we have the opportunity to accomplish something, and this develops our talents, our productive capacity, as well as forms a web of relationships in our lives. I realize that by their very nature, some professions have less apostolic opportunities than others. The housewife who spends her day busy with housework has fewer apostolic possibilities than a social worker. A university professor has generally more apostolic opportunities than a civil servant. However, no CLC member should ignore his duty, not only to live his work with a Christian attitude, but to bring a message, through his profession, to all those around him.

Pope Paul VI said that not only can one sanctify one's profession, but that the profession itself is a source of sanctification (Allocution to the Union of Catholic Jurists: 15th Dec., 1963). This mutual interaction is a very fruitful one.

Permit me to cite a concrete case: those who come from Italy know well the name of Giuseppe Moscati — a doctor, who carried out marvellous apostolate both in academic circles and in the hospitals of Naples. He was beatified in 1975, just 40 years after his dath, and Paul VI said in his homily on that occasion: "He was a layman, a simple Christian, who gave a mission to his life; a doctor who made his profession his apostolate, a school of love; a university professor who extended to his students and colleagues the high ideal — and example — of moral rectitude and total devotion to one's profession." (Homily on the Beatification of Giuseppe Moscati: 16th Nov., 1975)

This is certainly a famous example — from one man's professional apostolate — of that service we can render our brothers and sisters, through our occupation, so that our profession itself becomes an excellent means for apostolic service.

6. The Civic and Social Sector

"The apostolate of the social milieu, that is, the effort to infuse a Christian spirit into the mentality, customs, laws and structures of the community in which a person lives, is so much the duty and responsibility of the laity that it can never be properly performed by others." (A.A. 13) These are peremptory words from the Council which do not allow for divergence or diminution. It is the lay person's responsibility to make sure that the temporal order is organised according to the Christian precepts of charity and justice. And there are so many things to be done!

— in the area of labour: unions, employment, assistance for workers;
— in the legal and structural order: justice, equality, freedom, participation, political parties;
— in the area of public service: housing, schooling, environment, health, the elderly, energy, public safety;
— in the national and international order: international relations, colonialism, independence, development, spheres of influence.

As you can see, our world is beset by many problems, and if we were to enumerate them all, our list would grow longer and longer. In all of this, there is a theoretical level on which the Church can shed the light of its doctrine. However, political action as such falls within the competence of the laity. (A.A. 13) Naturally, there has to be a sense of responsibility with regard to the means by which this apostolate is exercised by each individual, according to his own circumstances. But over and above that, there is a common avenue of service open to all — the promotion of the common good, special attention to the most needy and support for those in high office who can promote a more just order.

The Second Vatican Council encourages those who are properly qualified, to assume public offices. By doing this, such people can exercise influence in conformity with the spirit of the Gospel, and accomplish great good. I would say that in your CLC groups, where you have men and women inspired by faith and a spirit of service, there is a reservoir of people who, within their area of activity, however modest it might be, try to render this kind of service. You should not fail to become involved through apathy or fear of commitment.

In short, you cannot disappoint the hopes of the Church and of the world that await the apostolic help of those lay

people who, through their Christian faith, are well qualified
to serve. Listen to how Paul VI expressed it in his apostolic
exhortation *Evangelii Nuntiandi,* of December 1975 (E.N. 70):
"Lay people, whose particular vocation places them in the
midst of the world and in charge of the most varied temporal
tasks, must for this very reason exercise a very special form of
evangelisation...Their own field of evangelising activity is
the vast and complicated world of politics, society and economics, but also the world of culture, of the sciences and the
arts, of international life, of the mass media. It also includes
other realities which are open to evangelisation, such as human
love, the family, the education of children and adolescents,
professional work, suffering."

Over the years I have had many experiences with members
of the Society of Jesus, and other religious orders, which
enable me to share this confidence with you: there is an
appreciable lack of lay people who are prepared to commit
themselves apostolically in those areas of life that I have been
speaking about. This means there is a great imbalance between what actually is done and what is left to be done,
and such a state of affairs constitutes a serious temptation for
not a few priests, especially those who are zealous, extremely
competent and see in a secular profession innumerable possibilities for evangelisation. Let us not make the mistake of having
priests take on vocations that you can and should undertake.
Are there few priests at the moment? If, as real apostles, your
numbers increase, so will ours; and the better apostles you are,
the better servants of the Word shall we priests be.

7. The Christian and Politics

I throw out an invitation to Christian lay people, to encourage them to assume, in a spirit of service, political responsibilities in different areas. They should follow this course,
which is a way to sanctity and evangelisation, especially if
they experience a call in this direction, and have the necessary qualifications.

However briefly, let me give you an image of the Christian
in politics:

— a man of profound faith and prayer, who through his love

for Christ, puts himself at the service of his brothers, to achieve the common good at different levels;

— a man who is not an opportunist, and yet can see beyond his own party;

— a man with a strong sense of the Church, who is enlightened by its social and political doctrine;

— a man who exercises power as a service, without ever falling into the idolatry of power;

— a man who inspires confidence in others — they see a man engaged in politics who speaks the truth and keeps his word;

— a man who studies problems and their human context;

— a man who is realistic in the choice of possible solutions;

— a man who is humble and knows how to consult and listen to others — and not only those of his own party or electorate;

— a man who, when faced with difficulties, has confidence in the power of God;

— a man who, as his very life witnesses, seeks to incarnate in society the evangelical values of respect, brotherhood, human progress, justice and special devotion to and concern for the poor;

— a man who is aware of the way that others, with the help of the Lord, have followed — St. Fernand of Castile, St. Louis of France, St. Thomas More and St. John Fisher in England.

Certainly, none of these traits coincide with the image of "The Prince" of Machiavelli, nor with that of "The Courtier" Castiglione — both of whom have been an inspiration for so many of their illustrious disciples! But they do follow the model of "The Universal Lord" who said He came "not to be served, but to serve." And doubtless, these traits I have mentioned might prove helpful to certain powerful politicians who claim to be Catholics: they might open their eyes and see the need to change or to stop calling themselves Catholics — which is at least one step towards conversion.

For the Christian in politics, we must insist on the necessity of prayer, the sacraments and the ability to love Christ in others. For the whole political arena to be sanctified, the people involved there must aspire to sanctity.

8. The Church

I would say this is the privileged area for your apostolic activity and service. Without in any way detracting from what I have said concerning other areas, it is clear that your co-operation with the life and work of the Church is indispensable, and so much so that "without it the apostolate of the pastors is generally unable to achieve its full effectiveness." (A.A. 10) You are the "multiplying agents" which the Church needs to make itself present in society.

It is not enough to say that in belonging to a CLC group, you are giving life to a movement in the Church. The CLC is not an end in itself, but rather a means "to form committed lay people for service." (G.P. 3) You have not fulfilled your goals when your groups are running smoothly — meetings held regularly, members feeling closely united around the Eucharist — but have not yet extended their apostolic service into the areas of need I have already mentioned. You must "collaborate with the pastors, share their concern for the problems and progress of mankind... (and offer a) concrete personal collaboration in the work of building up the Kingdom of God." (G.P. 5) The parish, the diocese, or possibly even higher levels of official Church structure, together, with other kinds of specialised activities, such as charities, missionary work, preparation for marriage, counselling, the press, radio — all these areas offer unlimited possibilities for your apostolic service. And unless something quite extraordinary and obvious should occur, each one of you will surely be able to find some apostolic activity suitable to his expertise and his circumstances.

9. Pedagogical Value of the Groups

I would not like to finish without mentioning a certain point which I feel is essential to the CLC's — the indisputable value of the group. The group structure falls in between an undifferentiated mass of people and the isolated individual. The group helps to create a homogeneous cell of "people of like qualities" (G.P. 3), and facilitates, in conformity with a healthy pedagogy, the spiritual growth and apostolic zeal of the individual. Without implying the acceptance of class structures, and various forms of segregation, the CLC's enable groups to form, capable of handling diverse situations. These groups are like cells in the Mystical Body of Christ in which he is present, for they are gathered in his name. In other words, the group experiences a basic community, and the beginnings of a fellowship which has to be extended to all who share our common faith and also to all those who have not yet experienced the vision which belief in Jesus offers.

But let me also add a few words on the duties of a CLC group. Do not ask: "What can the group give me?" Ask instead: "What can I contribute to the group?" Passivity is like a cancer in a group. The group lives off the life of its members, each of whom, in turn, receives back many times over his or her own contributions. For the group — ideally — helps a person to be open, teaches the art of dialogue and the virtue of tolerance; enriches an individual's point of view and introduces such an individual to a healthy pluralism. A group, moreover, deepens an individual's faith by challenging him or her to explain it and share it; creates a climate of trust in which persons can offer or receive help; and names the deep fellowship experienced in the group as a revelation of the fatherhood of God.

These days are very important for you and for all the CLC's throughout the world. I ask the Mother of God, whom you venerate with "filial love" (G.P. 6), and whose intercession you rely on in fulfilling your vocation (G.P. 8), "to place you with her Son" — as St. Ignatius himself asked her. I am sure that with her help your efforts and work throughout these days will bring to the CLC's a renewal of and even greater commitment to your vocation of service.

ROLE OF A LAYMAN
IN THE CHRISTIAN LIFE COMMUNITIES

Open Forum with Father Arrupe

Villa Cavalletti, Grottaferrata
September 13, 1979

After Father Arrupe's address to the General Assembly of delegates of the National Federations of the Christian Life Communities, held near Rome (see previous document), there was a question hour during which Father General in answer to questions from his audience clarified a few points referring to the role of the CLC's.

The questions touched the integration of the role of a Christian as a professional man and a member of the CLC's, the involvement of a CLC member and a priest or Jesuit in politics, institutionalized and armed violence, the distinction between the priest and the lay person in the Christian Life Communities.

*

1

Q: *A young Christian (a member of the Christian Life communities), at the end of his studies enters into a whole new world; on the one hand, there is his family, his work and new responsibilities; on the other hand, there is the pull of ambition, professional expertise, money, power. What genuine help can the CLC's offer him so that this stage of transition is not a break with, but a confirmation of his service and mission?*

A: This question presupposes a dichotomy which, in fact, should not exist. Our personal reality does not consist in being

either a Christian or belonging to a CLC group and exercisng
a profession. No; it is the integration of these two. A Christian
who exercises a profession does not divide his life into two
parts — one part given to being a Christian and the other
part given to his profession. Not at all. We see this clearly,
and it often happens, in the life of a priest, who can be a doctor,
a professor or engaged in research. It is not that one part of
him is priest and the other part is engaged in research; no —
it is the personal integration of both of these that achieves a
true unity in his life.

For you lay people, the danger is to want to turn yourselves
into religious, forgetting that you are the laity. When I see
40 Jesuits at this Assembly, I can also see there is a danger of
your wanting to be Jesuits in the world. Please, no! Something
quite different is called for, whch is why I am insisting that
you must take stock of what your position should be. And to
do this, you will find it very helpful to meditate on "*Apostolicam
Actuositatem*", other Council documents, and many of the
statements that the Holy Father John Paul II has made from
the first months of his pontificate.

2

Q: *When you spoke of professional life, Father, did you say
that it was not so much a question of sanctifying one's profession
as of making of one's profession a means of sanctification?*

A: That is not exactly what I said. What I did say was that
we must sanctify our profession, but sometimes our very
profession will also sanctify us. The members of the CLC's
must sanctify their profession, and that is a major apostolic
perspective. Someone who belongs to the CLC's has the mission
of exercising his profession which he has taken up for that
very reason; he or she must sanctify their profession, but the
profession itself could sanctify them, too. Take the case of a
doctor. There is no doubt that a doctor must sanctify his
profession of medicine, but the constant exercises of this kind
of humanitarian work, the effort to remedy suffering and to
help people — all these things oblige him to renounce selfishness,
to grow in sanctity, to think of the service of others; in a word,
to exercise charity. There really is no conflict between the two.

3

Q: *Could a housewife — if, for example, she is a member of the CLC's — be as apostolic as some other people you have mentioned?*

A: A housewife, especially if she is a member of the CLC's, has to be apostolic. And her apostolate is immensely important because she helps form the nucleus of human society, which is the family. Yet even though her apostolate is so very important, her apostolic activity is not of a "more universal" kind. We have to sanctify every profession we are engaged in, and sometimes some professions are more universal in their effects than others. For example, a man who is in radio or TV could have a tremendous impact; or someone who is a university professor or school teacher has the opportunity for a wider influence on society than someone whose apostolate centres on his or her own family.

4

Q: *We see that many Jesuits are engaged in political questions. What is the place of the CLC'Cs in this kind of option?*

A: It is true that we have many Jesuits in different countries who are very much engaged in political questions. In some places there will be exaggerations, just as in other places our presence is very much required. And so it is important to make some distinctions here. If you understand "politics" in the sense that it is used in *"Mater et Ecclesia"*, *"Populorum Progressio"* and other Church documents, everybody — Jesuits and non-Jesuits — has to engage in "politics", understood in that broad sense. That is the doctrine of the Church. However, a priest's involvement cannot be identified with any particular party, like the Christian Democratic Party, nor any human ideology, such as Socialism or Communism; a priest must be free of all this — he is only identified with the Gospel. It is true that we Jesuits think it is necessary today, precisely because we have to promote justice, to engage in many political questions — economics, community-organization, society and its structures, and so on. But we never engage in these areas as members of a political party — never! Some people have left the Society because they thought it would be better for them to be in a political party rather than in the Society. This stance is not peculiar to the Society; it is the doctrine of the Church. The Synod of Bishops of 1971 made this very clear in a press release they gave which stated that for any priest to be engaged in a political party, he must first have the permission of the local hierarchy.

Take the question of human rights. To defend human rights is not an ideology; human rights are a matter of concern to everyone, and so we have to fight for them. That is not party politics; it is something quite different. Sometimes a political party is fighting for the same human rights we are fighting for, and it might seem that we are both doing the same thing; but we are acting as human beings defending these rights, not as a political party. There is a possible source of confusion here; because Jesuits in some places are involved in political action, some young men who want to be involved in action have joined the Society. However, we have made it very clear to them, right from the beginning, that the Society will never, never be identified with any political party. And so if a young man wants that sort of action, it is better he join a party, not the Society.

In the same way the CLC's, cannot be identified with any political party, though individuals in the CLC's — as members of the laity — may have to make an option as to whether or not to join a political party.

But the CLC's as such could never make such an option — it would be completely wrong for them to become identified with a political party, in any country. And so prudence suggests that a man who is a leader in a political party, not be allowed to assume a leadership role in the CLC's, as this would only give rise to confusion. For instance, if a person is President of your Executive Council, it would not be right for him also to be a leader of a political party, as this would give the impression that the CLC's are fostering a particular political party, which is not true.

5

Q: *I fully agree, Father, with what you have said about the*

*importance of the laity being involved in political parties. But
many who do this do not feel that they are sufficiently supported by
the Church.*

A: It is difficult to reply to a concrete situation without
knowing all the facts. We should have to know why a particular Christian is not supported by the Church. We can say
that the Church supports the laity on a spiritual level, in their
professional and political activities, and encourages them,
but not in a political way because the Church cannot be
identified with a political party. In this area there have
been many misunderstandings. For example, a catholic
political party might sponsor some political action which
the Church judges to be inopportune at that precise moment;
naturally she will not support such action. That is why we
must take each case as it comes. People in the Church —
priests, Jesuits, Bishops — are sometimes very naive politica-
lly. This is one of the great misconceptions that exist in
several countries. But politics in the strict sense — party
politics — (not politics in the broad sense as used in *"Mater
et Magistra"*, for example) is not their role. When we Jesuits
work for human rights — a most important issue — it can
happen that some people in the Church think, 'That has
nothing to do with us'. We must always look for the reason
why a particular person does not feel supported by the Church.
We must always look at the concrete situation and see what it
all means; discernment is what is needed. The principles are
clear; it is the concrete application that is sometimes difficult.

6

Q: *How can we ensure that young people who engage in political action do not succumb to Marxism — particularly in Latin
America?*

A: To avoid this danger, it is very helpful if our young
people are instructed and study Marxism. There are many
distinctions to be made here: as an ideology, Marxism ignores
the transcendent; the Marxist concepts of man and society
cannot be reconciled with the Christian teaching. Consequently, it is important for young people to have a properly

nuanced instruction in these matters. Please do not misunderstand me. For even admitting that although there are many good points in the Marxist social analysis, and in many of the things that Marxists do, true Marxism is unacceptable as an ideology since it denies the transcendent, and the fundamental principles of the Christian vision. People must know why Marxism is unacceptable; otherwise you will never get anywhere. And why? Because so much is said on this matter that if we do not know, in an intelligent and scientific way, what is true and what is false, we can very easily be misled.

7

Q: *How do you think a member of the CLC's should react to institutionalized violence?*

A: With a non-violent resistance — hunger strikes, public denunciations, political action, discussions, meetings, demonstrations. All these are acceptable: violence, no. We should be pacifists in this regard — using non-violent resistance and confrontation; and protesting, too, but not with arms.

8

Q: *Do you think then, Father, that we should react as pacifists before violence, or resign ourselves to it?*

A: When it is clear that there is an injustice — we cannot support injustice — we must first of all look at the concrete circumstances. Take, for example, the countries of Eastern Europe. There is injustice in those countries, but no one can do anything because resistance has no effect. Some cases are very clear, others not so clear. Action in Czechoslovakia, Poland or Hungary is quite different from action in El Salvador or Peru. We must see the circumstances in each case. We cannot accept injustice or resign ourselves to it. But it is quite a different thing to know and to do. And that is why it is so important for us priests to be free in matter of politics.

9

Q: *Should a member of the CLC's, in this commitment to the transformation of structures, be ready to take up an extreme position — like that of the Sandinists in Guatemala?*

A: That is a matter for the individual conscience. We Catholics cannot be engaged in violence; that is against the doctrine of the Church. In other words, violence is anti-evangelical, and so no Catholic should engage in it. There could be exceptions, and these are also mentioned in the Council and the Synod; but the matter has to be discerned by the individual conscience. So, as a matter of principle, since violence is antievangelical, no Catholic — no CLC member — should engage in violence. There can be exceptions, but the individual has to judge whether his case really is exceptional, and it is his own conscience — not the CLC's — which must decide.

10

Q: *I know you are aware of the situation of violence in Latin America. I agree with what you say — that armed violence is not Christian, granted certain exceptions. And so my question is: how should we react, especially as members of the CLC's, when institutionalized violence (which is the predominant one in our society) produces effects analogous to or even worse than armed violence? Don't you believe that often the only way to get rid of institutionalized violence is by means of armed violence?*

A: I do not believe so. There can be exceptions, as the Council and Synod note, but these are exceptions, not the general norm. As I see it, to attack institutionalized violence with armed violence simply prolongs the problem. On the level of principle I think that is quite clear. There was a Jesuit who became a guerrilla, but he is no longer in the Society because he could not remain a Jesuit. He thought he could be both a Jesuit and a guerrilla, which is a matter we leave to his own conscience; it is not for the Society to judge his *conscience* (as distinct from his *decision*). He was obliged to follow what his conscience told him, and perhaps the moment came when he judged the way before him, though an exceptional one, was the one to take. His conscience will keep telling him what to do.

11

Q: *Returning to the theme of violence, and granted that in many of our countries we have the Military who exercise violence, unfortunately* *some times with the collaboration of Military Chaplains; could we say, along the same lines, that just as it is not right for a member of the CLC's to participate in revolutionary violence, so members of the CLC's should join the Military?*

A: I think there is a difference between being a Military Chaplain and collaborating in violence. The Military Chaplain is engaged in the spiritual direction of people, which can be one means of sanctifying this profession. Consequently, I do not think we can say that a Military Chaplain, even in countries where the Military behave in a violent way, is collaborating in their violence. They have the spiritual role of a priest, and a priest must care for marxists, soldiers, assassins, drug-addicts, adulterers, prostitutes. A priest must have a universal heart, and try to direct and sanctify people who have taken a wrong path. So — I do not believe we can say that a Military Chaplain is a formal collaborator in violence. It is rather like the case where the Church is accused of collaborating with the rich, with capitalists. No, the Church tries to convert capitalists; she gives them retreats; she gives retreats to communists. In a word, she tries to bring the spirit of the Gospel to people who, concretely, have gone astray; but we should not think of her as collaborating with these people. The same thing holds good for the CLC's where likewise we should apply the criteria of the Gospel.

12

Q: *The distinction between the priest or religious (Jesuit) and the lay person, in the CLC's, is not clear. Are there any areas of common action?*

A: It is clear that the CLC groups are lay associations in which the initiation, working through and completion of projects belong to the laity. If a priest or religious (whether he be a Jesuit or not) is a member of a CLC group or wants to work in one, he should be there by way of providing inspiration, or counselling, in such a way as to make the distinction quite clear between himself and others in the group. The priest is not an official member, or a member properly so-called, of a CLC group; rather he is an assistant, a consellor, a source of inspiration for the group — the CLC groups are specifically lay associations.

13

Q: *Could you explain this idea a little more, Father Arrupe?*

A: I think it would be very good to reflect on what I said, though I can see it has caused a certain amount of astonishment. The reason for what I said is that there seems to be a certain lack of clarity, and some doubts need to be clarified.

The principle is true (the distinction between the CLC's and the Jesuits or priests), but many of you do not have clear ideas about it — I can see that from your reactions. It is very important we clarify who we are; the identity of the CLC's is different from the Jesuits; absolutely! That has to be clear. What is your identity? What are the distinctive qualities of the CLC's? You should be able to discover that because you have the grace for it. Through your own growth and development, through the inspiration of the Spiritual Exercises and consequently through your work, your own experience, you have to discover what is the real spirituality and identity of the CLC's. It is a great role you have; and it is very important. I am speaking of this with such conviction because you have a tremendous role to play.

The Council explained the role of the laity, and what the Council said has to be developed. The Council, Vatican II, is not the end of the Church, nor the end of the history of the Church. On the contrary, it is the beginning for many things, and therefore you laity, with such a spirituality, with such a good spirit, have to contribute to develop more and more the role of the laity in the Church. And that could be a tremendous role for the CLC's — to help illumine the role of the laity in the Church. It is not a question of minimising your position — I was very careful there. I do not say the religious is higher than the lay person — no! "Higher" applies to the person who follows the will of God. You have the vocation of a layman, we have the vocation of a priest or Jesuit. The heights we reach depends on our fidelity to accomplish our vocation.

You should not have a complex of inferiority — by no means! In certain areas you are much better than we are, naturally, and therefore we have to learn from you. As was said before, when we speak of family life, we have to go to the

family itself and see what the parents are doing here, what
they think about; we are not specialists in family life. We have
had a certain experience of family life with our parents, but
we do not have the concrete experience of being responsible
for the lives of children; to know about that, we have to hear
from the parents and from the family in action today. In the
same way we how are priests, we how are Jesuits, have to
learn from you in many aspects of human life.

You are not the servants of the priest: you are collaborators
on the same level as the priests, for the People of God, the
Church, is not the Hierarchy, nor the priests, nor the laity —
it is all those together, with every one in the group having
a special role which he has to develop and grow in. For me
this is essential, and it is one of the essential points for you to
develop. Perhaps you have to study, observe how things go,
and when you come across some points which are not clear,
you will need to discuss them; if you find you have different
opinions, that is all right — it is all part of your pilgrimage
as the People of God. And if some times things do not go well,
then you get advice from people who can help. We may not
be clear about something today, but in a year's time, or after
10 years — wonderful, everything is crystal clear, and the
CLC's are in perfect form! I do not mean altogether perfect,
because we are never really perfect — we must keep moving
on for the whole of our history.

14

Q: *Can we say a priest is a true member of a CLC group, but
because the CLC's are essentially a lay movement, he is not present
in the way other members are?*

A: No; I do not think so. A priest can be very active; he
can contribute a great deal and collaborate in many areas.
But as you see from your General Principles, the CLC's are
a lay movement, and a priest is not a layman.

THE JESUIT
AND THE CHRIST
OF THE SPIRITUAL EXERCISES

Reflections of Father General Pedro Arrupe in various talks given to Jesuits in Rome, Spain, the United States, East Asia, and India in 1970 and 1971.

Bombay
April 23, 1971

In May 1970, Father Arrupe toured the Jesuit Provinces in Spain, and in 1971 he visited the United States and several countries in East Asia, and participated in the meeting of Provincials of India and Sri Lanka in Bombay. During these journeys he often addressed groups of Jesuits on various topics of their spiritual and apostolic life in the midst of rapid changes and the feeling of uncertainty among some.

Some salient points in these talks were collected into one coherent whole in the following text, which Father Arrupe approved for circulation.

The solution to some of our problems in the present situation is to be sought in making our own the living experience of the person of Christ through which Saint Ignatius went in the Spiritual Exercises he bequeathed to the Society.

*

I.   THE JESUIT AND JESUS CHRIST

With these presuppositions, let us try to answer the fundamental question: "What can the Jesuit be or ought to be today? What can the Society of Jesus be or ought to be today?"

1. Special Approach to the Gospel

We all know well how the consciousness of the vocation to
the Society was awakened in each one of us. We know also
that the Society itself originated historically in the same way.
The decisive element of our own particular charism resulted
from an access to the light of the Gospel and to the Person of
Jesus Christ, afforded us by the Spiritual Exercises of St.
Ignatius.

In the Exercises St. Ignatius foresaw his future dedication
to the Church and to the neighbour. From the exercises sprang
forth the group which one day was to offer itself to Paul III
"desiring to be called Company of Jesus" and asking "to be
sent to any part of the world where there was hope of greater
service of God and greater help for the neighbour". From the
Exercises have come forth, one by one, all the Jesuits, from the
beginning until today. This is what marks them and constitutes them, before any law or constitution. The Constitutions
and the rules are to be understood always as the concrete
application of the spirit of the Exercises to the exigencies of
an apostolic Order, flexible and available for the service of
the Church and of men.

The Exercises are not a stereotyped mould, a machine to
fashion wholesale men completely uniform, with subdued
personalities. They constitute a simple method of prayer, of
meditation and contemplation of the life of Jesus Christ, of
examination to know oneself and conquer oneself, "to order
one's life without being affected by any inordinate attachment".
They are a spiritual experience, which ought to be personal,
though under direction, and allow oneself to be guided by the
Spirit, learning to discern Him; tarrying where one meets Him
"without being anxious to go further". It is not strange,
then, if within the common inspiration, the Exercises engender, in each of those who make them and in each epoch
of their application, a diversity of orientations and of concrete
determinations in the Christian and apostolic life. Just as
personal experience, the experience of the Exercises is historical
in character, always old and always new, ever the same and
changing with the circumstances.

In reality, this variety stems from the infinite efficacy

of the Gospel, to which the Exercises give access. The Exercises have, certainly, their own special manner of access to the Gospel. They suppose on the part of the man the personal decision, the generous commitment of himself even to the "folly" of the third degree of humility, the reflection and maturity, the apostolic dynamism of love. They lay stress on the humanity of Jesus Christ, on the appeal to the love of friendship and to following Him closely, on the enterprise of the Kingdom. But all these particular features have not limited much the spectrum of possibilities opened up by the Exercises. In fact, though holding the Exercises as a family treasure, the Jesuits have not guarded it jealously; they have understood that it was a common good, and they have offered it to the Church. And much of recent spirituality has been fostered by the Exercises.

2. Jesuit Formula: Universality and Adaptability

Thus we come to a paradox, very enlightening when one thinks of the essential nature of the Society: it is the fruit of the Exercises, and yet the Exercises are in fact universal. Logically, the Society had to mark its particular nature by some communitarian rules to realize the spirit of the Exercises; she did so from the beginning by the "Formula of the Institute", and then by the Constitutions. But, as one could hope, granted the source of the inspiration, these rules are very flexible and adaptable. It is perhaps the most distinctive characteristic of the Society. And we know how many afflictions it cost St. Ignatius and his first companions to break as they did with many of the ordinances judged essential in the tradition of the existing religious Orders.

With certain limits, the Society possesses an undeniable universality. Its concrete history has involved the forging of a series of determinations on the manner of procedure, with rules and customs. No society can subsist without a minimum of regulation and discipline; much less still an apostolic society of men, who profess obedience and wish to be disposable for common enterprises. It would be suicide, therefore, to wish to simply prescind from these concrete determinations, the fruit of tradition (often going back even to the beginnings) and sanctioned as rules. But with respect to these it is the charism of the Society to possess a great liberty and flexibility, a great power of accommodation. No other Institute could have understood or welcomed more the appeal of the Second Vatican Council to seek renovation and accommodation to the changing circumstances of the times. In the 31st General Congregation the Society has taken great steps in that direction, in tracing out very broad norms.

Perhaps we cannot say that the whole of the Society has already assimilated them. Some Jesuits pay attention only to what is precise and restrictive in these norms, without accepting the new spirit that animates them. Others, on the contrary, seem attentive only to the horizons they open up, in order to launch out boldly towards these, without heeding details, which are prescribed quite precisely. Both of these attitudes are understandable, at the present time; in both cases, the Jesuits ought to know how to understand themselves in their own manner of viewing the common ideal. It is necessary to be on guard that our social reality is not rent by extreme tendencies, and that a bad example in not thus given others, in the present difficult circumstances.

But perhaps the best way of understanding and experiencing our deep unity, and correcting thereby what could be a deviation towards one or other extreme in our positions, is to return to the spirit of the Exercises, from which everything has grown; to return to what is most essential in spiritual experience, from which our vocation sprang, and what had fostered it and advanced it from year to year. To return thus to the Exercises is to return to Jesus Christ.

3. Christ's Saving Message to the Man of Today

Jesus Christ is all in all for the Jesuits; it is the only key possible for the understanding of his life, of the enterprise to which he has consecrated himself. Here again we meet with the paradox of universality. For Jesus Christ belongs to all Christians. The Jesuit knows this, and he is not jealous or disconcerted. Some follow Christ by seeking Him in a special way by contemplation, others in the practice of corporal charity towards the neighbour, others in the rigour of poverty...

The Jesuit would exclude nothing save in so far as his clear dedication to imitate Jesus in one of these aspects would suppose the necessity of neglecting the others. The different features of the figure of the historical Jesus centre about His prophetic mission as messenger of salvation. This is the Jesus which the Jesuit puts in the first place before his eyes.

Today the prophetic mission of the announcement of salvation will undoubtedly have to be exercised in conditions very different from those of Palestine of the first century; conditions diverse too, when there is a question of peoples with an old Christian tradition of peoples in the missions; of developed countries or of underdeveloped countries, which constitute the vast majority of the Third World, so important today. In all these cases it is necessary to follow Jesus with complete generosity, in the renunciation of marriage for the Kingdom, in poverty (according to circumstances and one's specific work), in obedience (since there is question of forming a group active and available to its milieu, like that group of disciples whom Christ formed and sent "to all towns and places he himself was to visit").

Enthusiastic, captivated by Jesus Christ, the Jesuit of today, as always, will try to realize in the midst of the men of today something comparable to what He Himself realized among the men of His day. He will try to imitate not so much this or that particular aspect as the essential profile of His historical figure. Thus, in union with companions who have conceived the same ideal, he will continue the group of those who were attracted by Jesus to share in His life and mission.

4. Subordinate Service in Anonymous Role

The Jesuit knows very well that he has no monopoly on this continuation of the evangelizing mission of Jesus. He knows that in the Church which He founded there is a Hierarchy established by Him on which primarily falls the duty of continuing His mission, and at its head the Successor of Peter, the Vicar of Christ on earth; for this reason the Jesuit makes a special vow of obedience with regard to the concrete aspects of his mission, to be more sure of ascertaining what Jesus Christ wants of him. The Jesuit also knows today more than ever, that the whole ecclesial community has the duty of continuing the mission; he knows the importance of the role which falls to the laity; he knows that only he who lives within the structures of human life (those of the family, marriage, paternity, those of the economy and of politics, those of the civil professions in all their variety) can give therein an authentic Christian witness; and he is called too to deliver a message which can be more authoritative because of his greater involvement.

The Jesuit has contributed historically to the advancement of the laity; and he is happy, today, to cooperate fraternally, without paternalism, in the enterprises which are properly those of the layman. But he remembers that his vocation always is to follow Christ more deeply and closely in the absorbing work of the prophetic vocation. This vocation implies the leaving to others tasks that are truly important and urgent; but, keeping to his own place, the Jesuit does not forsake them completely, since he animates the laity who bring them to realization.

The Jesuit knows, finally, that many others, priests and religious, concur with him today in the fundamental conception of his prophetic vocation to imitate Jesus. If in his day the Society conceived by St. Ignatius was an innovation, this ideal of life has since become, fortunately, that of many other Institutes, and is even shared and lived by the best priests. The Jesuit of today feels himself in fraternal cooperation with all, without any privilege or advantage. His identity, in this respect, comes to him simply from the historical involvement and from the fidelity to Jesus Christ, in the Institute founded by St. Ignatius; this involvement is a family affair, a tradition fashioned by some norms, certain works undertaken in common, and — this is truly decisive — guidelines of an obedience lived in the faith.

5. Specialization: Total Availability

Should the Society aim at specialization among the many Institutes which today profess dedication to the prophetic mission and to the kind of life which Jesus lived? As a group, there will be no better "specialization" than is universal availability to the orders of the Church and the Pope. But it is certain also that this very availability disposes it for some arduous missions which we would speak of today as being "on the frontier." This orientation is already underscored in the Formula of the Institute: "For the defence and the propagation of the faith": it is thus that in the first place the end of the new institution was formulated. And to express the content of the special vow of obedience to the Sovereign Pontiff, the words speak of the sending "to any provinces whatsoever", "whether it be to the Turks or any other infidels, even in the regions called the Indies, and to any heretics or schismatics, as well as to any faithful whatsoever". In these words can be felt throbbing the desire to work "under the standard of the Cross", the disposition to what is most arduous and difficult, the participation in the social ostracism of Christ and of him who wishes to work with Him, "to follow Him in suffering" and in His humiliation. It is a way of expressing the search for "the greater service", which in most cases is the most arduous and difficult, which demands the exaltation of love, the only force that can give the key to this rational involvement. The history of the Society has not been unfaithful to this engagement.

In our days, Pope Paul VI has said very explicitly where the new frontier has to be for us: "To the Society of Jesus, whose principal duty is the defence of the Church and of holy religion, we entrust in these calamitous times the mandate of vigorously opposing atheism". It is an immense task, which obviously we cannot realize alone. But it is to this that the Society of today will have to consecrate its best efforts. The last General Congregation, accepting the mandate of the Pope, has demanded that "all of Ours, resolutely though humbly, with prayer and action, devote themselves to this task" — the task of all and in all places, although not in the same degree nor in the same manner. It will be necessary to take account of this mission in the choice of ministries. It will be necessary to devote Jesuits to the serious study of the causes and the methods of atheism. But, more universally, all Jesuits will have to recognize and perceive that they are in a world whose spiritual crisis goes as far as atheism. They will have to reckon with this reality in all their apostolic works. They will have to prepare believers to meet this crisis. Above all, they will have to give living testimony of their faith in God, so that "in their whole manner of living and acting there may appear, as far as possible, that which is God".

The same Decree of the 31st General Congregation on atheism contains and important allusion to another field very appropriate for the apostolic preoccupatoins of the present-day Jesuit, towards which his love for Jesus Christ ought to call him at once today: it is that which we are wont to call under the general name of "the Third World", Numerically, it is the greater part of mankind; in its immense majority it is in a state or economic and cultural under-development, subject to flagrant injustice due to the selfish structures of our world. On the other hand it is also the part of humanity with the most vigorous potential on the spiritual level, and capable of giving lessons of faith and hope to the old world with its skepticism and inclination to atheism.

In looking at the map of the distribution of the Society, one should ask if it is sufficiently orientated towards this Third World, or too firmly entrenched in the western world. Would it not be a way of solving its crisis, and particularly the decrease of vocations, by a more real and more generous opening to the immense Third World? Is it not there that Christ calls today?

II.   CHRISTOCENTRIC THEOLOGY:
THE DEVELOPMENT

6.   Christ the Key to Human History

To enter more profoundly into the present reality of our vocation as Jesuits — and thus help us more to surmount what constitutes a "crisis of identity" in our time — we ought to consider above all these realities and these pressing problems of atheism and the Third World, which ought to be the centre of our attention. But besides, we must engage in a serious Christological reflection, derived likewise from the vital experience of the Spiritual Exercises.

If up to now, to get an insight into the image of the Jesuit of today, we have fixed our attention particularly on the historical figure of Jesus — and we have evoked thereby the spirit of the "Second Week" of the Exercises — we must now go beyond this view and the perspective of the personal imitation of Jesus, to consider, according to our faith, the integral reality of Jesus Christ at the centre of the whole creative and salvific plan of God. Jesus Christ, key of creation and of the history of the human community.

Such is the orientation of the Exercises in their Third and Fourth weeks. After "knowing Jesus Christ intimately, in order to love and follow Him more" comes the identification with His redemptive Death and with His Resurrection.

The Jesuit seeks not only to imitate Jesus Christ; he seeks also to *Christify* the world, to contribute in the small measure of his powers and of the grace with which God calls him to the realization of the plan of God who wishes "to recapitulate all things in Christ."

It is from hence, from this Christocentric theology, assimilated in the contemplations of the Third and Fourth Weeks, and crowned in the total vision of the "Contemplation for obtaining love", that he looks at the world, attempting to explain the crisis of development which he sees in the world, and by which he feels himself affected — from hence he catches a glimpse of what he can offer by way of solution.

It is a theology of history, theology of a world in development that is thus unfolded before our eyes. It is a theology not only of the creative Logos, but also of the incarnate Logos in exaltation, and of the incarnate Logos as redeemer. It is necessary to consider all the aspects that the vision may not be one-sided. We are attempting to evoke that balanced vision of the world in the faith, and then draw the consequences for our concrete vocation. It is best to fix our attention first on the aspect revealed to us by the Resurrection and the Contemplation for obtaining love: it is the theology of the incarnate Logos in exaltation. We will then find the unforgettable place of the Cross, and the theology of the Logos redeemer.

If the ultimate end of all things is "the glory of God", this glory is realized in man and through the medium of man. "The glory of God, it is living man", as "the life of man, it is the vision of God". It is man who really gives meaning to the world. "All things were created for man". The world receives its destiny from man; the relation of the world to God depends entirely on man as intermediary.

This elemental theology of the Logos creator is in no way annulled but *elevated* by the Christian theology of the Logos incarnate. What this adds — leaving out the question in what sense God destines man for Himself — is that in Christ, Son of God incarnate, God calls each man also tobe his son. The grace of Christ, Head of all mankind, has been given to all of us to share, to each one in the measure of the generous plan of God.

This grace, which unites us to God as Christ, makes us His Mystical Body, His "brothers", sons of the Father, possessors of the Spirit; this grace is a *reality* for the faith.

Our whole vision of things, of our possibilities and aspirations, ought to take account of this; otherwise, we will be fearful, and lose courage in the face of a world which, after having felt itself immensely great and powerful by the unfolding of its science and technology, finds itself often helpless to realise love and justice. The believing Christian has the consciousness of being immensely strong by the grace of God that lives in him, and capable of following the infinite example of love given him by the whole life of Jesus Christ.

And as we know by faith, grace is destined to culminate after death and beyond all the bounds of human life, in the vision of God, in which finally will be revealed also what we are, in love without limits and without selfishness; God will be all in all, and we shall realize ourselves in Him, the Total Christ attained in plenitude.

7. Harmonious Development: Individual and Community

Perhaps in times past Theology considered these realities of faith in a manner excessively individualistic, as well as in a dualistic manner, exaggerating the separation of the world from nature and nature from grace. We have reacted today against both excesses; yet we must be careful not to fall into another extreme, the naturalistic abolition of all distinction, or the reduction of grace to nature.

The principle of balance was always present in Catholic theology, though all the consequences were not drawn. "Grace does not destroy nature but supposes it and perfects it". In this light we see today clearly that the supernatural elevation and grace do not have to be thought of as realities external to man, like artificial additions. It is not necessary to imagine the history of salvation as if it were subsistent by itself, and absolutely independent of human history, as if the facts of human history were indifferent, and salvation followed another road, purely individual and internal, which was to appear only at the end, at the hour of judgment and sanction. Against this whole conception, in the measure in which it permeates spirituality and apostolic activities, there have arisen today the just protests of those who see in it a rending of the unity of the plan of God, a division between "God Creator" and "God Saviour" and finally, a disparagement of the work of salvation. The universal primacy of Christ, of which St. Paul speaks, seems to them to demand another vision of history.

And it is this theology, now not dualistic, this integral theology, which permeates and governs the splendid developments of the Constitution *"Gaudium et Spes"* of Vatican II; it is particularly evident in the explicit references to Jesus Christ concluding the different sections.

Such theology is very important for the thorough understanding on the part of the Society today of its mission in relation to atheism and in relation to the Third World. It will be good to assemble some underlying features of the image of man. For to realize "the Glory of God" in Christ and by the grace of Christ implies fundamentally the *harmonious personal and communitarian development of man*. And the believing Christian and the apostle ought to feel themselves today as the promoters of this development.

Personal development. It is in effect by his interior and spiritual world that man is superior to all the universe; he comes back to this interiority when he enters into his heart, where God, the searcher of hearts, awaits him. Development *in the world*. Man has need of the world for his own improvement, for the development of his creative power and for the indefinite increase of his liberty. To aid man to accept and to realize his obligation to transform the world is to prepare him to go towards God; it is the "Christifying" labour of pre-evangelization.

Communitarian development also. For man is essentially a social being, and for that reason the development of his own person and the growth of his society condition each other mutually. Finally, development *of the social structures*, according to the postulates of personal dignity, and of justice founded on the recognition of the rights of all men and of their fundamental equality.

All this, we insist, is not simple humanism in the eyes of those who have faith in Christ and a correct theology. According to faith, man exists only to have his end in Christ. The world exists only to have its end in Christified man, and in ultimate term, in Christ. The transformation of the world by human action is really ordained to bring about the participation and the expression of the glory of Christ; to go further, from this moment on there is preparation and anticipation of that glory. For the believing Christian the progress of man in history attains its final dimension in the plenitude of Christ.

8.   The Concrete Reality of our Vocation

This theology, at once encouraging and exacting, enlightens us all today in the search for the concrete reality of our vocation. It is surely that which stimulates our youth, when they wish to see the Society less bound to structures which permit such general injustice; on the contrary they would like to see the Society more involved in effective activities along the lines of progress. Who could deny that in this aspiration there is a profound Christian impulse, completely in keeping with the spirit of the Jesuit? All of us have to revise our action continually; perhaps the Society ought even to abandon some of its activities to undertake others; or else, proceed to transform profoundly the spirit of current activities.

Before the impatience of the young, fundamentally sound, often importune in its forms, frequently a little unrealistic, it is necessary to ask them to remember this: it is impossible to do everything quickly, and things should not be done lightly; further, it is necessary to keep in mind always those theological principles which will prevent the proposed vision from leading to contradictory consequences:

i) One cannot simply identify progress and the history of salvation, as if the latter would automatically follow from the former; we would run the risk of reducing salvation to something natural and immanent; besides this would destroy the best hope of nature itself, which aims always beyond itself. Natural progress is basic and Christian salvation cannot disassociate itself from it, nor promote it as a simple instrument, in an apologetic manner; but it is necessary to recognize that, in promoting it, it goes beyond it.

ii) Terrestrial realities have their autonomy and should be developed according to their internal laws, without outside interferences.

iii) If these two reasons are combined, it follows that a distinction is necessary between the *natural* service of humanity and its progress (which we have already said is per se a service in keeping with the plan of God in Christ) and a service more specifically supernatural; this consists in aiding men to discover the ultimate meaning of all their activity, in cultivating in them Christian faith, hope and charity, in realizing the sacrament which is the Church in their community life.

The prevailing note in the vocation of the Jesuit and in his service of the neighbour for love of Christ, goes under the heading of the most supernatural service. We ought not to forget it, even when involved in the actual undeniable urgencies of other more immediate services. It is true that the Society has always assumed many of these, and in the very formula of the Institute the list of our activities concludes with the very broad expression: "the other works of charity". We exclude nothing except what, in definite circumstances, prevents greater good. But if we seek a true and ordered effectiveness, we should learn rather to divide the tasks, by favouring the advancement of the laity and leaving to them the most direct promotion of human development, reserving for ourselves the duty of animating them with Christian sentiments, in keeping with the specific nature of our vocation.

This is what they expect most from us, and anything else could cover anew a paternalistic activity. It is true that there are many ambiguous situations, where it is impossible to define the boundaries clearly; it is true that at times temporary expedients are necessary, and we must make an effort to give visible witness, in order to dissipate prejudice. But perhaps it is not good to stabilize and perpetuate what is provisional; today we have to experiment continually in the search for new ways; let us learn also to revise them without cease, in the light of our ideal. In any case, the many Jesuits, who must still employ a good part of their energies in the human advancement of their neighbour, should be happy in the consciousness that this also is necessary for the edification of the total Christ.

Perhaps it is fitting to conclude our reflections on the Christian meaning and value of human development — in the frame-work of an integral Christology, of a theology of the Word incarnate — with a consideration of the integral development of the Jesuit himself. The honest search for a full growth of one's natural powers and talents is in the Ignatian tradition. Identified in heart with Christ and with the humanity he wishes to integrate in Christ, the Jesuit will not consider his own development as something private, with a selfish view that would belittle and tarnish it. He regards it as a patrimony of Christ and the Church, as something sacred, which does not belong to him, and which he cannot let lie fallow. His desire will be to be able to make the maximum return, according to what Jesus Himself did. But by doing this without egoism, he will be disposed to sacrifice definite aspects of his own development for the greater development of other superior values, in himself or in others; and he will not refuse to share in the mutilation that underdevelopment imposes today on so many men.

III. CHRISTOCENTRIC THEOLOGY: THE CROSS

9. Christ and Him Crucified

Thus we come to the second aspect of the Christology, which St. Ignatius has made live for us in the Third Week of the Exercises, and which we could in no way neglect without betraying the Gospel. It is the theology of the Logos Redeemer, theology of the Cross.

If there has been, in the past, a defect in emphasizing one-sidedly this aspect, in the theological presentation of the figure and the role of Jesus Christ, it would be likewise a fault and harmful to fall into the opposite extreme, and forget that only through the death on the Cross did Christ come to the exaltation of the Resurrection, which merited for Him the name of Lord. Whoever wishes to follow Him in glory has to follow Him in humiliation and in sorrow. For the humanity to which we belong, and in which the divine Logos became incarnate, is a sinful humanity, which dwells in a world beset with evil. It is not possible to disregard this nor to release oneself from that situation. Only by accepting it such as it is, by confronting evil and struggling against sin, even to the Cross and even to death, do we share in the Redemption, for our own personal profit as well as for the good of all mankind.

Evil is an undeniable feature of our world. And man can and ought to struggle against it always, by trying to overcome it and convert it into a good of a higher order; but very often he makes it worse, for himself and for his fellowmen, by the very selfishness with which he pretends to escape from it. Called to love by the best part of his very nature, made by God to His image, called to a higher vocation of love by grace and the example of Christ..., man, inherently low-spirited and cowardly, evades that call, withdraws within himself and, "wishing to gain all, loses all". Such is the drama of sin, present in human history from the beginning. Since his appearance upon the earth, man is a sinner.

The ascetic Christian tradition has never forgotten this. And it has understood, that for that reason the believer must turn ever anew to God by sincere conversion, from his condition as sinner. He has to struggle, inspired by grace, to bring about, in himself and in others, the triumph of good over evil, of love over selfishness. But, above all, he must feel himself identified with the death of Jesus, in which He offered Himself to the Father in expiation for the sin of the world, that man might thus be reborn with Him to new life.

10. Steering between Two Extremes

We have no reason to forget this today, quite the contrary. Is there less selfishness in our world? Is it more free from the dominion of sin?

What offends the young, perhaps, in the classic presentations of sin and penance, of the ascetic necessity of mortification and the cross, is its one-sidedness in not putting forward the integral plan of God, the elevation of mankind by the Incarnation and the Resurrection of Christ, the call to the love of charity. Taken by themselves, certain aspects of that classic presentation and certain ascetic examples of the past appear individualistic, manifesting obsession with individual salvation, without sufficient perspective for the more complete reality of the Total Christ.

These defects have been overcome today. Starting from the new perspective, more sound, more profound and more comforting, it is necessary to recover the whole insuperable truth of the cross and its redemptive value, the necessity of struggle and mortification, to put an effective limit to selfishness, to recognize the necessity of profound humility and continual conversion towards the Lord.

There is an aspect of sin, which used to be put less in relief, but whose importance we see today more than ever and whose comprehension can help us to understand better the mystery of the Cross, and what is demanded of us today by way of participation in this mystery. In its strictest sense, sin is an act of the personal will, which, called to good by grace, deliberately closes itself to that call under the impulse of selfish attraction. But this sin of man, by the inevitable social projection of all that is human, tends to "objectify itself", and in union with the similar sin of others, to establish social structures which perpetuate and protect the selfish attitude of individuals; these structures engender situations difficult for others — in which they can with difficulty retreat even from the temptation to sin — and they go so far as to make very difficult or even practically impossible the practice of good and the following of the voice of conscience.

11. The Problem of Collective Sin

Does not that description, unfortunately, fit great aspects or sectors of the social reality of our time? Do not the miseries of the Third World come from there? The young often feel it very keenly. That is why they consider hypocritical the diatribes against certain individual sins, when these omit these other greater social sins. They are not right in what they deny, but right in what they affirm, that is to say: the existence of that other greater sin. Every sin ought to be denounced and combated by those who wish to share in the prophetic vocation of Jesus. The Church and the Society ought to be very clear in the position they take in the face of the grave collective sins of today.

It is clear, however, that if it is not a question of concrete personal sin, the remedy is more difficult. Besides, everything is not resolved by denunciation, unless it is followed with personal example and with concrete action opposed to sin. "The mystery of iniquity" is in the world, and it will not leave it tomorrow or the day after tomorrow. It is necessary to take account of it, and to undertake against it an action that is broad in scope, patient and well directed.

Such an action should not neglect any support that the human sciences and techniques, especially psychology, sociology, economics and politics, can offer. It is necessary to know how to cope with the psychological defects of man, and remedy them in the measure possible. It is necessary to know how to convince men that their happiness does not lie in selfishness; it is necessary, however, to know how to reckon with those cold laws of sociology and economics that emanate from the selfishness of man — without remaining prisoner, on the other hand, of this motif, but trusting that there are in man better resources than those he has manifested up to now. It is necessary to make a prudent effort, combining the techniques of realism and possibility with the courage essential for renewal. None of these things can be neglected. But it would be extremely naive to believe that all that is going to establish order in the world at once, or that it is going to settle it in a definite way.

The way of the Cross of Christ continues, then, to open up

for us the other way, that of participation in the redemptive suffering. We will all meet it in our life, as He met it, however little we may feel ourselves honoured to struggle with Him against our own selfishness and that of others, and provided that we do not flee cowardly when it knocks at our door. Traditional asceticism has a repertory of concrete forms of mortification the result of positive research, and has presented them, with insistance, as exercises of penance and as participation in the Cross. We have come to realize today that the important thing is to accept the evil that comes our way and which makes us share, conjointly with our brothers, in the suffering caused by injustice and selfishness. If we wish to be ready for this participation, we will certainly find it opportune, and essential, in addition to the voluntary asceticism which prepares us for it, to accept the suffering that will come to us, with a view to being faithful, as Jesus Christ, to our vocation, and in order to feel our solidarity, with Him and as He does, with the suffering endured by mankind.

An exaggerated preaching of resignation to evil — above all to that caused by human selfishness — would be judged, and with reason, by men of today as evasion and culpable complicity. It is necessary to struggle against injustice in the name of God, and of man, son of God, and of the solidarity of the total Christ. But it is necessary also to continue to teach men that evil can be transformed into good through love, fidelity, sacrifice and even death. Jesus of Nazareth was not a politician. But with His death on the Cross and fidelity to His prophetic mission, concentrating against Himself the forces of sin and of human selfishness, He vanquished them more effectively than by any political action, through His redemptive love and His example. One does not, for that reason, exclude the vocation of politics for the Christian; quite the contrary. But the Jesuit ought to leave to the laymen action more specifically political, and illumine for him with the light of the faith the principles to guide that action; and, at the same time, he will confront evil on the level of those who suffer it, by his solidarity with them, as far as that is possible.

Jesus "being God, did not wish to present Himself as God, but emptied Himself, to assume the condition of a slave —

and became a man as all men are, and humiliated Himself even unto death, and death on the Cross". It is thus that He was able to redeem us, sharing with us the structures of evil in which we found ourselves. The Jesuit will do honour to the name which he bears when he knows how to renounce the privileges that are not strictly necessary for his mission and his work, and when he shares the lot of the majority of the mankind that he wishes to save. In a world in which the poor are still a majority — look no further — you have a decisive reason for being poor.

CONCLUSION

To bring this reflection to an end, we could conclude by saying that if anyone seeks a definition of a Jesuit, he will encounter a fundamental difficulty: no one wants to answer him and give a definition, according to "genus and specific difference". Besides, such a definition would not free him from his doubts nor would it resolve the problem. The difficulty comes undoubtedly from the fact that it is impossible to rationalize anything vital. The manner of being a Jesuit comprises elements that escape cerebral speculation: all those which proceed from a generous attitude of radical and permanent commitment to Christ and to the service of the Church.

Such attitudes are not "definable". And still less would they be expressed by an identification which would attempt to conform to the logical effort of a definition. There is question of something completely alien to such schematism. The very design of seeking an "identity"through an effort of speculation on what is not a matter for reasoning but a life (or a form of life not subject to rationalization), can imply ambiguities or even apparent contradictions. It is difficult to succeed in expressing concepts which, like life, each one of us perceives in the ultimate experience of our own behaviour.

Ultimately, the Jesuit is he who is a member of the Society of Jesus. The Society of Jesus is a dynamic, not an abstract body. It is a reality embodied in men; that is why the Society is a Society, in the measure in which there are incorporated in it men who embody a concrete spirit, inspired by the Exercises and formulated in the Constitutions. The living source of this Spirit should be Jesus Christ, the Word of God lived in the Exercises (adapted vitally for a whole life-time), and the historical readjustment of that spirit to its own authenticity should be effected by the Constitutions.

The true Jesuit goes along under the interior guidance of that spirit. It is what in each situation inspires him and directs him. Neither is the "identity" of that spirit attained to by reasoning. It is something which is born to life in the Exercises, and which grows by the experience of each one incorporated into the life of the Society. The spirit is never completely realized since its formation, development and growth are perpetual, being continually fostered by the personal and corporate experience of the spirit itself. That is why Ribadeneira wishing to define the Jesuit, conceives it thus, descriptively, as an attitude and motive for life: "That we be men crucified to the world and to whom the world itself is crucified, that is what our rule of life demands; new men, I say, who have stripped themselves of their affection that they might put on Christ...etc.".

We can hope that the crisis in the world, in the Church, in the Society will lead to a happy end only if we count seriously and effectively on grace. Only by counting on grace can we put our shoulders to this difficult task which is the vocation of Jesuits. To count on grace is to pray, to be men of prayer, who come "to meet God in all things" and who can be called "contemplatives in action".. If there is to be any truth in what we propose in the way of bold and generous renovation and accommodation, in fidelity to our original charism and to our tradition, it will be necessary for each and all of us, with God's help, to find the way to make operative and joyously conscious in our inner being that presence of the Spirit, which translates itself into faith, hope and love.

25

THE EXERCISES AND THE JESUIT

(A)

Making and Directing the Exercises

Rome
September 8, 1972

At the end of 1971 Father General asked that all who were expected to write 'ex officio' letters in January — Superiors, Province Consultors and House Consultors — should give special attention in their report to three points: the steps taken in the Provinces and houses to determine apostolic priorities and to adapt their ministries; secondly, the life style of our communities; and thirdly, the practice of the Spiritual Exercises, both for Jesuits themselves and as part of our apostolate.

On September 8, 1972, Father Arrupe wrote a letter to all Major Superiors, to be communicated to those concerned, offering some observations and comments on the points treated in the annual letters. Here are his reflections on the Ignatian Spiritual Exercises.

*

The third question was intended to see how the Exercises of Saint Ignatius influenced our own lives as Jesuits and our apostolate today.

Most Jesuits are faithful to making their annual Exercises. My desire is that this should be applicable to all, because they are so necessary in this periodic renovation. I consider it very important that the duration of the Exercises should not be shortened, nor easily broken up into shorter periods without very special reasons that should be judged by the Superior.

The Exercises should be made annually, but it is also important to renew and revitalize this Ignatian practice. For some it could become mere routine. Others have tried to find a substitute for this spiritual exercise of personal discernment and renewal of their own life, having recourse to a more exclusively intellectual and less demanding reflection, assisted by a good preacher or a few fine books, sometimes also discarding the silence that is so indispensable.

I was very pleased to learn that in some Provinces a good number of Jesuits made the Spiritual Exercises personally under the guidance of a skilled director. In some Provinces a few Jesuits made the entire month of the Exercises, as actual circumstances dictated and allowed. Others have found it profitable to make the Exercises together with their community. What is clear from the information received on this and on other details is that these different forms of making the Exercises show a genuine spiritual renewal in an area that is of capital importance for our conversion. I strongly desire that this movement may continue to spread ever more widely.

Provinces in many countries report that the Exercises of Saint Ignatius, as a principal instrument of the apostolate, are suffering a setback. Certainly they are given to fewer groups and above all to fewer large groups. On the other hand, they are being given to persons who are more capable of making them individually and in a more exacting manner. With the Exercises we are still helping a good number of religious sisters, while on the contrary in some places we are giving them to fewer groups of priests. We should ask ourselves what, on our part, has caused this reversal, especially since it concerns an important service to the Church which the Society has always tried to render with particular dedication and consoling results, including some excellent vocations.

It will also be necessary to renew the methods and adaptations in giving the Exercises to younger generations, and in this area much remains to be done.

It is good to note that courses that prepare Jesuits as directors for the Exercises are on the increase, but I should like to observe that theological updating on the content and the presentation of the meditations is not sufficient. We must also go more deeply into the typical internal dynamism of the Ignatian Exercises, which apart from disposing a person for the action of grace, also yields its own special fruit...

(B)

Mission: Key to the Reading of the Gospel and of the Exercises

Loyola, Spain
September 2, 1974

In 1974 a Jesuit International Congress was held, September 2-7, on "The Spiritual Exercises and the Constitutions as instruments for renewal in the Society", at the ancestral home of Saint Ignatius at Loyola in Spain. Father Arrupe delivered then an address which he described as "my small contribution on the existential level: to share with you some simple reflections which stem from life and from experience." The subject of his paper was "Apostolic Mission: Key to the Ignatian Charism."

Inserted here are only two short excerpts on the meaning of 'mission' as the key to our reading of the Gospel and to our reading of the world today according to Ignatius in the Exercises.

*

I. MISSION: KEY TO OUR READING OF THE GOSPEL

1. Ignatius' Experience of the Person of Christ

If we want to understand what 'mission' signifies in all its dimensions in our Constitutions, we must approach the source from which it grew, which is nothing else than the Gospel, meditated upon in the Spiritual Exercises. The Constitutions are rooted in the experience of the Exercises.

The Gospel is an infinite treasure, something which gives rise to an innumerable variety of inspirations and experiences.

One of these experiences is that which came to be crystallized in the Exercises.

For Ignatius the key to the Gospel is to be found in the person of Christ, and in His condition as that of being one 'sent' from the Father in mission to man, and this implies the Incarnation — His identification of man with Himself — and His death for man. The whole of the Exercises revolves around the person of 'the Lord who has become man for me':[19] the life of Christ, especially His public life, His passion and His resurrection, are a living reality which the exercitant ought to meditate upon 'as though I were present there'[20] asking with insistence for 'an intimate knowledge of our Lord... that I may love and follow Him better'.[21] Christ appears to the eyes of the exercitant as the Eternal King to whom is present the whole world; and to the world, and to each man, He gives the same invitation to work for all others 'and thus to enter into the glory of My Father'.[22] For the exercitant, Christ chooses so many persons, apostles, disciples, etc., and sends them throughout the world to spread His sacred doctrines.[23]

2. The Kenosis of Christ

The Christ of the Gospel is seen and experienced in the Exercises as Christ who is poor, humble, the servant who is obedient to the Father; as the Christ of the *kenosis*, *'formam servi accipiens'*,[24] who has become one of 'the many', like unto a man needing redemption. He is the Christ of the Beatitudes and the Christ of the cross. When He sends His disciples to continue His mission, He sends them as neighbours to man, as unconditional servants of all men in fulfilment of the will of the Father. He sends them in poverty, to be humiliated as He was and like Him to suffer and be laden with injuries, for the redemption of the world.

Well, then, what is formulated as an individual experience

---

[19] *Spir. Ex.* 104.
[20] *Ibid.*, 114.
[21] *Ibid.*, 104.
[22] *Ibid.*, 95.
[23] *Ibid.*, 145.
[24] Philip. 2. 7.

in the Exercises is subsequently crystallized in the Constitutions as a communitarian experience — the same charismatic experience of Ignatius and of his first companions. "The Constitutions are writ through with the spirit that God our Lord inscribed in the hearts of our first Fathers, and this the Lord communicated to them by means of the Exercises'.[25]

All these companions had lived the same basic experience of the Exercises, but to experience themselves as 'friends in the Lord' they planned, if it was the will of that same Lord, to form a body. At the end of their deliberations of 1539, they became convinced that they should always be united not only by the bond of charity, but also by that of obedience to one who was to be elected from among themselves. This was truly the expression of the 'group', in which all participated in one and the same grace, and in one and the same vocation.

3. The Experience re-lived by the Jesuit

This lived experience is repeated, according to degree, in each Jesuit: the intimate, personal perception of his vocation and the realization that this special charism includes essentially the pertaining to a body—in as much as all the members arrive, through one and the same experience, to one and the same mission.

This charismatic experience of Ignatius and his companions has been approved by the Church. We are dealing, therefore, with an authentic experience since the authoritative mark of the genuineness of charism is always its approbation by the Church.

Thus the Constitutions come to be the inspiration of an authentic way of life; they come to be a *situs* if you will, a hermeneutic instrument, one that offers us a specific key for reading the Gospel, one that is ours, one that belongs to those who desire to live according to the 'founding' charism of Ignatius, a vocation the essence of which is apostolic mission.

This key to the reading of the Gospel and of the Exercises is also evident in the Constitutions: Christ as Saviour— humble servant, obedient—He who sends His disciples.

[25] La Palma, *Camino Espiritual*, Bk. 5, c. 3.

4. The Jesuit a Man with a Mission

The obverse of this coin is the key to the life of the Jesuit:
'I am the one to be sent—by Jesus—in poverty and humility—
in service—and in obedience—in salvific mission'. Truly this
is an admirable key, fashioned in the mould of St. Paul and of
St. John. It is specific, rather than general, and is at the
same time open to all of the possible correlationships which
are to be found in the context of the Gospel.

This key is both traditional and original, because it does
not represent the whole, but rather a means of coming into
contact with the whole. 'The key must be distinct from the
door: therefore it must be something that, while taking up a
part of Scripture, permits us to read it and to make of it, as
from a rather shapeless material, a two edged sword'.[26]

In order to deepen and renew his vocation which contains
in itself the reality of 'mission', the Jesuit must read the Gospel
from this particular perspective: namely that of one who is
sent by Christ to continue His redemptive work, one who is
sent to be an 'apostle', *one who is sent*. This will be like an
intense light for his life. He will reflect upon history 'in order
that he may derive some fruit',[27] and this method of reflection
will involve asking himself in each Gospel passage that he
meditates: how can he better fulfill the mission he has received
from Christ through the Society; what concrete lesson can
he take from each passage to help him in his life as an apostle.
This will always be the key which opens to him the 'jewels
of wisdom and knowledge'[28] which are contained for him
in the Gospel, comprehended within the specific charism of
his vocation, a charism which he must ceaselessly go on
discovering for himself.

II.   MISSION: KEY TO OUR READING OF THE WORLD TODAY

5. Sent to the World

The Constitutions lead us to consider the world as the

---

[26] Cf. Martini, *Gli esercizi spirituali*, cited by I. Iparraguirre in CIS, *Subsidia*, no. 5.

[27] *Spir. Ex.* 114.

[28] Col. 2. 3.

object of our mission and its purpose. If we are 'sent', it is for the sake of serving and saving the world, and this fact makes it obligatory that we know the condition of the world, that we become involved with its needs and its opportunities—if we are to make real the kind of service that we can offer it.

Destined by his vocation to the world, to 'the help of souls', to be 'dispersed to any part of Christ's vineyard, to labour in that part of it and in that work which has been entrusted to him',[29] the Jesuit ought to be a co-worker of Jesus Christ in the salvation of this world. The Constitutions, which describe our vocation, give emphasis to this character of mission, and, at the same time, they determine its modalities.

The Jesuit must look on this world, the world to which he is sent, with love; he must look at it with the eyes and under the light that are proper to his charism; with eyes that are full of love for men and for all other creatures in function of man, a love which 'proceeds from the divine and highest Goodness', by reason of which he experiences himself as 'sent', as a companion of the Word, and from whom there descends this love which extends itself to all his neighbours;[30] he looks on this world with the eyes of a universally loving one who 'embraces all kinds of persons',[31] 'even though they are adversaries one to another',[32] who knows how to serve them without offending them, 'for it is proper to our Institute to serve all in our Lord'.[33]

6. Incarnation for Universality

In order to understand and complete his mission, the Jesuit must see the world with the breadth and depth and *nearness* of God:

"How the three Divine persons were looking upon the whole extent and space of the earth, filled with human beings;[34] to see the great extent and space of the world,

---

[29] *Const.* 603.
[30] *Ibid.* 671.
[31] *Ibid.*, 163.
[32] *Ibid.*, 823.
[33] *Ibid.*, 593.
[34] *Spir. Ex.* 102.

where dwell so many different nations and peoples;[35] to see all the different people on the face of the earth, so varied in dress and behaviour. Some are white and others black; some at peace and others at war; some weeping and others laughing; some well and others sick; some being born and others dying, etc.[36] to consider what the people throughout the world are doing; how they are wounding, killing, and going to hell, etc."[37]

In the face of the depth and universality of this field in which he must realize his 'mission', the Jesuit experiences in depth the meaning of the phrase: "that I may more closely follow and imitate our Lord who has just become incarnate",[39] in obedience to the decree of the Trinity.[40] Mission and Incarnation are inseparable; that is to say, mission involves making his own in as far as possible, the reality of the man he must save.

For the Jesuit then, all human history, all his personal life is thus focused through the optic of his 'mission', of his more effective collaboration with Christ in the salvation of the world. The world is, as it were, the 'field'[41] in which he must make real his mission of service to God through men with the means and the manner that is 'in conformity with our Institute'.[42]

---

[35] *Ibid.*, 103.
[36] *Ibid.*, 106.
[37] *Ibid.*, 108.
[38] *Ibid.*, 109.
[39] *Ibid.*, 102.
[40] *Ibid.*, 107.
[41] *Ibid.*, 102, 138, 140, 144, 145.
[42] *Const.* 134; Cf. also Nadal, *Schol.* p. 147.

THE EUCHARIST AND YOUTH

Address of Father Arrupe to Teenagers of the "Youths' Eucharistic Movement"

Basilica of St Francis, Assisi
September 6, 1979

It is three o'clock in the afternoon. Some 1400 boys and girls of the " Youths Eucharistic Movement" have entered into the lower Basilica of St Francis. They are members of the two senior sections of the Apostleship of Prayer for children and young men and women in Italy. In the present assembly there are some 950 from the groups of "Community 14", that is of boys and girls from 14 to 16; and 400 from the groups of "Witnesses", that is young men and women of 17 and over. (The younger groups will only come in at the end of the talk. They will be about 400 from the "Emmaus Groups", from 9 to 10 years, and another 750 of "Ragazzi Nuovi" or New Youths, 11 to 13 years old).

Father Arrupe will speak to them as a part of the celebration of " Youth Festival 1979" which has for its central theme: "Eucharist, Bread of the World". This meeting marked the 35th anniversary of the Movement, which was set in motion by Father Virginio Rotondi when he began the work of the Apostleship of Prayer among students.

Father Arrupe captured the attention of the crowd of Italian "ragazzi" by telling them a number of his own Eucharistic experiences at Lourdes, Loyola, on the summit of Mount Fujiyama, following the atomic explosion in Hiroshima, during his month in a Japanese jail, in a Peru slum, and also by appealing to the teenagers' idealism and generosity.

*The English translation of the talk was edited and publish-
ed in the monthly "Prayer and Service" of the General
Office of the Apostleship of Prayer in Rome.*

*

1. Life's Prospects for the Young People of Today

Some time ago I was making a long trip on a train when
three young fellows of around eighteen entered into my
compartment. They were accompanied by a man who was
somewhat older, and after a bit I learned that he was the
director of physical education at their school.

They were tired, and after some remarks on their winning
a soccer game, they dropped off to sleep, one after the other.
A couple of hours later they began to speak again and to take
down a good number of cokes, orange sodas, etc. Their conversation became lively, and they looked at me with a certain
curiosity as if they were asking themselves:Who in the world
is this priest? I did not join in their conversation since I had
to prepare a conference which I was to give as soon as I
reached my destination.

At one point, when their talk seemed to be dying down, the
teacher asked: "Now that you have finished school, what do
you plan to do?" One of the boys answered without much
thought: "I don't know. I suspect that my father will tell
me; I have no thoughts about anything. Who knows? It's
a tough problem. It's better that they tell me what to do.
Besides, I don't care to be bothered."

The second then broke in: "I've thought a lot about it, and
I don't know whether I should go into business or work in the
stock market. I don't know which of these two pay the better
without too much work. What I want is an easy and peaceful
life. I don't care for much more."

The third seemed to be a bit ashamed. He said nothing,
and it looked as if he wanted to avoid giving an answer. The
two others looked at him with some perplexity, and after a
few seconds the teacher asked him: "And you, Frank, what
are you going to do? "To tell the truth, I'm not sure myself.

I have been thinking about going for some years to some spot in the Third World to see its greatest need. I could then be a help to many who are suffering in it."

The eyes of the other two started to pop out as if to ask: "Frank, are you crazy?" The teacher then queried him: "How did you get that idea?" "I don't know", Frank replied a bit embarrassed, "but the idea has been floating around in my head for some months. Do you think it a crazy idea?" "No, not crazy, just a bit strange. Still, Frank, I really admire you."

At this I was no longer able to keep quiet. In a low voice I said what I was thinking "It's great, Frank. Follow that tugging of your heart since it must be a heart of gold." My four travelling companions looked at me and then began to speak about soccer.

I also gave up the theme, but I began to think how these three young fellows clearly manifested different attitudes shared by youths today:

There are those who are not much on thinking. They let themselves be carried along by circumstances. They don't want to be bothered. And why? You live very well if you have no worries.

There are those who have no other ambition than to make money, and this with the least effort possible. They are self-centered at heart: "I go my way; and others can think what they want." They believe that they can find their happiness in money. They let themselves be carried off by appearances, by what they see in ads, by the fascination of the world of entertainment.

But there are also those of noble heart who are moved by a desire to be of help to others, to console those who are afflicted, to be of service to others even at the cost of personal sacrifices.

2. My encounter with Christ

Dear members of the Youths' Eucharistic Movement, you have invited me to share in this festival of yours; and I would like to speak with each one of you about the plans which you are cherishing in your hearts for your future life. Are you waiting for someone to tell you what you should do? Do you want to make money most of all in order to be happy? Do you feel a longing to serve your brothers? There is perhaps no one of you that has ideas that are firmly fixed, but certainly you are more or less inclined to one of these three general tendencies.

To you, to your questions, and to your expectations, I am today telling you in all simplicity what I have myself experienced in meeting Jesus Christ. A few weeks ago in Rome a group of pilgrims, boys and girls, came to pay me a visit after the Wednesday audience of the pope. At one point, one of the younger of the group asked me point blank: "Why did you become a Jesuit?" — "Because I believed that it was my vocation?" — "And why did you believe it was your vocation?" "Because I felt that God was calling me." — "And why was He calling you?" "Well, the Lord wished to have another who would consecrate himself completely to Him, and He chose me" — "What did you think?" "I thought that it would cost me much to abandon my career as a doctor, but that by becoming a Jesuit I could labour even more for others. I would be able to cure not only bodies, but also souls."

Another boy broke in: "Father, I have heard that different Jesuits have been killed." "It must be a rather risky vocation." — "You are right. Six Jesuits have been killed in Rhodesia, four in Lebanon, one in Chad, two in Latin America." — "Why don't you defend yourselves? Why don't you use weapons?" — "There's not even a thought of that. We want to be of service to all without discrimination. We live to serve. If we are killed for our service, it is a great honour for us!" — "But if you are hated and you let yourselves be killed, you have to have a lot of courage. I don't get it." "Right you are, but the Lord gives one strength since it is done for Him, and it is He who gives us strength." — "So". The boy exclaimed in amazement, and his face showed that he had failed to understand; and the same expression could be seen on the faces of the rest, who were listening in silence.

I then tried to explain myself: "Look at it this way. We Jesuits became such and continue to be such simply out of our enthusiasm for Jesus Christ and from our desire to work for Him and for others. Jesus Christ is most faithful. He does not abandon those who are dedicated to His service. Jesus Christ lived two thousand years ago, but he still lives today in the Eucharist and in the depths of our hearts.

One of those present suddenly exclaimed: "What? I'm getting less now than I did before!" The rest began to laugh.

I believe that this conversation, simple and straight-forward as it was, revealed a whole series of feelings, questions, and attitudes that are prevalent among young people today. And I am certain that you who have already become familiar with Jesus Christ will understand me better than the boy who said: "What? I'm getting less now than I did before!" I am certain that you will understand me.

3. One Same Jesus: the Jesus of the Gospel and the Jesus of the Eucharist

It is a fact that Jesus Christ, especially in the Eucharist, is a source of energy for all: for us Jesuits, for you young people, for all, since Jesus Christ is present and lives for us in the Eucharist. He becomes our Friend, our Ideal, our Model, our Strength, our Way. You should know Jesus Christ. The more you know Him, the more you will love Him, since He is in addition to being God — nothing less — He is also a perfect man, one who is both simple and congenial.

During the course of history there have been, and even today there are, many leaders, many individuals who represent different ideologies and who seek to attract us and to convince us that it is worth the effort to follow them and to dedicate ourselves to their cause, but there is no one who can be compared in this regard with Jesus Christ, even from a distance. Those who dealt with him said: "No one has ever spoken as this man." "You have the words of eternal life." "Let us follow him and stay with him." "For him I have accepted the loss of everything, and I look at everything as so much rubbish if only I can have Christ" (Philip 3:8).

What can we do to gain an ever better knowledge of Jesus Christ? It is really very simple. In the Gospels we have a true picture of the historical Jesus, of the Jesus as he lived in Palestine. And in the Eucharist we have Jesus Christ living today in the midst of us. In neither case can we see him with our eyes, but the Gospel narrative is the word of God which gives vitality to what is said. When we read the Gospels we realize that the person of Jesus, who lived two thousand years ago, is still alive; and we feel Him very close to us. It is as though Jesus of Nazareth continues to live now as He did then. And on the other hand, the Eucharist is the same Body and Blood of the risen Christ. He is alive and present though hidden under the sacramental species. He lets himself be perceived. He speaks to us. He inspires and strengthens us.

Saint Teresa arrived at such a living faith in the presence of Jesus Christ in the Eucharist that she used to say: "If they told me that Jesus was in the house next to mine, I would not go to see Him since I already have Him with me in the tabernacle and He visits me daily in Holy Communion. I do not have greater faith in the eyes of my face than in those of my faith. The eyes of the body can be deceived, but not those of faith."

By bringing together the two figures, that of the Gospel and that of the Eucharist, we shall obtain the precise image of what Jesus was and is today. Do you really wish to know Jesus Christ, to be transformed by Him? Read the Gospel before the tabernacle, receive Him in Holy Communion, ask Him with His disciples: "Lord, teach us! Lord, we do not understand what you are saying. Explain it to us!"

There is no doubt that in this way each one of us can obtain a true concept of Jesus, even though He is endowed with an infinite richness which no one can completely comprehend, assimilate, or imitate. Each one of us understands or imitates some aspects of the figure of our Lord. All the saints have sought to imitate Jesus and they are all different from each other; St. Paul is different from St. Peter, and both of these from St. John. St. Francis of Assisi is different from St. Dominic, and both of these from St. Ignatius, and all three from St. John Bosco.

Nevertheless we should all seek to make for ourselves an image of Jesus Christ and to grasp as surely as we can His personality. The path which we follow in our lives should be one that brings us ever closer and ever more dedicated to Him, the Jesus of the Gospel and the Jesus of the Eucharist, who is the same and only Jesus, the Jesus who has risen and is alive, who loves us and seeks us as He does the whole of mankind.

To explain what I want to say, I shall relate some of my own experiences which were connected with the Eucharist and in which I recognize the hand of the Lord who led me and still leads me in my way of life. But I am sure that you also can reflect on your own experience up till now and on the way in which the Lord is guiding you on the path of your life.

4. Jesus, the Worker of Miracles, the Healer of the Ill, is Calling Me and Is Sending Me on a Mission

The first of my Eucharist experiences was closely connected with my vocation as a Jesuit, the same vocation about which those boys asked me as I observed earlier. The experience was that of a miracle which I saw at Lourdes during the procession of the Blessed Sacrament on the esplanade that lies in front of the basilica. Some weeks after the death of my father I had gone to Lourdes with my family, since we wished to spend the summer in quiet, peaceful, and spiritual surroundings. It was the middle of August. I stayed at Lourdes for a whole month; and since I was a medical student, I was able to obtain a special permission to study closely the sick who came seeking a cure.

One day I was in the esplanade with my sisters a little before the procession of the Blessed Sacrament. A cart pushed by a woman of middle age passed in front of us. One of my sisters exclaimed: "Look at that poor boy in the cart." It was a young man of around twenty, all twisted and contorted by polio. His mother was reciting the rosary in a loud voice and from time to time she would say with a sigh: "*Maria Santissima,* help us." It was a truly moving sight, and I remembered the plea which the sick turned towards Jesus: "Lord, cleanse me from this leprosy!" She hastened to take her place in the row which the bishop was to pass carrying the Blessed Sacrament in a monstrance.

The moment came when the bishop was to bless the young man with the Host. He looked at the monstrance with

the same faith with which the paralytic mentioned in the
Gospel must have looked at Jesus. After the bishop had made
the sign of the cross with the Blessed Sacrament, the young
man rose cured from the cart, as the crowd filled with joy cried
out: "Miracle! miracle!"

Thanks to the special permission which I had, I was later
able to assist at the medical examinations. The Lord had
truly cured him. There is no need to tell you of what I felt
and my state of mind at that moment. I had come from the
Faculty of Medicine in Madrid, where I had had so many
professors (some truly renowned) and so many companions
who had no faith and who always ridiculed miracles. But I
had been an eyewitness of a true miracle worked by Jesus
Christ in the Eucharist, by that same Jesus Christ who had
during the course of His life cured so many who were ill and
paralytic. I was filled with an immense joy. I seemed to be
standing by the side of Jesus; and as I sensed His almighty
power, the world that stood around me began to appear
extremely small. I returned to Madrid. My books fell from
my hands. The lessons, the experiments which had so thrilled
me before now seemed so very empty. My comrades asked me:
"What's happening to you this year? You are like one who has
been stunned!" Yes, I was like one stunned by that impression
which every day grew more disconcerting. The one thing that
remained fixed in my mind and in my heart was the image of
the Host as it was raised in benediction and of the paralyzed
boy who had leapt from his cart. Three months later I entered
the novitiate of the Society of Jesus of Loyola.

The teaching of our Lord was the same as that of the
Gospel. Through his miracles and His teaching He awakened
in me a faith and love for Him so that He could finally say:
"Leave everything and follow me!" The Lord of the monstrance was the same Lord as that of the Gospel. His powers were
the same, and His wishes were as they had then been: "May
the workers, who are few, become more numerous since the
harvest is great."

Once this voice is heard today as it was twenty centuries
ago, it cannot be forgotten. One is of course free to follow
it or not, but one with judgment or reason, as St. Ignatius of

Loyola says, will end with following it. There is not doubt
that the force which goes forth from Jesus in the Eucharist,
and which went forth on that unforgettable afternoon at
Lourdes, is the same that went forth from Jesus in Gospel
times. That experience at Lourdes was a repetition of what the
contemporaries of Jesus saw when the crowds surrounded him
and he cured all (Mt 9:18; 14:14; Mk 2:13; 3:20; Lk 5:17-26,
etc.). Certainly it is a question of the same Jesus, now hidden
under the sacramental species, but with the same love and
the same power. These are experiences which leave an indelible
trace and bring it about that we also can say with the apostle:
"That which we have seen and heard and touched of the
Word of life, that is what we preach to you" (1 Jn 1:1).

Our vocation as Jesuits is essentially missionary. It is thus
normal that a Jesuit should go to one of those countries known
as a mission country. From the time that I became a Jesuits in
1927 until 1937, when I was destined to Japan, I had conti-
nuously asked to be sent there since it seemed to me that it
was the place for me. This conviction had its origins in a deep
feeling within me, but the Lord had confirmed it in circumstances connected with the Eucharist. Once when I had just
finished serving Mass for our rector in the novitiate, his name
was Cesareo Ibero, I told him that I had received a negative
answer from the General of the Society of Jesus to my request
to be sent to Japan. The rector, who was descending from the
altar where he had finished celebrating Mass, told me: "You
will go to Japan." At that moment I felt as if the Lord who
had been offered upon the altar had said through the lips of
my rector: "Your vocation is to go to Japan, millions of souls
are waiting there for you. That is the field of your apostolate."
It was Jesus who told me from that hour what would be offi-
cially decided ten years later. It was the same Jesus who called
His disciples from among others (Jn 1:40-45) so that He might
personally send each one of them on his own way.

I also remember that in October, 1938, when I was sailing
from Seattle to Yokoama, that as I was celebrating Mass
alone in the cabin of the ship, I recalled that incident when
the rector of Loyola spoke to me when I was still a young
Jesuit student. At that moment, when I was now a priest, I

held in my hands, in the Host which I had myself consecrated, Him who had destined me for that same country in which another great Jesuit, St. Francis Xavier, had begun to preach the Gospel four hundred years before. There in my hands was that Saviour who had said to his apostles: "Go and preach to all men; I shall be with you till the end of time." On the ship, I experienced great joy and was inspired with the thought of the work which I was about to begin in Japan. It seemed to me that Jesus Himself, whom I held each day in my hands, was teaching me as He had taught the crowds from the prow of the ship on the lake of Tiberias (Mt 13:1-3). It seemed to me that it was that same wisdom which had then spoken in parables that had spoken also to me but in a manner which I could not fully understand as yet: It was that "for the moment you cannot undersatnd" (Jn 16,12), as Jesus told His disciples. There were in fact things that would have then been too hard and difficult for me, but He who was speaking to me was the same Master who had said: "I will give you rest" (Mt 11:28).

5. The Body and Blood of Jesus for the World

The mission which the Lord entrusts to us, though it has its origins in a personal encounter with Him, is always open to others, to the entire world, since the Lord has shed His blood "for the multitude", that is for all men. Every Mass is a Mass for the world and in the world. I remember the Mass which I celebrated at the top of the famous Mount Fujiyama, at a height of more than 11,000 feet. I had climbed it with one of my religious brothers. At that time it was made almost entirely on foot. One could only go on horseback to a height of about 3,300 feet. It was necessary to reach the summit by four in the morning to be able to see the marvellous panorama since by six the peak was covered with clouds and could no longer be seen.

We arrived on time and celebrated Mass in the most complete solitude. It was shortly after I arrived in Japan. I was living through the first impressions of a new environment and my mind was bubbling with a great number of projects for the conversion of the whole of Japan. We had climbed Fujiyama so that we might be able to offer to the Eternal Father the Sacrifice of the Immaculate Lamb for the salvation of all Japan at the highest point in all that country. The climb had been most tiring since we had to hasten in order to arrive on time. Several times we thought of Abraham and Isaac as they climbed a mountain to offer their sacrifice. Once we had reached the top, the sight of the rising sun was stupendous. It raised our spirits and disposed them for the celebration of the Holy Sacrifice. Till then I had never celebrated Mass in such conditions. Above us the blue sky expanded like the cupola of an immense temple — brilliant and majestic. Before us were all the people of Japan, at that time some eighty million who did not know God. My mind ranged out beyond the lofty vaulting of the sky to the throne of the divine Majesty, the seat of the Blessed Trinity. I seemed to see the holy city of the heavenly Jerusalem. I seemed to see Jesus Christ and with Him St. Francis Xavier, the first apostle of Japan, whose hair had become white in the course of a few months because of the sufferings he had to endure. I also was being confronted by that same Japan as Xavier had been. The future was entirely unknown. If I had then known how much I would have to suffer, my hands would have trembled as I raised the sacred Host. On that summit so near to heaven it seemed to me that I understood better the mission which God had entrusted to me. I descended from it with a renewed enthusiasm. That Eucharist had made me feel the grandeur of the everlasting God and universal Lord. At the same time I had felt that I was an "assistant", a sharer in the labour of Jesus Christ in the great redemptive mission entrusted to Him by His Father. I could repeat with more sincerity and conviction the words of Isaiah: "Here I am, send me" (Is 6:8) or those of St. Francis Xavier: "I am! Behold me."

Our Lord also, as is told in the Gospel, went up a mountain with His disciples and was transfigured before them (Mt 17:1ff). I also experienced the longing to remain there and not to leave so that I might continue to relish those heavenly moments, as St. Peter had when he exclaimed." "It is good for us to be here. If you wish I shall prepare three tabernacles one for you, one for Moses (my companion, Moses Domenzáin, bore this same name), and one for Elias" (cf Mt 17:4). That same Jesus who had filled St. Peter with joy and admiration, so much so that he had adored Him "falling with his face to the earth" (ibid. 17:6), had also shown Himself to me in the sublime sight of our Eucharist — the sacred Host, illuminated by the white light of the rising sun seemed to be transfigured before my eyes, and I believed that I heard with St. Peter the voice of the Lord which said to me: "Have no fear" (ibid. 17:7). It was a word most necessary for me as I was descending from those heights to the harsh life that was waiting for me during those years in Japan. How many things can Our Lord teach and make one feel in a single Mass.

From this it is almost natural for me to pass on to another remembrance of the Eucharist, to a Mass celebrated in very different circumstances from those just mentioned. This Mass taught me how Jesus, who suffers and dies for us, can bring about His plan of salvation through the mysterious ways of sorrow and suffering.

The atomic bomb had exploded at 8:10 on August 6, destroying the whole of Hiroshima, reducing it to ashes and killing at one blow eighty thousand people. Our house was one of the few that remained standing, even though it was badly damaged. There were no windows or doors left, all had been torn away by the violent wind caused by the explosion. We turned our house into a hospital and assembled there around two hundred who were injured in order to nurse and assist them. The explosion had occurred on the sixth of August. On the following day, the seventh, at five in the morning before beginning the work of helping the wounded and burying the dead, I celebrated Mass in our house. It is certain that in the most tragic moments we feel nearest to God and the importance of His assistance. Actually, the external surroundings were not much adapted for fostering devotion during the celebration of the Mass. The chapel, half destroyed, was packed full of those who had been injured. They were lying on the floor close to each other and they were obviously suffering from the torments of their pains. I began the Mass as best I could in the midst of that crowd which did not have the least idea of what was taking place upon the altar. They were all pagans and had never seen a Mass. I cannot forget the frightful impression I had when I turned towards them at the "Dominus vobiscum" (Mass was then said with one's back to the congregation) and saw that sight from the altar. I was unable to move and remained as if I were paralyzed with my arms stretched out as I contemplated that human tragedy: human knowledge, technical advance used for the destruction of the human race. All looked at me with eyes filled with anxiety, with desperation, as though expecting that some consolation would come to them from the altar. It was a frightful scene! Within a few minutes there would descend upon the altar the one of whom John the Baptist had said: "There is one in the midst of you whom you do not know" (Jn 1:26).

I had never sensed before so greatly the solitude of the pagan ignorance of Jesus Christ. Here was their Saviour, the One who had given His life for them, but they "did not know who was in the midst of them" (cf Jn 1:26). I was the only one who knew. From my lips there spontaneously went forth a prayer for those who had had the savage cruelty to launch the atomic bomb: "Lord, pardon them, since they do not know what they are doing", and for those who were lying before me, tortured by their pains: "Lord, grant them faith so that they may see; give them the strength to endure their pains." When I lifted the Host before those torn and mangled bodies there rose from my heart: "My Lord and my God: have compassion on this flock without a shepherd!" (Mt 9:36; Mk 6:34). Lord, may they believe in You. Remember that they also must come to know You (1 Tim 2:4).

Certainly from that Host and from that altar there poured forth torrents of grace. Six months later, when all, already cured, had left our house (only two persons died), many of them had received baptism, and all had learned that Christian charity can have compassion, can assist, can give a consolation that is above all human comfort, can give a peace that helps one to smile in the midst of pain and to pardon those who had made us suffer so much.

Such Masses as these are moments replete with a sacramental intuition which arrives at understanding what is so difficult or so impossible to understand without faith, that is, the value of suffering, the beauty and sublimity of the sacrifice of charity.

6. Jesus Friend and Consoler

Another type of Eucharistic experience is that which shows us the value that the Most Blessed Sacrament has for us when we have been in intimate and prolonged contact with Him during our life and we sense the lack of this sacrament when we are not able to receive it. At such a time we appreciate the great role which Jesus, our friend, companion, and consoler has in our life if we have been and are habitually nourished by the Eucharist.

I remember a Japanese girl of around eighteen whom I had baptized three or four years earlier and who had become a fervent Christian. Every day she received Communion at the six-thirty Mass in the morning, which she promptly attended every day.

One day after the explosion of the atomic bomb, I was passing through streets clogged with masses of ruins of every kind. On the spot where her house had formerly stood, I found a kind of hut supported by some poles and covered with pieces of tin. I went up to it. A wall about a foot and half high marked off a place within its interior. I tried to enter but an unbearable stench repelled me. The young Christian, her name was Nakamura, was lying stretched out on a rough table raised a bit above the ground. Her arms and legs were extended and covered with some burned rags. Her four limbs had become along their whole length a single sore from which pus was oozing and falling down upon and penetrating the earth. Her burned flesh seemed to be little else but bones and wounds. She had been in this state for fifteen days without being able to take care of herself or clean herself, and she had only eaten a little rice which her father, who was also seriously injured, gave her. Her back was already one gangrenous mass since she had not been able to change her position. When I sought to clean her burns, I found that the muscles were rotten and transformed into pus that left a hollow into which my hand entered and at the bottom of which was a mass of worms.

Appalled by such a terrible sight, I remained without speaking. After a little, Nakamura opened her eyes and when she saw me near, and smiling at her, she looked at me with two tears in her eyes and sought to give me her hand which was only a purulent stump and she said to me with a tone that I shall never forget; "Father, have you brought me Communion?" What a Communion that was, so different from that which I had given her each day for so many years! Forgetting all her sufferings, all her desires for physical relief, Nakamura asked me for what she had continued to desire for two weeks, from the day on which the atomic bomb had exploded. She asked for the Eucharist, for Jesus Christ, her great consoler, to whom she had months earlier offered her body and soul to work for the poor as a religious. I would have given anything to have been able to hear her speak of that experience of her lack of the Eucharist and of her joy at receiving it after so much suffering. Never before had I experienced such a request, from one who had been so cruelly reduced to a "wound and ulcer", nor such a Viaticum received with such an intense desire. Nakamura San died soon after, but she had been able to receive and embrace Jesus whom she had loved so much and who was anxiously waiting to receive her forever in His home in heaven.

The absence of Jesus is something like that which Martha felt when after the death of Lazarus she said to Jesus: "Lord, if you had been here, my brother would not have died" (Jn 11:32). It was precisely then that Jesus performed one of the greatest miracles of His public life. Like Martha, Nakamura also was able to feel that Jesus, though absent exteriorly, had not abandoned her and that He would come to meet her again to take her to Himself and make her completely happy for all eternity.

I have frequently thought of that scene of Nakamura San. How much it taught me! The value of the Eucharist for souls who have truly experienced it, the desire to receive it that causes one to forget every other kind of suffering and need, the joy of receiving it, all the greater the longer that one has been deprived of it, the strength that Christ gives us under the sacramental species, communicating to us His love and His incomparable joy.

A religious who, because of her work with the poorest people of Peru, could only assist at Mass every six weeks, since she had to remain far from a place of worship, told me: "It is just in this situation that I feel more what the Eucharist means for me." If we must leave our Lord to serve the souls of others, He makes Himself felt more deeply even in His physical absence since He is always living in the depth of our soul.

I myself personally experienced this deep sense of pain for the lack of the Eucharist during the thirty-three days that I was imprisoned in Japan, but there was also at the same time a feeling of the faithful and consoling presence of Our Lord. The enemies of Christianity had made a thousand accusations against me. They were angry, since they saw that while they were trying to put obstacles in the way to conversions, a good number of young people were turning to the Church and were receiving baptism. The war broke out in Japan on the feast of the Immaculate Conception, 1941, with the attack of Pearl Harbor. The military police immediately put me in jail, in a cell with an area of four square metres. I did not know why they had put me there, and I was not told why for a long time, and only at the end of my confinement.

I passed the days and nights in the cold of December entirely alone and without a bed, or table, or anything else but a mat on which to sleep. I was tormented by my uncertainty on why I had been imprisoned. This provoked a kind of self-torture because of the presumptions, suspicions, and fears that I had done something that could have been a source of harm to others. But I was above all tortured by not being able to say Mass, at not being able to receive the Eucharist. What loneliness there was! I then appreciated what the Eucharist means to a priest, to a Jesuit, for whom the Mass and the tabernacle are the very centre of his life. I saw myself dirty, unshaven, famished, and chilled to the bone without being able to talk with anyone. But I felt even more anguish for my Christians who were perhaps suffering because of me. And above all there was no Mass. How much I learned then! I believe that it was the month in which I learned the most in all my life. Alone as I was, I learned the knowledge of silence, of loneliness, of harsh and severe poverty, the interior conversation with "the guest of the soul". who had never shown Himself to be more "sweet" than then.

During those hours, those days, those weeks of silence and reflection I understood in a more illuminating and consoling way the words of Christ: "Remember what I have told you: a servant is not more important than his master. If they have persecuted me, they will also persecute you" (Jn 15:20).

I was interrogated for thirty-six hours in a row. I was asked matters that were very touchy to answer and I was myself astonished by the "wisdom" and the fitness of my replies. It was a proof of the saying of the Gospel: "Do not be concerned about what you must say to defend yourselves. I shall give you the right words and I shall give you such wisdom that all your adversaries will not be able to resist and much less defeat you" (Lk 21:14-15).

When my sufferings were becoming more cruel, I experienced a moment of great consolation. It was Christmas night. My mind went back to so many happy Christmases, to the three Masses which I was able to celebrate that night. What remembrances filled my mind! But none of all this was now possible. I was alone, without Mass. Instead of Christmas it seemed more like Good Friday! Just then when my Christmas was being changed into the Passion and that blessed night into a sad Gethsemani, I heard a strange sound near one of the windows. It was the soft murmur of many voices which with muted accents sought to escape detection. I began to listen. If any of you have been in prison waiting for a sentence, you would appreciate the anxiety with which I followed those sounds which were now of themselves becoming an immediate source of suspicion. Such are the fears that one feels within the four walls where one is detained.

Suddenly, above the murmur that was reaching me, there arose a soft, sweet, consoling Christmas carol, one of the songs which I had myself taught to my Christians. I was unable to contain myself. I burst into tears. They were my Christians who, heedless of the danger of being themselves imprisoned, had come to console me, to console their Shimpu Sama (their priest), who was away that Christmas night which hitherto we had always celebrated with such great joy. What a contrast between that thoughtfulness and the injustice of senseless imprisonment!

The song with those accents and inflections which are not taught or learned poured forth from a touching kindness and sincere affection. It lasted for a few minutes, then there was silence again. They had gone and I was left to myself. But our spirits remained united at the altar on which soon after would descend Jesus. I felt that He also descended into my heart, and that night I made the best spiritual Communion of all my life.

From then on the Eucharist became for me something new and different. I sought never to lose it. The moment when one loses something is also the moment in which its worth is best known. And so, my dear young men and women, the Eucharist is a treasure, a great treasure which the Heart of Christ was able to give to mankind.

There is still another incident that has been most instructive in my life and which made me understand more fully the intimacy which we should have with Jesus in the Eucharist and that the simpler one's manner of prayer is the more profound it becomes.

I was once in Yamaguchi in charge of a group of boys and girls. Among these was a girl of about twenty who without any show went to the chapel and remained on her knees before the tabernacle at times for hours on end. She seemed to be absorbed, as she remained there motionless. I was struck by the fact that though she was a young woman like all the others, very charming and cheerful, she went to the chapel with such persistence, though she was living together with her companions who held her in the highest esteem. One day I met her, or rather, I made it a point to meet her as she was leaving the chapel. We began to speak as usual and our conversation fell upon her constant and long visits to the Blessed Sacrament. She had hardly given me the chance to speak about this when I asked her: "And what do you do in so much time before the tabernacle?" Without hesitation, as if she had already prepared her answer, she told me: "Nothing." "What? Nothing?" I insisted. "Does it seem possible to you to remain so long without doing anything?"

This sharpening of my request, which wiped out all possibility of doubt, seemed to upset her a little. This time she was a little more slow in answering me. At last she said: "What do I do before the tabernacle? Well, I am there." Then she was silent again. And we took up again our ordinary conversation.

She seemed to have said nothing, at least nothing particular. But in reality she had not concealed anything and had said everything with a word replete with content. In a single word she had condensed the whole meaning of being present before the Lord: "To be", as Mary, the sister of Lazarus, was at the feet of the Lord (Lk 19:39), or as His Mother stood at the foot of the cross. They also *were there*. Hours of friendship, hours of intimacy, during which nothing is lost and it seems that nothing is said, since that which is given is everything, one's whole being. Unfortunately there are too few who understand the value of this "being" at the feet of the Master in the Eucharist, of this apparent loss of time with Jesus.

Would you like to have some good advice from me? Look upon Jesus as your friend, as your confidant. Learn to go and see Him, to visit Him, to "remain" with Him, and you will see how many things you will learn. It is a wisdom which He alone can give you, the true knowledge which makes men wise, holy, and even happy. All that we need for our life is gradually attained with a pouring forth from heart to heart. "Tell me with whom you associate and I shall tell you who you are." If you go with Jesus, if you remain with Jesus, you will certainly become yourself another Jesus. Do you not recall that the principles of your association tell you that you should become personal friends of Jesus and that you should speak with him?

7. Jesus has a Special Love for the Poor

Certainly Jesus, the same Jesus of the Gospel and of the Eucharist, can say profound and precious things to those who have cultivated for a long time an intimacy with him, but we should not think that he cannot speak to all men, even though they are living in the most difficult conditions and in utter poverty. Rather, it is precisely that Jesus who gave His blood for them, that can find secret and wonderful ways for reaching their hearts.

A few years ago I was visiting a Jesuit province in Latin America. I was invited, with some timidity, to celebrate a Mass in a suburb, in a "favela", the poorest in the region as they told me. There were around a hundred thousand people living there in the midst of mud since the town had been built along the side of a depression and became almost completely flooded whenever it rained.

I readily accepted since I know from experience that visits to the poor are most instructive: they do much good for the poor, but one also learns much from them.

The Mass was held in a small structure all patched together and open. Since there was no door, cats and dogs came and went without any problem. The Mass began. The songs were accompanied by a guitar which was strummed by one who was not exactly an expert, but the results seemed marvellous to me. The words were as follows: "To love is to give oneself, to forget oneself, by seeking that which can make another happy." And they continued: "How beautiful it is to live for love, how great it is to have to give. To give joy and happiness, to give oneself, this is love." "If you love as you love yourself, and give yourself for others, you will see that there is no egoism which you cannot conquer. How beautiful it is to live for love."

Gradually as the song went on, I felt a knot in my throat and I had to force myself to continue with the Mass. Those people, who seemed to have nothing, were ready to give themselves to share their joy and happiness.

When we arrived at the consecration and I raised the Host in the midst of a absolute silence, I perceived the joy of the Lord who remains with His beloved. As Jesus says: 'He has sent me to bring the good news to the poor" (Lk 4:18), "Blessed are the poor in spirit" (Mt 5:3).

Soon after, when I was distributing Communion and was looking at their faces, dry, hard, and tanned by the sun, I noticed that large tears like pearls were running down many of them. They were meeting Jesus, their only consolation. My hands trembled.

I gave them a brief homily in dialogue. They told me things which are heard with difficulty in lofty discourses. They were very simple things but at once human and sublime. One old woman asked me: "You're the superior of these priests, aren't you? Well, 'Señor', thanks a thousand since your Jesuit priests have given us the great treasure which we lacked, and of which we have the greatest need, the holy Mass." One young man said openly: "Señor padre, you should know that we are very thankful since these priests have taught us to love our enemies. One week ago I had prepared a knife to kill a comrade whom I hated much, but after I heard the priest explain the Gospel, I went and bought an icecream and gave it to my enemy."

At the end a big fellow, whose fearful looks could have inspired fear, told me: "Come to my house. I have something to honour you." I remained uncertain, not knowing whether I should accept or not, but the priest who was accompanying me said: "Go with him, father; the people are very good." I went to his house which was a half falling shack. He made me sit down on a rickety chair. From where I was seated the sun could be seen as it was setting. The fellow said to me: "Señor, see how beautiful it is!" And we remained silent for some minutes. The sun disappeared. The man added: "I did not know how to thank you for all that you have done for us. I have nothing to give you, but I thought that you would like to see this sunset. It pleased you, didn't it? Good evening." He then gave me his hand. As I was leaving I thought: "I have met very few hearts that are so kind." I was about to leave that street when a small woman very poorly dressed came up. She kissed my hand, looked at me and said with words filled with emotion: "Father, pray for me and for my children. I was at that beautiful Mass which you celebrated. I am running home. But I have nothing to give to my nine children. Pray to the Lord for me: He must help us." And she disappeared almost running in the direction of her house.

I learned many things with one Mass among the poor. How different from the great receptions of the leaders of this world!

8. The "Eucharist Person", the "New" Person Modelled upon Jesus Christ

I would be able to continue on telling you of other experiences which I have had, but the time does not permit it. Let us therefore sum up what I have sought to tell you up till now. Our Lord, through contact with Him in the Eucharist, has entered into the project of my life. He has revealed Himself to me in different and ever new ways and He has transformed my plan of life into his own plan of life, the plan which He made known in the Gospel, for He, the Jesus of the Gospel and the Jesus of the Eucharist are the same Jesus risen from the dead and living.

He, the worker of miracles, the *almighty Healer of the sick*, met me on the esplanade of Lourdes in the Host that was blessing the ill. He *chose me* and *sent me personally with an apostolic mission* to continue His work, when the rector of Loyola at the end of his Mass confirmed me in my aspiration to ask for the mission in Japan, and when during the Mass on the ship He made me feel that I was near the apostles whom He sent into all the world and to St. Francis Xavier. He, the *Anointed-Victim* who offers Himself upon the cross to His Father for the salvation of the world, for all the men who do not yet know Him, at one with all those who suffer, offered Himself in my hands on the highest peak in Japan and in the midst of those who had been tortured and wounded by the atomic bomb. And again, He has always shown Himself to me as a most faithful friend. He, the *great consoler in suffering* fulfilled the hunger and the longing of Nakamura as she was rent with pain. He, the *true and sole companion* able to remain united with us even in the most absolute solitude never abandoned me in the days when I was in prison. He, *the friend who communicates Himself* in silence to those who "remain" near him as to that girl in Yamaguchi. He who *has a special love for the poor* and knows how to fill them with joy and to bless them with great gifts that are hidden to us, as to those Christians of the Mass in the "favela" of Latin America.

We should now reflect on all this and strive to draw some practical results for our own personal lives. I shall limit myself to some brief points. You yourselves will later, during the next days, continue to think upon them.

The central ideal which your movement presents to you is that of "a man of the Eucharist", that is, of a man who like Jesus carries to the very end the plan of the Father, dedicating himself totally to others, letting his heart be broken for them on a universal level open to all the world, to all men. This man of the Eucharist is the new man, the man who wishes to build a new world with Jesus. In the midst of the present culture with its advances and limitations, you wish in fact to be new, that is to be modern among those who are modern. The problem consists in knowing the criteria of this newness and in remaining constant to it.

If the newness is measured by the style of dress, by the length of hair, by "jeans", by guitars, by the songs of rock and pop, the use of drugs, by confrontations and by the recourse to violence, I believe that you will certainly not be "the newest" young men and women.

But the true criterion of what is new is that which is described by St. Paul. According to him, to be old men means to be slaves to sin, to have that hardness of spirit of one who has lost his moral sense, who lets his conduct become disordered and delivers himself over to the unbridled practice of every kind of impurity (cf Eph 4:22-24). According to this criterion, many young people who claim to be "modern", and "new", are precisely those who are most "old".

A man who is truly "new" is the one created by God after the model of Jesus Christ "in justice and in holiness' (Eph 4:24), "renewed (by God) to bring you to perfect knowledge and to make you like to Him who has created you" (Col 3:9-10)" "with sentiments of mercy, kindness, humility, patience, and sweetness, supporting one another, pardoning one another... And above all may you have love, which is the bond of perfection" (Col 3:12). This perfection in charity brings a great joy, the serenity which is the fruit of the Spirit. Because of this you of "Community 14" and "Witnesses", should always be the most cheerful of those who are young, with the joy and the smile most solid and profound, that joy which, as St. John says, no one can take from you (Jn 16:22).

The criteria for recognizing men who are "new", are those which were spoken of the first and true "new" man, Jesus of Nazareth, the Christ, the man-God. He is that charming friend who spoke in such a way that one who heard Him exclaimed: "No one has spoken as this man" (Jn 7:49), "He did everything well" (Mk 7:37), "To whom shall we go? You have the words of eternal life" (Jn 6:69), "Let us also go with him to die" (Jn 11:16). He is that friend who has so given Himself for us that He offered His life in the terrible tortures of the cross, but who, having risen, lives for ever, not only at the right hand of the Father in heaven, but also much closer to us in the Eucharist.

The Eucharist gives some very precious characteristics to Christ's complete giving of Himself. They are a source of inspiration for your life as "Community 14" and "Witnesses", and they renew you each day, making you ever more "new" and ever more "men of the Eucharist". Jesus Christ becomes our food in the Eucharist, a new food, so that He may be united in the most intimate measure possible with us and to give us new strength to plan and build a new world. Jesus Christ in the Eucharist, hidden under the sacramental species, remains near us in the tabernacle as a faithful friend to encourage us and to teach us to be "new" as he was.

Strive to become intimate with and to obtain a knowledge of Jesus Christ in the Eucharist. May He be the force which moves you along the path of the new world. Christians should not only be new for themselves but also witnesses, leaders, precursors of the truest modernity, heralds of Christ, always new and always modern.

All this that I wish to say to you can be summed up in your being friends of Christ, but true friends. He has chosen us as His friends; "You are my friends" (Jn 15:14). Now we are those who must choose Him as our friend, but as a true friend, as our best friend. And to be converted to Him, to be more closely united with him, to be identified with Him, to continue His life in ours, there is no more direct route than that which passes through the Eucharist.

Lord, You have before You this group of young men and women who have heard Your invitation: "If you wish to be perfect, sell all that you have, and give it to the poor, then, come and follow me" (Mt 19:21). They long to be faithful to You, to follow You wherever you go and to give their lives for You. They are so filled with enthusiasm for You that they say, as Ittai said to king David: "By Yahweh and your life, my lord king, where my lord king is, living or dead, there also will your servant be." (2 Sam 15:21).

True "men of the Eucharist," who are engaged in building a new world, are those who follow their Lord wherever he goes and who, to follow him, are nourished by his Body and Blood, and are thus transformed into "other Christs." From here, from Assisi, You shoud leave with a heart on fire, on fire with the love of Christ, who is the only one who can transform the egoism of the heart of stone of the old man in the man of today.

27

MISSION AMONG THE WORKERS

Father General's Directives to Jesuits Working among Workers (MO)

Rome
February 9-10, 1980

On the 9th and 10th of February, 1980, Father Arrupe welcomed in Rome a group of Jesuits belonging to the 'Mission Ouvrière'. They were 16 in number from 6 European countries: Germany (1), Belgium (1) Spain (4), France (5), Holland (1) and Italy (1).

This meeting, long looked forward to and carefully prepared, was designed to give Father General first-hand information on the surroundings, activities and life-styles of Jesuits committed to this presence among workers.

Father General took an active part in the discussions which were held in an atmosphere of prayer, brotherhood and trust. At the end of the meeting he spent some time summing up his own impressions. He expressed, however, the desire of developing later more fully the reflections he had communicated to the participants and which their own interventions had inspired and enriched. The result was the following 'restrospective reflections'.

As stated by the Secretary of the Society when he sent this document to the Provincials, "these notes are of interest not only to Jesuits belonging to the 'Mission Ouvrière' but to all of us, whether our apostolate is among workers or not, who have been called by the 32nd General Congregation to the service of faith and the promotion of justice."

*

FATHER GENERAL TO THE 'MISSION OUVRIERE'(MO)

Introduction:

(1)   As I set out to write these notes on our recent meeting my first thought is the happy memory of the days we spent together. I am grateful to you for giving me so much spiritual joy by accepting my invitation to meet in this House of the whole Society and spend two days in reflection, exchange and shared prayer. I regret only that your work commitments obliged us to have so short a meeting; by I nourish the hope that this meeting will be followed by others. I really look forward to this and have great interest in it.

(2)   Searching for the reason why I was so happy to be with you — because on the outside it was just one meeting more among the many I have with representatives of the different apostolates in which the Society is engaged — I believe I can identify two: first, the special circumstances of your mission which, while perhaps no more arduous than others carried out by so many companions in the Society, does present, as I shall explain later, certain especially problematic characteristics and, therefore, merits particular care and consideration on my part.

(3)   Secondly, and I want to be frank about this, because paradoxically — for several reasons and different people being responsible — the MO has been somewhat out on a limb and neglected. I will not be telling you anything new when I say that in some quarters – jesuit, ecclesiastical, lay — feelings about it are more violent, both for and against, than for most other types of apostolate. This is something understandable; but there is room for much improvement, especially in favour of the MO itself. Here I think meetings like the one we have just finished can do much to bring out the authentic values of the MO and help dissipate the cloud of vague suspicion that emanates from some quarters, partly due to lack of communication and information.

1: NATURE

(4)   Perhaps the first misunderstanding to be cleared up concerns *the very nature of the MO*. Like any other mission given by the Society, and to the extent it is given by it, the MO is a form of apostolate the Society recognises as its own, promot-

ing, directing and taking responsibility for it. The worker
Jesuit, priest or not, is a member of the Society from whom
he receives the specific mission to insert himself into the world
of manual labour and carry out there an apostolic activity.
Obviously this mission carries the same guarantees and
conditions as any other in the Society with regard to origin,
duration, dependency, disponibility, co-ordination, etc.

(5)   The worker Jesuit serves in a distinctive form of apostolate which *has its place in the wide range of activities undertaken
by the Society* to serve those whom St. Ignatius referred to in
general terms as "souls" and who today constitute the vast
masses of men and women in the working world, in special
need of understanding, promotion and evangelization. It
is an advanced form of the Society's effort to serve faith and
promote justice, which our Jesuit identity requires of us and
which, at different levels, inspires other social apostolates, of assistance, reflection and, to some extent, shapes all our ministries.

2: IMPORTANCE

(6)   It would be a mistake to measure the importance the
Society attaches to your type of apostolate by *the number of
Jesuits engaged in it*. There are many and obvious reasons why
this mission can be entrusted to no more than a well prepared
minority. The   MO's importance stems from a different
series of considerations.

(7)   It is a *vanguard apostolate* since it tries to carry the
witness of manual labour to areas not penetrated by other
forms of evangelization and where circumstances can even
prevent or advise against any open proclamation of your task
to spread the Gospel. The importance of your work from this
point of view is twofold: on the one hand you are like a bridge-
head to a continent still awaiting discovery; on the other
your experience is of great value and should be integrated in
the sum of experiences feeding the Society's reflection and
discernment at all levels.

(8)   It is an apostolate directed towards *vast masses of men
and women in today's world*. The universality of the Society's
apostolic action is not only a question of availability to go
anywhere and carry out any mission. It has a geographic and

even a demographic dimension as well: large numbers should carry a proportionate weight in the Society's planning. The Exercises and the Constitutions are built round this twofold notion of subjective and objective universality. And the Society's history abounds, especially in its most glorious pages, in pioneer missions to huge masses of hostile or indifferent people, in full knowledge and awareness of the great disparity between means available and objectives pursued. (Counter-Reformation Europe, the 16th century missions in Africa and Asia, etc.).

(9)   It is *a privileged apostolate* according to Ignatian norms for the selection of ministries. No one could deny that the world of the worker, the rural or industrial proletariat, the huge numbers of hired and unskilled labourers, of immigrants, of part-time or occasional workers, of unemployed, of drop-outs incapable of holding a stable job... all categories found in different degrees in every country in the world, fulfill perfectly what St. Ignatius described as the first criterion for choice of apostolate: "that part of the vineyard ought to be chosen which has *greater need*, because of the lack of other workers or because of the misery and weakness of one's fellow-men in it". (*Constitutions, 622*).

(10)   The same can be said of that other Ignatian criterion to discern priorities: "to labour more intensely in those places *where the enemy of Christ our Lord has sown cockle*". (*ibid.*). The world of the worker has been and still is a seedbed of ideologies whose character is a-christian and, to a larger extent, directly atheist and materialistic as well. The working masses are wooed by ideologies opposed in many things but sharing one in common: the promise of a liberation in which any spiritual dimension is absent. People are thus instrumentalised through their material, social and political needs while being deprived of the one thing that, in the final analysis, provides their strongest guarantee and justifies all other claims: their very human dignity as sons of God.

(11)   It is an apostolate which in many countries is counted among those where "it is seen that *there are not others to attend to them.*" (*Constitutions,* 623, d). For this reason it should be preferred by the Society. What can I say to you about abandon-

ment when I see you each day alone, like drops in the ocean, left more to your own fate than perhaps my own responsibility or that of your immediate superiors should allow? When sometimes in cities and highly cultivated environments disproportionate care is given to little circles of the devout, here are these immense multitudes with nobody "to attend to them". I don't know how history will judge our post-conciliar Church, but I would not like to see the same reproach as was made to the Church of the past 100 years: that of having lost the working classes. It is a difficult apostolate: agreed. There are many risks: agreed again. You know this as well as I. But can we maintain that the Church and the Society are not obliged to do more than they are doing at present?

(12) Lastly, as I mentioned above, your apostolate is important because *it offers an additional and very valuable reference point* for the rest of the Society. It sensibilizes us whose mission is carried out in "safer" (*Constitutions* 623, e) circumstances and exemplifies an openness to the challenge of unbelief and insertion among the poor. In this way it will help fulfill what GC 32 asks of us: "Relying on the unity we enjoy with one another in the Society and our opportunity to share in one another's experience, we must all acquire deeper sensitivity from those Jesuits who have chosen lives of closer approximation to the problems and aspirations of the deprived. Then we will learn to make our own their concerns as well as their preoccupations and their hopes". (Decree 4, § 49).

3: CHARACTERISTICS

(13) The same thing that makes this mission important and meaningful also makes it difficult in that it gives a special characteristic to elements common to other missions of the Society. I shall mention a few of the main ones:

(14) 1 — *It is a Jesuit mission.* Though I have said this already, I want to say it again expressly. With this affirmation I want to answer those who raise their eyebrows at the very mention of 'MO', who tend to look on our work as a spurious apostolate in the Society and maliciously establish a causal link between occasional failures or defections that have taken place among priest-workers and the basic theory or concept

behind this apostolate. "This priestly ministry, within the unity of the presbyteral order, embraces various functions: evangelization of non believers ...participation in the life and toil of workers...". (GC 31, d. 23, n. 2. Cfr. also *Presb. Ord.*, nn 4 and 8).

The past and recent history of the Society, and also its present apostolic labours, abound in examples of apostolates that are no different from yours except in respect of the social or working class among which they are conducted. It would not be just to accept a pioneering apostolate among intellectuals or of assistential nature with full insertion and inculturation, yet show reticence or disapproval if the medium of insertion is the working proletariat. Is such suspicion the remnant of a mentality and class prejudice we have not yet succeeded in ridding ourselves of ? The carrying out of this mission (like that of any other), inexperience due to new forms and recent developments, the circumstances of certain specific cases — all these can be discussed and should lead to a healthy, christian and thoroughly Jesuit form of self-criticism. But no one should reject a priori a form of apostolic insertion and inculturation in the world of the worker which has as its model Jesus of Nazareth and Paul the tent-maker. The worker Jesuit is not a Jesuit apart. It would be offensive and intolerable to compare him unfavourably with other Jesuits engaged in more directly apostolic work. What holds us together in the Society is our mission in whatever field it is carried out. And because the Society imparts the mission and assumes responsibility for it, it should also support and encourage those who bear its weight to persevere. And it has both the right and duty to terminate the mission should it consider this fitting in the Lord.

(15)   2 — *Insertion.* Full insertion in the working class seems a necessary condition for achieving the objectives pursued by the worker Jesuit. This means place and type of dwelling, disposal of working day and life-style in general must be as far as possible the same as those of the people among whom one works. Such identity conditions the value of witness given and the possibility for apostolic work. The worker Jesuit is like the gospel leaven which cannot ferment the mass unless

it is mixed and dissolved into it. There is no question here of an apostolate by remote control or juxtaposition: what is required is identification and assimilation. The worker Jesuit has to experience for himself the uncertainties of the labour market, the poverty and limitation of cramped living quarters, social pressures which undermine his dignity and rights as a person, insecurity, subjection to enforced time-tables and unreasonable production quotas, and the harshness of human relations that flows from all this, etc. Only at this price — and in spite of considerable distance from his companions due to cultural and spiritual background — can he consider himself less unfitted to spread from within the world of the worker the values he has come to offer. I say this because, without wishing to subtract in any way from the merit of your option, your status of workers by choice prevents you from total identification with those who belong to the working class by birth or through necessity. There are two insurmountable differences: you have joined the working class with the impetus that comes from a 'mission' fully accepted, with an intellectual baggage and development of your faculties that, interiorly at least, must set you somewhat apart. This is true even to the extent that you are more alive to situations your companions accept with a certain resignation and fatalism. Secondly, your spiritual life, maintained with that fidelity proper to a son of the Society in all situations, especially the more difficult, is a permanent source of faith and eschatological hope that gives meaning to your life. These things are lacking to many of your comrades.

(16)   3 — *Inculturation*. The purpose of insertion is to achieve inculturation. If this does not take place, the insertion is no more than make-believe. A purely phenomenological identification with the life and activities of the working class is not sufficient: it is necessary also to learn and assimilate its cultural or sub-cultural values: its mental paterns, its emotive feelings, its typical reactions, its behavioural norms of loyalty and rejection, its moral values, its concept of man, family and society, its attitude towards anonymity, its use of leisure, its capacity for comradeship, in short, all those elements which make up the working-class culture, so rich in human

and spiritual values that are often not properly appreciated or developed. Only in this way, "if we have the patience and the humility and the courage to walk with the poor, we will learn from what they have to teach us what we can do to help them". (GC 32, D. 4, n. 50).

(17) As I have already indicated, this insertion and inculturation in depth enables the worker Jesuit to make a valuable contribution towards vitalizing with insights drawn from real life other forms of apostolate in the Society, especially those which, either through reflection or action, are trying to serve faith and promote justice. And in a special way it can serve as a stimulus for other Jesuits to insert themselves among the poor and experience poverty, things the last Congregation singled out as elements of renewed and ongoing training for the whole Society. (cf. D. 4 n. 49).

(18) 4 — The identification with the working class presumed by this insertion and inculturation must, however, be achieved leaving intact another previous and more important identity: our Jesuit identity and *sense of belonging to the Society*. Only in this context does our 'mission' make sense: in no circumstances should it degenerate into a breaking away from. The gradual and subconscious loss of this identity and sense of belonging has unfortunately taken place in more than one case and is one of the reasons why there are objections to the very idea of the MO. I had occasion to say something about this process of 'disidentification' in my talk on *Our way of proceeding* (n. 42). When a case occurs in which the mass seems to have absorbed the leaven to the extent of neutralizing it, there is only one thing to do: reverse the process. This is a task not only for superiors but also for those involved, individually and as a group. They have a more realistic notion of what is taking place and it is their duty to help superiors carry out their main responsibility which is the *"cura personalis"*. In this way they will be defending the true values of the MO.

(19) 5 — *Co-ordination with the Church and Society's pastoral planning*. Those sent to the MO are not there on their own responsibility. Like any other group of Jesuits in any other type of work, they should be and feel themselves to be part of an overall plan. The special characteristics of this apostolate

make regular contact with the hierarchy and superiors perhaps more difficult but, precisely because of this, more necessary. Such contacts should be seen as a service of support and help for individuals and the mission as a whole. They presuppose a sincere and open conscience, a genuine sense of companionship and team spirit, humility and constructive optimism. Opposed to these, on the other hand, is a certain sufficiency which disdains the advice of others, a messianical radicalism which looks on itself as complete and indispensable, and even a type of independence which is sometimes the result of total insertion in a different milieu. In the complaints one sometimes hears from worker Jesuits of abandonment and lack of interest on the part of 'established' communities, it is not always clear who was the first to cut or block channels of communication.

4: ATTITUDES

(20) From the importance of the MO and its special characteristics I have just listed, there follows logically a set of personal attitudes for someone assigned to it that I would like to comment with you. Obviously they are not exclusive to the MO but common also to other missions of the Society.

1 — *Mission, yes; self-destination, no.* In any mission, the selection of the person sent is a matter of enormous importance and responsibility. Normally it should be preceeded by a discernment in which the Lord's call is clearly heard, together with its acceptance and the Society's readiness to receive the offer made. This offer-obedience relationship should be determined in open dialogue with as many participants as are necessary. The superior's role is to verify the legitimacy of the call which, to be authentic, must be accompanied by the necessary qualities, human as well as spiritual, and their "proper use" (*Lumen Gentium*, § 12) in the light of the overall apostolic plans of both Society and hierarchy. Consequently, a natural inclination is not, of itself, enough; nor a strongly felt attraction; nor a prophetic stance within the Society or the Church lacking the first hallmark of any authentic prophecy, namely charity; nor even a generous urge stemming from the immense needs experienced in one's first apostolic ventures or from bonds of brotherly attachment to those already

engaged in this type of apostolate. The experience I wish to share with you tells me that, however sincere it may be, generosity alone is not enough for this type of mission. The responsibility for more than one failure must be attributed not only to the victims themselves, but also to superiors who haven't taken all the measures they should have in deciding on so important a destination. (Cf. *Constitutions*, § 619). On the other hand, I have been touched to hear your words of gratitude to the Society for the confidence placed in you by entrusting you with this 'mission'.

(21)   2 — *Adequate training*.   It is a gross mistake to think that a less rigorous form of training is required by those who carry the Gospel to the world of the worker. This is to undervalue that world unjustly and ignore the problems that are at stake. Whoever thinks in this way is already showing a certain lack of suitability for this type of mission. As a matter of course, the Jesuit in the MO will have to face discussions on basic issues and confrontations with other ideologies. He will have to promote the interests of the working class. To do all this, good will is not enough. Even for his own interior life (and not only spiritual) a solid foundation for integrating and reflecting on his experiences is essential. Furthermore such a preparation is indispensable if he is to contribute anything more than anecdotes or personal adventures, however intense, for the apostolic reflection of other Jesuits, as I mentioned above.

(22)   Speaking here of formation, I wish to place special emphasis on the religious, spiritual dimension of our training. I spoke before of my own experience, but perhaps I should appeal to yours: without spiritual depth, without an apostolic motive continually renewed through a genuine interior life, without strength to resist so many sources of attraction to which you are necessarily exposed, the MO, in so far as it is an apostolic mission, is, to say the least, nonviable. Every form of adaptation or accommodation required by circumstances is possible. But the maintenance of your sacramental life and of your lived religious identity is not negotiable. This responsibility can be a grave one. And not to take the necessary means when it is lacking can be a blameworthy act of omission on the part of superiors. On the other hand, I have been immensely

pleased to hear some of you say that your life of work is a valuable source of inspiration for your personal prayer and for meeting the Lord. This interaction between prayer and apostolic activity is the very essence of a ture Ignatian spirit. I exhorted the whole Society to this in my letter on the subject. (Cfr. AR XVI, pp. 953-962). Now I earnestly exhort you again.

(23) 3 — *Humility.* I wish to put you on your guard against a subtle temptation that can assail you; that of making comparative judgements between other forms of apostolate and your own and remaining satisfied with the results of your own evaluation. The apostolate you undertake — as long as it conforms with the conditions mentioned above — is certainly an advanced, arduous and praiseworthy form of that insertion among the poor to serve faith and promote justice which constitutes our modern expression of the Society's charism. But in no way does this justify any feeling of superiority or, still less, exclusiveness. Apart from other important considerations; such an attitude would indicate a certain ingenuousness and lack of perspective, not to mention a profound ignorance and deficiency of information. Nor would it help towards that brotherly contact and integration with other communities and the Province as a whole which is of special value to you.

(24) 4 — *Discreet charity.* The "discreet charity" of Ignatius or, in other words, discretion in charity is most necessary for you. This discretion will prevent you from becoming radicalized by ideologies and help you detect whether your apostolic outlook is becoming gradually weakened by a more secular approach or one based on an ideology of whatever tendency. I understand the tension you must experience as spectators, and sometimes victims, of heart-rending situations of all types, often massive and institutionalised. And I therefore also understand your generous feelings of solidarity with your comrades and your need to contribute to the search for a better realisation of the common good and for structural reform. Here the whole question arises of industrial, trade union and political action. You are aware what limits and conditions are imposed in this respect by your status as priests and Jesuits, which takes priority over your status as workers. But I feel obliged to remind you of something I have

said at greater length and to others, not always from the MO, about our political commitment. The general directives of the Church, those of the 1971 Synod of Bishops and of our 32nd General Congregation, bind us all, and it is my inescapable duty to see that the apostolic activity of the Society conforms to them. I do not intend to repeat them here. In addition, on several occasions, I have myself expressed in norms which, I believe, leave no room for doubt, what the Society thinks about the socio-political commitment of Jesuits, and I have endorsed documents and guidelines at Assistancy or Province level which apply these prescriptions even more clearly to a specific situation. (Cf. for example, AR XVI 690, 1086; XVII 186, 604). I wish to make one point clear: these directives and norms are for all Jesuits, not only for those of the MO, and they apply to political parties of all shades.

(25)   This same discretion in charity should be yours in other aspects and relationships of your life. Your living conditions, your contacts with neighbours, the use of rest and leisure time, the need to establish friendly relationships, dealings with persons of the opposite sex, entering a milieu that is new, etc., — all these put you in situations where discretion as well as charity is required. I don't think people consider me an alarmist. But I confess at times I feel worried by the 'indiscretion' which some Jesuits show in their professional life. Again this observation doesn't apply to you alone. I have made it about other Jesuits as well. For, when all is said and done, the MO is no more than another variety of the professionalization one finds in other types of activity such as, for example, teaching. What begins as a clear apostolic work — this is the only admissible starting-point — can degenerate into a professionalism totally lacking any Gospel message. Given the situations pertaining to some forms of professional work, if there is no 'discretion' with regard to limits and conditions, nor a continual counter-influence of a true spiritual life, the whole process naturally ends in secularization with all its consequences.

(26)   5 — *Love of the Chuch and the Society.*   Why not speak of this too? You are moving in a climate where the Church, its members and its teaching are often the object of judgements

ranging from disrespect to open hostility. Sometimes you yourselves encounter a lack of trust or a more or less disguised rejection from those who, affectively at least, should be sharing your concerns. Try to discern. Don't generalize. Know that this is perhaps an inevitable, though painful, part of the work which, on the surface, sets you apart from other apostolates. And carry on within the Society and the Church this evangelizing task which both need; let them see that the poor have the Gospel preached to them in the sector where you have been sent. I give thanks to the Lord for what I have heard you say during these two days about your identification with the Society and the gratitude you feel towards its superiors for the confidence they have shown in you by giving you this mission.

Conclusion

(27)   That is all. As I look over the notes I took during the many hours of our exchange, I am aware that each point I have touched on could be expanded with so many other things said and heard as we lived, worked and prayed together. The final impression I have of you is seeing you leave for your work, encouraged and — if I am not mistaken — with a renewed faith in your mission and deeper experience of what it is to be a Jesuit. I beg the Lord that, for this mission of yours and for the faithfulness and joy in being his companions, he gives you his abundant graces.

28

THE LITURGY
IN A JESUIT'S LIFE

A Letter of Father General
to all Major Superiors

**Rome
December 1, 1973**

*A the end of 1973, Father General Pedro Arrupe released
three liturgical books for the Society. The Jesuit Supplement to the Missal presented new prayers for use on Jesuit
feasts, together with appropriate antiphons for entrance
and communion processions; several of these Masses included special prefaces. The Jesuit Supplement to the Lectionary
lined up a wide variety of Scripture readings, meant to be
adapted to the group celebration. The third book was a
Supplement to the Liturgy of the Hours or Divine Office.
A fourth and larger volume in the series was not technically
liturgical but could be of interest to many: it was titled
"Spiritual Profiles of Saints and Blessed of the Society of
Jesus".*

*And why bother with the saints at all? Isn't this a relic of
pre-Vatican-II devotionalism, now happily defunct with the
liturgical renewal? The following letter of the General seems
to have taken these objections seriously. He shows that there
is a devotion to the saints, and for Jesuits to the Jesuit
saints in particular, that is altogether in line with Vatican
II and modern liturgical thinking.*

*While enthusiastic about the recent stress on Scripture and
the life of Christ (which should always hold pride of place
in our spiritual reading), the General suggests that there*

have been some losses in our discarding all reading of the lives of saints.

Father Arrupe goes on to remind his brother Jesuits that the renewal to which the Society is invited by the Church and by the evolving world cannot be achieved except by an interior conversion. Such a conversion can draw inspiration from Ignatius' own conversion, which was given an initial impetus by two books: The "Life of Christ" and that of His saints, the "Flos Sanctorum".

*

Reverend and dear Father, P. C.

Among the more weighty tasks which, in accordance with the Second Vatican Council, the Church of the present has to fulfil are also enumerated the renewal and development of the Sacred Liturgy, which "is the summit towards which the activity of the Church is directed and at the same time the source from which all its force flows" (Constitution *Sacrosanctum Concilium,* n. 10).

In its desire to live and think with the Church, the Society has always promoted the liturgical movement in a great variety of ways. With the freedom granted by the Church, the Society also from the very beginning worked at the proper adaptation of its own liturgical celebrations.

In conformity with the norms regualarly published by the competent authority over the past few years, I saw to it that the New Calendar of the Society was promulgated (in my letter of April 30, 1971, AR XV, 725), and I asked a special Commission to compose new texts and to prepare the necessary schemas for the liturgical celebrations proper to the Society.

In promulgating this new Liturgical Proper I would first like to stress the great importance we should attach to the liturgical life in the context of the broad and organic renewal programme of our life and apostolic activities.

The renewal to which the Society is invited by the Church and by the evolving world cannot be achieved except by an interior conversion: only through individual and collective conversion shall we be able to find both the method and the strength to transform our religious life and apostolic work.

As for conversion, there is today no other way to arrive at it than that which leads to our origins, that is, to Saint Ignatius' own conversion. Two books gave him the initial impetus: The *Life of Christ,* and the *Flos Sanctorum.* The love of the Word of God and the emulation of the Saints gradually led him to spiritual maturity: and when it was a matter of trying to find God's will, we see Ignatius undertaking pilgrimages, practising ascetical austerity, engaging in prolonged prayer, and finally describing the discernment of spirits in the book of the Exercises.

But our imitation is not concentrated on Saint Ignatius alone. If we consider that the Society and its presence in today's world should themselves be a recommendation especially by the witness of our fidelity, this same consideration will enable us to understand that in the course of more than four centuries it made itself known by other companions who followed God's will with great generosity. Among the companions who, in widely different circumstances, manifested through their splendid way of life the spirit of the Exercises and the Constitutions, the Church and the Society single out for us those inscribed in the calendar of Saints.

If we want the Society to rejuvenate itself we must — without neglecting the demands of our own times — continue to draw nourishment from the proper source, that is, from the pristine Ignatian intuition and from our whole tradition. Therefore we must return to that sound cult of our Saints and Blessed who in our days have, for a variety of reasons, unfortunately been relegated to the background.

In these circumstances it seems quite opportune to publish the Proper of the Society, which should be seen not as a mere implementation of the decrees of the Council, but rather as an excellent help to bring about that renewal to which all of us should sedulously apply ourselves.

While recalling the memory of the Saints, we do, in spite of our weakness and failures, render thanks to God for the accomplishments by which He graciously enabled our Society to serve the Church, and at the same time we fulfill the duty we have to work for His greater glory.

Further, in honouring the memory of our Saints, we collectively implore God to grant us to be like our predecessors who never strayed from the path which led to God, even with the total abnegation of their own lives.

Finally, in celebrating their memory it is given to us especially to find the word of God, the seed from which both they and the rest of the Society gathered a copious harvest. In fact,without this salvific word, we would try in vain to achieve renewal and bear fruit. That is why the new Proper contains an abundance of readings from Sacred Scripture, which can fittingly be used widely in a spirit of freedom and of truth.

When we reflect on the singular manner in which Saint Ignatius was impelled towards his conversion while reading those two books, we find that the example of the Saints and the readings from Scripture joined him inseparably to our Lord. Let us hope that the same will happen to us, for as Saint Francis of Sales once wrote, there is no greater difference between the Gospel and the life of the Saints than there is between written music and music that is chanted. Both are the living word of God. In fact, "In the lives of those who shared in our humanity and yet were transformed into especially successful images of Christ, God vividly manifests to men His presence and His face. He speaks to us in them, and gives us a sign of His kingdom." (Dogmatic Constitution *Lumen Gentium*, n. 50). But in all sincerity we should admit that at times we did not pay much attention to this music and that consequently those who were chanting it, were unable to help us much. Gradually we have discarded the reading of the lives of the Saints, thinking that Christ could be better reached directly; but we should acknowledge that this option was not without harmful effects. Actually, do not most of us have to admit that in the early stages of our life in the service of Christ, the example of one Saint or another, whose life we had read, has profited us greatly?

Therefore, when speaking of honouring the Saints, let us guard against being ignorant about their lives, lest we stumble into a mere ritualism, causing the liturgical renewal to desiccate for want of the necessary roots. It was for this reason that I saw to it that, while the liturgical texts were being composed, a volume should be prepared with the title "Spiritual Profiles of the Saints and Blessed of the Society of Jesus." It will surely help if we know those whom we honour, and to make them known to the faithful at large when occasion offers. These texts, prepared with special care by experts chosen from all parts of the Society, will assist us in our liturgical celebrations to unite ourselves more closely to God, and thus also to strengthen the union of souls which we are striving for.

The sacred liturgy is of the greatest importance and the most noble form of the service we can and ought to render to the Holy Trinity. But, as the Second Vatican Council indicated, our praise of God is enriched when we unite it to the worshipping Church in heaven, joining with and venerating the memory first of all of the glorious ever-Virgin Mary and of all the Saints (cf. Dogmatic Constitution *Lumen Gentium,* n. 50). At the same time, while on earth we continue our pilgrimage towards the Lord, and surrounded by infirmities and weaknesses, this worship shown the Divine Majesty becomes a prayer of petition, reaching the Heart of God, through the intercession of all our brethren who are with Christ in glory and who with Him, in Him, and through Him plead for us with God.

The liturgy also is an expression of the life we are hoping for, a life of constant sharing in the mystery of Christ, i.e. in the proclamation of the Gospel and in the supreme sacrifice which is the source of our life.

With all these considerations in mind, and having heard the opinion of the General Assistants, I promulgate with this letter the New Liturgical Proper of the Society of Jesus.

In this second part, Father General gives instructions on the composition, features and use of the three sections of the Latin edition of the new Jesuit Proper (Missal, Lectionary, Divine Office).

He then concludes his letter with his prayerful wish:

May God our Lord, through the intercession of the Blessed Virgin Mary, Mother of the Society, and through the prayers of our Father Ignatius and all our brethren who are with Christ in glory, bestow abundant blessings on this liturgical renewal, so that the spiritual progress and apostolic activity of all Jesuits may receive a new stimulus, for the greater glory of God.

Recommending myself to your prayers,

Devotedly yours in Christ,

Peter Arrupe
Superior General of the Society of Jesus

29

DEVOTION TO THE HEART OF CHRIST

A LETTER, AN HOMILY, AN ACT OF CONSECRATION

(A)

A Letter of Father General to the whole Society

Rome
April 27, 1972

This letter was addressed to the whole Society in 1972 which marked the first centenary of the Consecration of the Society to the Sacred Heart of Jesus by the General Father Peter Beckx. One year earlier, Father Peter Arrupe had disclosed to the Provincials his intention of writing this letter and renewing the Act of Consecration. In this document, that proves the intimate bond between this devotion with Ignatian spirituality and with the Society itself, Father General meets certain real problems concerning this devotion and outlines a theological position with regard to them.

During these hundred years circumstances and conditions in the world and in the Society have changed a great deal, but challenges of change today require the same firm adherence to Christ and His Church that external pressures and persecution demanded of the Society then.

During the 31 years of Father Beckx' generalate, the Society witnessed a remarkable increase in number, which rose from 5.200 to 12,000. This was a period of favourable developments linked with severe trials, including expulsion of the Society from Spain, the banning of Jesuit activities by the 'Kulturkampf' in Germany, and the sacrifice of five

Jesuit victims of the French Commune in Paris. The General himself had to transfer his residence from Rome to Fiesole, where it remained till 1895.

In the eyes of the Jesuit General, the consecration of the Society to the Sacred Heart of Jesus was a testimony of fidelity to the mission entrusted to the Society by Our Lord of the promotion of devotion to His Heart, a source of encouragement and hope in the midst of the troubles of that time. The solemn renewal of the Consecration took place during a Concelebrated Eucharist at the church of the Gesù in Rome on the Solemnity of the Sacred Heart of Jesus, June 9, 1972.

*

Dear Fathers and Brothers: Pax Christi,

As this year of 1972 marks the centenary of the Consecration of the Society to the Sacred Heart of Jesus by Fr. Peter Beckx, I would like to keep the promise I made in my letter of December 16, 1971 (AR XV 766), and share with each and every one of you my thoughts on one aspect of the Christocentric spirituality of the Society: the devotion to the Heart of Christ.

Dear to my heart though this subject is, I find it difficult to treat of because of the conflicting opinions found in the Society today regarding this devotion. I will therefore limit myself to expressing to you a desire I feel deeply as General: that of helping resolve the ascetic, pastoral and apostolic problems which the devotion to the Sacred Heart presents today.

Ignatian spirituality is, without a doubt, Christocentric. Like our apostolate, it is based on a deep knowledge and love of Jesus Christ the Redeemer, who loved His Eternal Father and mankind with a divine and human love, infinite and personal, with a love that reaches out to each and every man. It is this love of Christ, which a tradition of many centuries encouraged by the Magisterium represents in His Heart, which moulds the Ignatian apostolate, making it a response on the part of those who "seek to distinguish themselves in every kind of service" and attain to the self effacement of the Standard of the Cross, the "*kenosis*" of the "*vexillum crucis*" and so cooperate in the redemption of the world.

1. Two Conflicting Attitudes

On this fundamental point it is easy to find general agreement. But when one attempts to treat of the devotion to the Sacred Heart, one encounters two conflicting positions which may be summarized thus:

Some maintain that the spirituality which they unabashedly insist on calling Devotion to, or Cult of the Sacred Heart, is something so distinctive of, so essential to the Society, that it should be the characteristic mark of every good Jesuit. For them, the Sacred Heart Apostolate, that *"munus suavissimum"*, should be an essential feature of our pastoral activity, its inspiration and soul. The Sacred Heart, symbol of the divine and human love of Christ, is for them the most direct path to the knowledge and love of Jesus Christ.

Then there is a second position, that of those who feel a certain indifference, even some kind of subconscious aversion, to this type of devotion, and who will not speak of it. They hold that it consists merely of certain obsolete and anachronistic devotional practices. They find no inspiration in the symbol of the heart, because the word "heart" for many is charged with sentimentality; it excites distaste, even repugnance. The fact that in at least some cultures the heart is not considered a symbol of love except in a grossly sentimental context may contribute to this attitude.

These conflicting views have left not a few Jesuits greatly perplexed on the subject. They are convinced of the values essential to the Sacred Heart devotion, but they are at a loss as to how this devotion can be proposed in an acceptable manner to the faithful today. So they prefer to maintain a respectful silence and await further developments.

2. Reconciling the Two Positions

The first two attitudes may seem incompatible and mutually exclusive, but perhaps in their fundamental aspects they are not so. The first attitude is solidly based on the official documentas of the Church and on the tradition of the Society: decrees of the General Congregations, letters of the Generals and other similar sources. The formation which they have received along these lines from the noviceship onwards, and their own personal spiritual and apostolic experiences have convinced them that they have drawn great profit from the practice of this devotion. Many of them point to the extraordinary fruits of their apostolic action, *"ultra quam speraverint"* as an authentic sign of its efficacy.

The opposite attitude derives from a series of reasons which vary from case to case. It should be clear that I am not referring to the more fundamental difficulties based on a Christological problematic which can go so far as to distort our very faith in Christ and the personal relationship we ought to have with Him. I refer rather to the various other motives on which some base their serious reservations in this regard. Some in fact experience a difficulty in accepting any type of spirituality that could limit personal freedom or give the impression of being imposed indiscriminately from without. Others hesitate to commit themselves to a spirituality that seems to them excessively individualistic and subjective. Yet others are turned away by the exaggerated importance given to private revelations, and by the claim that the devotion to the Sacred Heart, even the very concept of consecration, is based solely on them. It may be added that many experience an instinctive revulsion to the over-emotional, inartistic, and often tawdry representations of the devotion.

If these two ways of thinking are calmly considered they are not as conflicting as might seem at first sight. If one analyzes the meaning of such reactions as, "Spare me your special devotions! Jesus Christ the redeemer, crucified and risen, is enough for me", it is immediately clear that they are intended as strong affirmations of a true love for Christ, who in the Paschal Mystery has achieved our salvation and calls us to identify ourselves with Him; and it is precisely this unconditional love for the person of Christ that has always constituted the essence of the Sacred Heart devotion.

When those holding the second position say they reject external practices as incompatible with the way people think today, those of the first group experience no difficulty in acknowledging that such things are incidental and of only relative and limited value. If the first group in turn insist that

Christocentricity and personal love of Jesus Christ are absolutely necessary to attain one's true vocation in the Society, those maintaining the second position accept this fully, but caution against being led to exaggerate the "horizontal" relationship if one loses sight of the indispensable "vertical" aspect.

One could continue citing other points which in the light of sound discernment shed their intransigence and even tend to disappear. We ought indeed to foster such an exchange of ideas, provided they are characterized by the following characteristically Ignatian features:

— a broad understanding, which seeks to evaluate the statement itself and the spirit in which it is intended (Exer. 22);

— a complete objectivity, which knows how to consider the positive values and put aside one-sided exaggerations or purely emotional reactions (Exer. 181);

— utter respect for the legitimate freedom of others, without seeking to lead all by the same road, but allowing the Spirit to guide each one according to His will (Exer. 15).

3. The Objective Value of the Devotion

The objective value of the Sacred Heart devotion is taught clearly in many documents of the Church and the Society. It would be very difficult to maintain, and even more difficult to justify scientifically, the opinion that the fundamentals of this devotion are outdated or lack a theological basis, if one presents in its essentials the message which it offers and the response which it demands.

Christ, the God-man, by very virtue of being the incarnate Son of God, possesses all genuinely human values in their fulness. He is God, and at the same time the most human of men. He embodies in his person love in its fullest measure, because it expresses the Father's gift to us of His Son incarnate, and because it is in itself the perfect synthesis of his love for the Father and of his love for all men.

It is this mystery of divinely human love, symbolized in the Heart of Christ, that the traditional Sacred Heart devotion has endeavoured to express, and which it has sought to emphasize, in a world ever more eager for love, ever more in need of comprehension and justice. Between the Word of God and the pierced Heart of Jesus Christ on the cross lies the whole humanity of the Son of God, and the eclipse of sound theological understanding of that humanity has been one of the reasons which has led to the depreciation of the heart as symbol. To bypass the total humanity of Christ means to leave a theological vacuum between the symbol and the object symbolized, a vacuum which anthropomorphism and pietism are always ready to fill. To neglect the humanity of Christ means, above all, to lose the communitarian and consequently the ecclesial dimension of Christocentric spirituality.

The Church is born of the Incarnation. Rather, it is a continuing Incarnation; it is the mystical body of God made man. Hence there is nothing less individualistic than a genuine love of Christ: the very concept of reparation proceeds from an authentic communitarian demand, that of the Mystical Body.

Overcoming the psychological obstacles which the external forms of this devotion may present, the Jesuit should revitalize it with the solid and virile Christocentric spirituality of the Exercises which, integrally Christocentric and culminating in total commitment, prepare us to "feel" the love of the Heart of Christ giving unity to the whole Gospel. The life of the Jesuit is perefctly integrated in his response to the call of the Eternal King and in the "Take, O Lord, and receive" of the Contemplation for obtaining love, which is the crown of the Exercises. To live that response and that offering will be for each one of us and for the whole Society the true realization of the spirit of Ignatian consecration to the Heart of Christ.

From this intense living of the Spirit of the Exercises issues, with a certain inescapable apostolic urgency, the pledge to live and offer one's own prayer and work in union with the Heart of Christ and so attain to a life profoundly centered in Christ and the Church. The Apostleship of Prayer has long animated, and still continues to animate, the priestly perspective of many Christian lives, drawing them onwards to the Eucharistic sacrifice of Christ and the consecration of the world to God (LG 34). This instrument of the Apostleship of Prayer, which has so greatly helped the People of God in the past can, with appropriate renovation and adaptation, render new and greater service today, when the need is so keenly felt to establish apostolic groups of prayer and earnest spiritual commitment.

4. Summary

It is a fact that the Providence of God has, at different times, provided the Church with the most appropriate spiritual means. For the Society of Jesus, one of those means has manifestly been the devotion to the Sacred Heart. None can deny the excellent fruits which have resulted from it for a Christocentric spirituality and the apostolate of the Society.

It is a theological certainty confirmed by the tradition of the Society, that the devotion to the Sacred Heart by its very nature possesses great values which can and should be applied to present day needs.

It is a fact that there are today many good Jesuits who experience no special attraction to this type of devotion; they may even be repelled by it. And an Ignatian principle tells us that we cannot impose on anyone a form of spirituality which does not help him in his life as a Jesuit (Cf. *Fontes Narrativi* IV, 855).

We find ourselves then in an historic moment of contestation; of criticism, even of rejection, of traditional attitudes. This entails great dangers, but it also has the advantage of compelling us to go to the very heart of things.

It follows that the Society, if it is to remain faithful to its tradition, has the duty of reflecting seriously on what is essential in the Sacred Heart devotion and of finding ways to channel and present it to the world of today. Simplistic solutions are unacceptable, both those which ignore the necessity of constant adaptation and theological development of its essence and exercise, and those which openly reject the devotion because it does not happen to possess an appeal for them.

A thorough investigation of this spiritual, pastoral and apostolic problem should lead us, on the one hand, to discover its true solution, which should be of great service not only to ourselves but also to the many, religious and lay, who in their perplexity are looking for concrete direction in this matter; and on the other hand it should help us to attain a deeper understanding of Him in whom are hidden all the treasures of wisdom and knowledge. (Col 2:3).

Profound meditation on the pierced heart of Jesus on the cross (Jn 19, 34) becomes a source of fruitful and very timely theological reflection. The Evangelist who expressly emphasizes the love of Christ in His passion and death (Jn 13, 1; 15, 13), seems to want to call our attention to this love as the keystone of His redemptive work by showing us the open side of Jesus, from which gushed forth blood and water, those mystical symbols of the gifts of the Spirit to the Church.

5. Conclusion

I would like as General, to add a personal word. I have felt an obligation to speak out on this subject so vital to our spirituality. Apart from the centenary celebration, apart from my own personal conviction of the intrinsic value of the Sacred Heart devotion and its extraordinary apostolic efficacy (to which both theology and experience testify), I also believe that it can be defined, with the Supreme Pontiffs, as "a compendium of the Christian religion", and with Paul VI as "an excellent form of true piety for our times".

I therefore wish to recommended to all, particularly our theologians and our specialists in spirituality and pastoral care, to study the most effective way of presenting this devotion today, so that we may reap in the future the plentiful harvests of the past. I am convinced that by insisting on this recommendation I am rendering great service to the Society, and that the more perfectly we comprehend the love of Christ the more easily shall we find the authentic way to describe it and to express it. The graces promised *"ultra quam speraverint"* avail for us as well.

In the Church of the Gesù in Rome, where Fr. Beckx first consecrated the Society to the Sacred Heart of Jesus, I hope to renew that consecration on the 9th of June, the feasat of the Sacred Heart, using the formula which I enclose with this letter. I would like all of you to join me in spirit in this consecration, in whatever manner each province finds most convenient.

May the Father, "who has hidden these things from the wise and the prudent and revealed them to the humble" (Mt 11:25), grant to us, to you and to me, to know and experience more deeply day by day the inexhaustible riches hidden in the Heart of Christ. I consider this grace of the greatest importance at this moment in the history of the Church and of the Society. Ask, and it shall be given you.

Yours in the Lord,

Pedro Arrupe
General of the Society of Jesus

Rome, April 27, 1972
On the Feast of St. Peter Canisius

(B)

The Spiritual Experience of La Storta and the Consecration of the Society to the Heart of Christ

From the Homily at the Concelebration Church of the Gesù, Rome June 9, 1972

After the space of a hundred years since Father Peter Beckx, General from 1853 to 1884, had consecrated the Society of Jesus to the Sacred Heart of Jesus in the Church of the Gesù, Father Pedro Arrupe, who has always shown a very personal attachment to this devotion, renewed this act on the solemnity of the Sacred Heart in 1972, in the same Church which evokes so many undying memories to the Society and the city of Rome.

For the Prayer of the Faithful the intentions were read in a variety of languages by five Jesuits representing as many continents: there was a Novice, a Scholastic studying philosophy, another doing his theology course, a Priesst, and a Brother.

Shortly before Communion, a special 'rite' introduced the act of consecration which Father General was going to read

> *in the name of the Society. For Saint Ignatius and his compa-*
> *nions, the pledge to "service" confirmed at La Storta took*
> *its actual form in the religious profession which the group*
> *made on 22 April 1541, in the Basilica of St Paul-outside-*
> *the-Walls. Each pronounced his vows in the presence of*
> *the Sacred Host before Communion, and this practice has*
> *always been kept in the rite of Final Vows for Jesuits. It*
> *was in like manner, before the Host and the Chalice, that*
> *Father General pronounced the consecration of the Society*
> *to the Sacred Heart.*

My dear Brothers,

. . At La Storta, a little chapel, solitary and abandoned, on the extreme outskirts of Rome, a poor pilgrim stops to pray with two other companions. There the Most Holy Trinity communicates to Ignatius, in the inmost depths of his soul, a grace of the highest magnitude which will be like a synthesis of all his past mystic life and will become one of the most decisive graces in the foundation of the Society of Jesus.

The Consecration of the Society to the Sacred Heart took place here, three centuries later, in this church of the Gesù, at the initiative of Father Beckx. Father General acted in the name of thousands of Jesuits, and the echo of his Consecration was repeated in all the houses of the Society spread throughout the world.

But if we examine these two happenings in their interior reality, we shall discover an intimate relation between the grace of La Storta and the ceremony in the Gesù. There is no better key than the spiritual significance, the depth and the richness of the grace of La Storta, in order to interpret in an Ignatian way the meaning and the scope of our Consecration to the Heart of Christ. . .

*

The grace of La Storta, a true compendium of the mystical experience of Ignatius, marks and illumines the spiritual trajectory of the Society. It also helps us to understand the meaning of our vocation: in every historical perspective, our life must be a ceaseless service of the Trinity with Christ poor.

And what other meaning can be given to the "*munus suavis-simum*" entrusted to the Society, to live and spread the devotion to the Sacred Heart, if not that of a total and unconditional commitment to the service of Christ and of the Trinity?

La Storta helps us to penetrate more profoundly into the true Ignatian meaning of our consecration: it is meant to be a public confirmation that our life will be an unflagging service of God and of our brothers. Our Consecration to the Heart of Christ, in its turn, helps us to penetrate more deeply into the message of La Storta; it makes us know more intimately the person of Christ, makes us steep ourselves into the import of our mission, and finally it makes us more Ignatian and better and more authentic "*socii Jesu*".

The '*Suscipe*', the synthesis and climax of the Exercises, is meant to signify the personal element of our commitment, the concrete realization of a holocaust, which, united with that of Christ on the altar, we shall offer in the presence of the Consecrated Host, as on the day of our vows "*in odorem suavitatis*" (Const. 540).

The spirit of our consecration is thus identical with that of the Exercises and of the Constitutions. And the most adequate testimony of our Consecration will be that which will the better achieve the ideal of the true son of Ignatius and authentic "Companion of Jesus".

(C)

Consecration of the Society to the Sacred Heart of Jesus

Heavenly Father,

As Ignatius prayed in the small chapel of La Storta, you willed by a singular grace to grant the petition which he had been begging of you for a long time through the intercession of Our Lady: to be placed with your Son. In your words to him you assured him of your support: ' I shall be with you". You asked Jesus carrying his cross to take him as your servant, and this he did in turning to Ignatius with those unforgettable words: ' It is my will that you serve us".

As the followers of the handful of men who were the first "companions of Jesus", we in our turn address to you the same prayer, asking to be placed with your Son and to serve "under the banner of the Cross" where Jesus is nailed out of obedience, with his side pierced and his heart opened as a sign of his love for you and for all men.

We renew today the consecration of the Society to the Heart of Jesus, we promise you all our fidelity and we ask for your grace to continue to serve you and to serve your Son with the same spirit and the same intensity as Ignatius and his companions.

Through the intercession of the Virgin Mary who received the prayer of Ignatius, and before the Cross where Jesus Christ gives to us the treasures of his open heart, through Him and in Him, we say from the very depths of our being: "Take, O Lord, and receive all my liberty, my memory, my understanding, and my entire will. Whatever I have or hold, you have given me; I restore it all to you and surrender it wholly to be governed by your will. Give me only your love and your grace, and I am rich enough and ask for nothing more".

On the Feast of the Sacred Heart
Church of the Gesù, Rome
June 9, 1972

30

MARIAN DEVOTION
IN THE SOCIETY

**A chapter by Father General Pedro Arrupe
in the book "Companions of Jesus: Spiritual
Profiles of the Jesuit Saints and Beati"**

Rome: 1973

*At the time in 1973, when Father General promulgated the
Jesuit Supplement to the new Missal, the Lectionary, and
the Liturgy of the Hours, a book was also published,
"Spiritual Profiles of Saints and Blessed of the Society of
Jesus". This book contained biographical sketches of the
canonized and beatified Jesuits in the new Calendar. The
brief accounts were written by Jesuits of different countries
and cultures in the language of their choice.*

*One year later, the English Jesuit Province brought out
an English edition of the original polyglot collection.
Among the special feasts in the Jesuit Calendar, there is,
on April 22, that of "Our Lady, Mother of the Society
of Jesus." The task of writing this chapter was undertaken
by Father Arrupe himself.*

*

Mater Dei mater mea est : this expression of St. Stanislaus
Kostka represents the conviction and the experience of every
member of the Society of Jesus:

All members of our Society have rightly had an outstanding
devotion to Mary our mother...No mother ever had more
sons, none was ever more blessed or showed such fidelity ..
For none was ever so holy, beautiful and fair, none so

honoured or endowed with the gifts of the Holy Spirit. No
mother ever had more love for her Son...Mother of the
living, means of grace, begetter of life, Mother of God, our
mother, who therefore loves us and out of love prays to
God on our behalf and begs for us...([1])
Mary is indeed the mother of the Society.

1. The Blessed Virgin Mary and Saint Ignatius

Mary played her part in the conversion and training of
St. Ignatius:

'One night, while he lay awake, he saw clearly the likeness
of Our Lady with the Holy Child Jesus, at the sight of
which he received most abundant consolation for a considerable period of time. He felt so great a disgust with his
past life, especially his sins of the flesh, that he thought all
such images which had formerly occupied his mind were
wiped out'.([2])

She also had a role in the composition of the Exercises([3])
and the Constitutions([4]). The young Society saw Mary as
*Virginem Dei Matrem, quae Societatis universae patrocinium suscepit
universale*([5]) (the virgin Mother of God who has undertaken
the patronage of the entire Society).

Ignatius' devotion, which was *non secundum scientiam*([6]) (not
according to knowledge) at the beginning, was gradually
purified, from the time when he wanted to avenge the honour
of the motherhood of Mary with a dagger'([7]) directed against
the Moor who had insulted her, and then left his dagger and
his sword on Our Lady's altar([8]) and gave his clothes to a
poor man on the eve of Our Lady's Annunciation by night([9]),

---

[1] St. Peter Canisius, *De cultu Beatae Virginis*.

[2] St. Ignatius, *Autobiography*, n. 10.

[3] A. Codina, S.J., *Los orígenes de los Ejercicios Espirituales de S. Ignacio de Loyola*,
pp. 85-93.

[4] St. Ignatius, *Autobiography*, n. 100.

[5] Nadal, *Scholia in Constitutiones et Declarationes S. P. Ignatii*.

[6] *Fontes Narrativi*, I, p. 76.

[7] St. Ignatius, *Autobiography*, n. 15.

[8] Ib. 17.

[9] Ib. 18.

until he attained the heights of mystical prayer, when his Mother 'interceded for him before her Son and the Father'[10]. His entire life is marked by her presence 'whom he saw with his inner eye'[11].

Ignatius' constant petition 'to the Mother' was 'that she would place him with her Son'. This grace was granted, and 'he felt such a change in his soul that he saw clearly that the Father placed him with his Son in such a way that he could not doubt it'[12].

In Ignatius' writing Mary always appears together with her Son, as in the offering at the end of the Exercise of the Kingdom, and in the companions' last vows at St. Paul's-Outside-the-Walls. While Ignatius was deliberating about the poverty of professed houses, on 14 February 1544, he said the Mass of Our Lady, who offers her Son to the Father. On the following day he notes in his Spiritual Diary that 'at the consecration I could not help feeling or seeing her, as though she were a part, or the gateway of all the grace that I felt within my soul. At the consecration she showed that her flesh was in that of her Son'[13].

The figure of Mary was always prominent in Ignatius' life, especially while he was writing the Exercises and the Constitutions, appearing to him repeatedly both at Manresa and in Rome. Those documents form the basis of the Society and Mary played her part in their development.

2. The presence of Mary in the Society's history and in the life of every Jesuit

Mary always appears in the light of her Son's work[14]. Mother and Son belong alike to the mystery of our redemption, into which we were born as sons of God. Between Mary's immaculate conception and her glory comes the sacrifice of the cross. It was for the cross that Mary had been given her Son, and for the cross that she had to give him up again to God.

---

10 *Spiritual Diary*, 8th Feb. 1544.
11 St. Ignatius, *Autobiography*, n. 29.
12 Ib. 96.
13 *Spiritual Diary*, 15th Feb. 1544.
14 *Lumen Gentium*, 61.

'This maternity of Mary in the order of grace began with the consent which she gave in faith at the Annunciation, and which she sustained without wavering beneath the cross' [15]. The Virgin Mother is seen as indissolubly linked to the work for which Christ desired to be born of her. And so Mary is mother also to the Companions of Jesus; she brings them forth as sons of Christ, and places them under his standard.

Throughout its history the Society has been linked to Mary in this way, in its individual members and as a body. The Jesuit's vows are made to the Son of Mary, Jesus who is God Almighty, and 'Eternal Lord of all things', in the presence of his mother[16]. She has always been regarded by Jesuits as mediatrix of all graces, and the Society has loved her at different times as Lady, Queen, and Mother. It can be said of every Jesuit that *tenerrimo affectu ferebatur in Beatissimam Virginem tamquam in Matrem suam* (he is most tenderly attached to Our Blessed Lady, regarding her as his mother) [17], but, like Ignatius, without being excessively emotional about it. There is not a Saint or a *beatus* of the Society of whom it cannot be said that he cultivated Mary's love with the affection of a son. *Numquam quiescam donec obtineam amorem tenerum erga dulcissimam matrem Mariam* (I shall never be at peace till I have achieved a tender love for our most sweet mother Mary) [18].

The Society has always defended the glories of Mary in a number of different ways, by theological study, preaching and teaching the Faith, in art and architecture, in its missions and its Marian Congregations, but above all in its daily life. In all these ways the Society's apostolic activity has been such that the Jansenists said that, under the influence of the Jesuits, Christianity had degenerated into 'Marianity'[19]. This was a false interpretation of the maxim *Ad Iesum per Mariam* (to Jesus through Mary) which the Society has made its own.

---

[15]   Ib. 62.
[16]   Constitutions 532.
[17]   E. Villaret, S.J., *Marie et la Compagnie de Jésus: Etudes sous la direction d'Hubert Du Manoir, S.J.*, vol. 2, p. 946, note 11.
[18]   V. Cepari, S.J., *Vita di S. Giovanni Berchmans* (Rome, 1921), p. 211.
[19]   *Litterae a nonnullis protestantibu. theologis Groninganis ad S. Patrem Pium IX datae,* d.d. 1 Dec. 1868.

It is true, however, that we have always regarded Mary as Mother, as the way (Strada), and as 'Advocate, Auxiliatrix, Adiutrix, and Mediatrix' ([20]), but always in such a way as to draw attention to Christ, as Ignatius would insist([21]).

3. Marks of the Society's Devotion to Mary

One pre-eminent feature of the Society's devotion to Mary is a remarkable trust([22]), as of a son for his mother, a mother who showed complete submission([23]) in order to give a mother's service to her son, becoming 'the handmaid of the Lord', which for Ignatius was always the expression of man's ultimate end([24]).

The theologians present Mary to us as the immaculate one, the fairest of creatures, who is exalted above all the angels and saints put together (Suarez, Bellarmine and Canisius), since Jesus Christ is the only man who was able not merely to choose his own Mother, but actually to create her, in his omniscience and omnipotence, as the most perfect creature, 'raised up by the Lord as Queen of the Universe'([25]).

Mary was the fruit of God's omnipotence and was placed at the service of his infinite love, and therefore as daughter of the Father, mother of the Son, and spouse of the Holy Spirit 'after her Son, was exalted above all the angels and above all mankind'([26]) and is closest to the Trinity, so that we can use of her the words of Leo XIII, quoting St. John Damascene, that *eius in manibus sunt thesauri miserationum Domini* (she carries in her hands the treasures of the Lord's mercies) ([27]).

Scripture complements this picture, telling us that Mary was the creature who was closest to the mystery of Christ, since she alone gave him his humanity and shared most fully in his Cross. Mary is the *mater dolorosa*, who suffered as no one else

---

20   *Lumen Gentium*, 62.
21   *Fontes Narrativi*, II, pp. 9-10.
22   *Spiritual Diary*, 2nd, 4th and 5th February, 1544.
23   Sp. Ex., 108.
24   Ib. 23.
25   *Lumen Gentium*, 59.
26   Ib. 66.
27   *Diuturni Temporis*, ASS 31, pp. 146-147.

in the world suffered, and thus became 'our mother in the order of grace'([28]), inspiring compassion in us and at the same time encouraging us to be what we really are. When we see her suffer so much 'with no wavering at the foot of the Cross'([29]), and realise that Jesus gives her to us: 'Woman, behold your son. Son, behold your mother'([30]), when we consider 'the loneliness of Our Lady with so much suffering and weariness'([31]), we can be sure that the Queen of Heaven, exalted as she is, and powerful as she is, knows our sufferings, since she brought us forth in pain, with a love inferior only to the love of God. She is the Virgin 'who gave an example of that maternal love'([32]) with which she is willing and able to come to our aid. 'She cares with a mother's love for the brothers of her Son who are still on their pilgrimage, surrounded by dangers and difficulties'([33]). For that reason she is a sign of hope and consolation, and so in our difficulties the cry that is forced from us is *monstra te esse matrem* (show thyself our mother) ([34]).

This spirit of sonship, like that of a child with its mother, is a characteristic of Ignatius. It was this same spirit that made him see himself as 'an unworthy little servant' of Mary at Bethlehem, that made him feel, when he failed in something, 'a certain shame or something like it before the mother of God', as he says several times in his Spiritual Journal.

'I saw a likeness of Our Lady, and realised how serious had been my fault of the other day, not without some interior distress and tears, since it seemed that I was in disgrace with Our Lady who prayed for me so often, after my many failings, so much so that she hid herself from me, and I found no devotion either in her or from on high'.

'As I was praying to the Son to help me with the Father in company with his Mother, I felt within me an impulse to go

---

[28] *Lumen Gentium*, 61.
[29] Ib. 62.
[30] John 19:26-27.
[31] Sp. Ex., 208.
[32] *Lumen Gentium*, 65.
[33] Ib. 62.
[34] From *Ave Maris Stella*.

before the Father, and in this motion I felt my hair stand on end, and also a very noticeable burning in my whole body, and following upon this tears and devotion at Mass.' ([35])

The Jesuit continues to look for help and protection from Mary as mother, just as Ignatius himself hoped and desired: 'May it please Our Lady to intercede between us sinners and her Son and Lord, and obtain for us that with the co-operation of our own toil and effort she may change our weak and sorry spirits and make them strong and joyful to praise God'.([36])

Pedro Arrupe,
General of the Society of Jesus.

[35] *Spiritual Diary*, 15th and 8th February, 1544.
[36] Letter of St. Ignatius to Agnes Pascual, 6th Dec. 1524.

EPILOGUE

A Prayer to Christ
the Model of our Apostolate

Rome
January 18, 1979

At the end of 1979 every Jesuit received a copy of a talk Father Arrupe had given in Rome earlier that year. It was on "Our Way of Proceeding" or the Jesuit Way of Life. As Father General says at the very beginning, "This talk is a further contribution to what I have said on other occasions about the renewal, updating and adaptation of the Society as called for by the last two General Congregations, in implementation of Vatican II."

Among the genuine traits of the Jesuit charism Father Arrupe includes a love for the person of Christ. He says: "Ignatian spirituality is eminently Christocentric. Love for Christ gives unity to everything in the life and work of Ignatius, and in our way of proceeding, for everything is a concrete application of that love on the level of attitudes and actions. Just as everything converges on Christ, so the love for Christ, in Ignatius's intuition, unifies the dialectical pairs into which our apostolic action is diffracted:

— prayer and action

— dedication to the perfection of self and neighbour

— use of supernatural and human instruments

— pluralism and unity

— one's own effort and total dependence on God

— poverty and having the most effective means

— local insertion and universality.

"To live that intense love for Christ the person, to aspire to a "mind of Christ" that will make us be, seem and act like him, is the first and fundamental trait of our way of proceeding. To attain this ideal, St Ignatius turns to the Mother, so that she will place him with her son".

At the very end of the same talk, Father General states that the Jesuit life and apostolate is based on the personal experience of the person of Jesus Christ:

"Associated with our way of proceeding we invariably find that sensus Societatis which Nadal mentions, a sort of sixth sense or conditioned spiritual reflex connatural in those who live to the hilt the Society's charism. This sensus Societatis is, after all, nothing but an Ignatian form of the sensus Christi that every Jesuit cultivates in order to identify with Christ, particularly through the profound Christological experience of the Exercises.

"Thus all Jesuits, whether young men in their first formation or the rest of us who are in permanent formation, must strive to maintain and quicken the sensus Societatis so as to preserve our identity as Jesuits and be able to meet the challenges of today. But we will never have this sensus Societatis unless we first have a deep and ingrained sensus Christi."

And Father General concludes his exhoration with this prayer:

A Prayer to Christ our Model in the Apostolate

Lord, meditating on "our way of proceeding", I have discovered that the ideal of *our* way of acting is *your* way of acting.

Hebr 12,2
For this reason I fix my eyes on you;* the eyes of faith see your face as you appear in the gospel. I am one of those about whom St Peter says: "You did not see him, yet you love him, and still without seeing him, you are already filled with a joy so glorious that it cannot be described, because you believe".*

1Pet 1,8

Lord, you yourself have told us: "I have given you an example to follow".* I want to follow you in that way so that I can say to others: "Be imitators of me as I am of Christ".* Although I am not able to mean it as literally as St John, I

Jn 13,15

ICor 11,1

would like to be able to proclaim, at least through the faith and wisdom that you give me, what I have heard, what I have seen with my eyes, what I have contemplated and touched with my hands concerning the Word of Life; the Life manifested itself, and I have seen it and give witness.* Although not with bodily eyes, certainly through the eyes of faith.

1Jn1
Cfr.Jn20,25-27;1,14;15,27
Lk24,39

Above all, give me that *sensus Christi** about which St Paul speaks: that I may feel with your feelings, with the sentiments of your heart, which basically are love for your Father* and love for mankind * No one has shown more charity than you, giving your life for your friends* with that *kenosis** of which St Paul speaks. And I would like to imitate you not only in your feelings but also in everyday life, acting, as far as possible, as you did.

1Cor2,16

Jn14,31
Jn13,1
Jn15,13
Phil 2,7

Teach me your way of relating to disciples, to sinners, to children* to Pharisees, Pilates and Herods; also to John the Baptist before his birth* and afterwards in the Jordan * Teach me how you deal with your disciples, especially the most intimate: with Peter,* with John,* with the traitor Judas.* How delicately you treat them on Lake Tiberias, even preparing breakfast for them! How you washed their feet!

Lk17,16

Lk1,41-45
Mt13-17

Mt10,2-12   Mk3,16
Jn19,26-27

Jn13,26   Lk22,48

May I learn from you and from your ways, as St Ignatius did:* how to eat and drink; how to attend banquets;* how to act when hungry or thirsty,* when tired from the ministry* when in need of rest or sleep.*

Mk2,16;3,20 Jn4,8,31-33
Mt9,19;Jn2,1;12,2Lk7,16
Mt4,2;Jn4,7;19,28-30
Jn4,6
Mk4,38

Teach me how to be compassionate to the suffering * to the poor, the blind, the lame,

Mt9,36;14,14;15,32;20,34
Lk7,13

and the lepers; show me how you revealed your deepest emotions, as when you shed tears* or when you felt sorrow and anguish to the point of sweating blood and needed an angel to console you * Above all, I want to learn how you supported the extreme pain of the cross, including the abandonment by your Father.*

CfrMt9,36;14,14;15,32; 20,34 Lk7,13;19,41

Jn11,33-38 Mt26,37-39

Mt27,46

Your humanity flows out from the gospel, which shows you as noble, amiable, exemplary and sublime, with a perfect harmony between your life and your doctrine. Even your enemies said: "Master, we know that you are truthful, that you teach the way of God in truth and care not for any man, for you regard not the person of men." * The gospel shows your virile manner, hard on yourself in privations and wearying work,* but for others full of kindness, with a consuming longing to serve.*

Mt22,16

Mt8,20

Mt20,28 CfrPhil2,7

It is true that you were hard on those in bad faith, but your goodness drew the multitudes; the sick and infirm felt instinctively that you would have pity on them * you so electrified the crowds that they forgot to eat;* with a knowledge of everyday life you could offer parables that everyone understood, parables both vigorous and aesthetic. Your friendship was for everyone * but you manifested a special love for some, like John,* and a special friendship for some, like Lazarus, Martha and Mary.* Show me how you expressed joy at festive gatherings; for example, at Cana.*

Mt9,36
Mt14,16

Jn15,15
Jn13,23;19,26

Jn11,36

Jn2,1

You were in constant contact with your Father in prayer, and your formal prayer, often lasting all night, was certainly a source of the luminous transcendence noticed by your contemporaries.* Your presence instilled respect, consternation, trembling, admiration, and sometimes even profound fear from various types and classes of people.

Mk1,35.CfrMt14,23;26,36
Lk5,16;6,12;9,18;11,1

Teach me your way of looking at people: as you glanced at Peter after his denial * as you penetrated the heart of the rich young man* and the hearts of your disciples.*

Lk22,61

Mk10,21
Mk10,23;3,34;5,31-32

I would like to meet you as you really are, since your image changes those with whom you come into contact. Remember John the Baptist's first meeting with you?* And the centurion's feeling of unworthiness?* And the amazement of all those who saw miracles and other wonders?* How you impressed your disciples * the rabble in the Garden of Olives,* Pilate* and his wife* and the centurion at the foot of the cross.*

Mt3,14
Mt8,8

Mt8,27;9,33Mk5,15;7,37
Lk4,36;5,26
Mk1,27Mt13,54
Jn18,6 Jn19,8 Mt27,19
Lk23,47

The same Peter who was vividly impressed by the miraculous catch of fish also felt vividly the tremendous distance between himself, a sinner, and you. He and the other Apostles were overcome with fear.*

Lk5,8-9

I would like to hear and be impressed by your manner of speaking, listening, for example, to your discourse in the synagogue in Capharnaum* or the Sermon on the Mount where your audience felt you "taught as one who has authority" and not as the Scribes.*

Jn6,35-39   Mt5,2

Mt7,29   Lk4,22

In the words of grace that came from your mouth the authority of the Spirit of God was evident.* No one doubted that

Jn7,46

the superhuman majesty came from a close bond between Jesus and God. We have to learn from you the secret of such a close bond or union with God: in the more trivial, everyday actions, with that total dedication to loving the Father and all humanity, the perfect *kenosis* at the service of others, aware of the delicate humanity that makes us feel close to you and of that divine majesty that makes us feel so distant from such grandeur.

Give me that grace, that *sensus Christi*, your very heartbeat, that I may live all of my life, interiorly and exteriorly, proceeding and discerning with your spirit, exactly as you did during your mortal life. Teach us your way so that it becomes our way today, so that we may come closer to the great ideal of St Ignatius: to be companions of Jesus, collaborators in the work of redemption, each one of us an *alter Christus*.

I beg Mary, your Most Holy Mother who contributed so much to your formation and way of acting, to help me and all sons of the Society to become her sons, just like you, born of her and living with her all the days of your life.

INDEX OF MATTERS

(References are to pages)

Church: love of the Ch., 320—
Ch needs us today—at the service
of the Ch, 242—ecclesial service of
CLC, 221—postconciliar ecclesiology, 212—situation of permanent
mission, 151—still at the beginning
of its history? 150—local Ch's
cultural experience—ecclesial sense
of inculturation, 178, 182, 183—
role of the laity, 222—'sensus
Ecclesiae'.

Collaboration: with the Hierarchy,
31—with clergy and laity, 31—
with laity, clergy and religious in
CLC, 31—among religious in the
Church, 132,—with other Churches,
201, 209—of friends and benefactors, xvi-xvii—inter-provincial and
international, 193—interdisciplinary and in research, 119-120;
need of teamwork in sciences 38—
for inculturation, 180—for education, 47, 72, 75, 94—for promoting
justice

Commitment: to mission 152—
to education, 60—to intellectual
apostolate 122-125—to Christ and
Church, 273.

Community: in teaching institution 64-71—of university presidents,
81, 94—dispersed, 81, 94—the
CLC a world C, 225-243—C.
development, 266.

Congregation of Procurators:
(1970) four apostolic priorities, 1
—voted 'non cogenda', but, 20—
(1978) progress reports of apostolates, 25-31; Ignatian criteria for
ministries, 157.

Constitutions SJ: cristallize Jesuit
identity, 17—rooted in experience
and the Exercises, 279—mission in
the C, 280—on service, 231—
the more universal good, 281—
universality and flexibility, 257—
and inculturation, 175—Part IV
and college rectors, 101—hermen-
eutics to Gospel reading, 277—
book at the altar of the Gesù,
97-98.

Conversion: need of inner and personal C, 107, 160—for renewal, 275
—for CLC action 232—of Ignatius,
228.

Cross: under the standard of the
C, 98, 101, 231, 261—Christ
crucified, 268—Jesus carrying the
C at La Storta,—mystery of the C,
270—participation in the C, 272
—folly of the C, 88—Mary's share
in the C, 345-346—theology of
Logos Redeemer, 263, 268—redemptive suffering, 254, 272—presence
of evil 269.

Culture: in Church documents,
172, 173—Christification of C,
183—faith incarnate in C, 165-166
—broad sense of C,—and inculturation, 84—respect for the particular,
147—assessement of modern C,
191—international apostolate, 190.

Decree 4 (GC 32): our mission today,
98—and evangelization, 141—an
agent of change in SJ, 25—integrity
and energy required, 88-91—in
international apostolate 190-191—
and CLC mission, 233-234—faith
and justice in Mission Ouvriére 311.

Development, Human: the whole
man and all men, 23—integral D
of a Jesuit himself, 268—and
evangelization, 29—in the Formula
of the Institute—total D aim of
education, 87—individual and community D, 264—often to be left
to the laity, 266.

Dialogue: germ of D in "Presupposition" of Sp. Exerc.—between faith
and cultures 173, 183 between
educationists, 43, 46—ecumenical
215-219.

Discernment: personal talents a
factor, 123-124—of Ignatius on
his ideal—and theological reflection, 34—by school community,
59—in intellectual apostolate,—
in inculturation, 176, 184.

Discreet charity: for inculturation,
178, 183—and worker Jesuit, 319.

Ecumenism: in 31 GC, 206, 215·—
formation for E, 203-207—gradual
awareness in SJ, 217—Jesuits and
non-Catholics, 216-217—and Cardinal Bea, 216—all-pervading dimension, 204—fields of E activity, 207—
among the young, 207—need of
united Christian witness, 211—in
social action, 217—ecumenical theology, 218—postconciliar ecclesiology, 212—theologates with other
Churches, 218—and the Holy
Spirit, 201, 219.

Education: a) apostolate of: Jesuit
commitment to E, 11-12, 60—high
priority, 5, 12, 23, 27, 39, 76-78—

139—integrated into our formation, 29—coordination of activities,
29—collaboration of all religious,
132—with other Christians,—with
other bodies, 132—local and global
task 133-134—international collaboration and research 133-135—
Jesuit Communications Research
Unit, 135-136. universal body, 18.

Society of Jesus: a clerical order,
21—grades, 20-21—fourth vow,—
Company of Jesus, 231, 256—the
least Society, xvi, 16, 194—its
charism, 16, 187—our way of
proceeding,—'sensus Societatis', 168
316—love for the person of Christ,
sense of community, 94-5—service
of the Church, 16, 187-188—
global mission, 153, 157—mobility
and flexibility,—apostolic goal, 17
—and pluralism,—love of the
Society, 320—the 'Hated' Society,
9—friends and benefactors,—expulsion of,—fitted for the apostolate,
39-41—for the international apostolate, 194—for ecumenical work,
207—for theol and multidisciplinary work, 93-94—its interest in
education, 23,—philosophy and
theology studies, 117—enlightened
fervour, 159—timing of impulse in
the young, and devotion to Sd
Heart, 329.

Solidarity: with the lowly by intellectuals, 119, 123—in international
apostolate, 194—with the poor in
CLC,

Spiritual Exercises: a) Christ:
and the Person of Ch. 17, 256,
258—personal experience of Ch,
223, 255-262—imitation of Ch,
257-259—to Christify the world,
259, 263.

b) Ignatius: Ignatian service, 227-
231—Ign. cosmogony and anthropology, 151.

c) the Book: its presupposition,
175, 183—man created, 151, 228
—three sins, 152—temporal king,
152, 222, 229—2nd week, 263—
divine plan of Incarnation, 148-
151—two standards, 229—3rd degree
of humility, 17, 222, 257—3rd and
4th weeks, 263, 268—contemplation for love, 'Suscipe', synthesis
and climax, 334, 339-340.—silence
indispensable,

d) Ministry: instrument of forma-

tion, 8—training school for apostolate, 222—preparing directors, 276—
making and directing them, 275-277
—instrument of pastoral work, and
the CLC, 232, 222—and the Church,
—influence on life and apostolate,
8, 275—proselytising and pluralistic,
152—and inculturation, 175—to
youth, Sisters, priests, 276—international congress on, 277.

Spiritual reading: for St. Ignatius,
325—for us,

Structures: changing or adapting
S, 23, 250—development of social
S, 266.

Survey, sociological SJ: 1-2, 21.

Television: for the millions, 24—
generates new values, 87.

Tensions: between education and
pastoral work, 47—evangelization
and development, 29—human needs
and Gospel message, 176—national
identity and world interests, 142-
143—local cultures and growing
interaction, 158, 166— long-term
evangelization and immediate conversion,—universality and adaptability—drudgery and mobility—faith
and profession in CLC,—balanced
faith-justice option, 160—in the
apostolates, 26—two attitudes to
devotion Sd. Heart, 331.

Theological Reflection: highest
priority, 2-4, 22-23—in faith and
justice, 195-197—for Ecumenism,
208, 248—on devotion to Sd.
Heart, 335-336—answer to human
problems, 33—points of faith, 33
—first rank theologians and exe-
gates needed, 33-34—attitudes and
manifestations, 34—object of TR,
34-35—interdisciplinary, 34-36—
human values, 35—man the centre
of world's problems, 35—revelation
and history, 35-37—opens avenue
to God and faith, 36—irruption of
God into human history, 36—
ministry proper of SJ, 40—particularly well equipped, 41—obstacles and difficulties, 41-42.

Theology: harmonious development
264-266—christocentric, 262-273 —
ecumenical, 218—theologates moved
to cities, 218—maintaining high
standards, incarnation of original
sin, 23.

Third World: and respect for the
particular, 144—prophetic mission,

A. M. D. G.

The Institute of Jesuit Sources
Fusz Memorial, St. Louis University
3700 West Pine Blvd.
St. Louis, Missouri, 63108, U.S.A.

This Institute consists of a group of Jesuits in St. Louis, Missouri, assisted by collaborators in many English-speaking provinces of the Society. The chief aim of the Institute is to make the sources of Jesuit thought more readily available to the scholarly world in English-speaking countries, especially by publishing English translations of important books written in other languages by or about Jesuits. The titles of the books published so far follow.

Pedro Arrupe, S.J. *Challenge to Religious Life Today. Selected Letters and Addresses—I.* Edited by Jerome Aixala, S.J. 1979, 310 pages.

Pedro Arrupe, S.J., *Justice with Faith Today. Selected Letters and Addresses—II.* Edited by Jerome Aixala, S.J. 1980, 336 pages.

Pedro Arrupe, S.J. *Other Apostolates Today. Selected Letters and Addresses—III.* Edited by Jerome Aixala, S.J. 1981, 384 pages.

Series I. Jesuit Primary Sources, in English Translations

No. 1. Saint Ignatius of Loyola. *The Constitutions of the Society of Jesus. Translated, with an Introduction and a Commentary,* by George E. Ganss, S.J. 1970, 432 pages.

No. 2. *Documents of the 31st and 32nd General Congregations of the Society of Jesus.* A translation of the official Latin texts, prepared by the Jesuit Conference, Washington, D.C., and edited by John W. Padberg, S.J. 1977, 608 pages.

No. 3. *Jesuit Religious Life Today. The Principal Features of Its Spirit, in Excerpts from Papal Documents, St. Ignatius' Constitutions, the 31st and 32nd General Congregations, and Letters of Father General Pedro Arrupe.* Edited by George E. Ganss, S.J. 1977, 190 pages.

No. 4. *Letters from the Mughal Court. The First Jesuit Mission to Akbar (1580-1583).* Edited by John Correia-Afonso, S.J. 1981, 150 pages.

Series II. Modern Scholarly Studies about the Jesuits, in English Translations

No. 1. Joseph de Guibert, S.J. *The Jesuits: Their Spiritual Doctrine and Practice. A Historical Study.* Trans. by W. J. Young, S.J. 1964, 717 pages.

No. 2. *Ignatius of Loyola: His Personality and Spiritual Heritage, 1556-1956. Studies on the 400th Anniversary of His Death,* by F. Wulf, S.J. (Ed.), Hugo Rahner, S.J., Karl Rahner, S.J., and others. 1977, 318 pages.

No. 3. Josef Franz Schütte, S.J. *Valignano's Mission Principles for Japan, Part I: The Problem (1573-1580)*. Trans. by John Coyne, S.J. 1980. 452 pages.

Note: *Part II: The Solution (1580-1582)* is planned to be published in 1982.

No. 4. Edouard Pousset, S.J. *Life in Faith and Freedom. An Essay Presenting Gaston Fessard's Analysis of the Dialectic of the Spiritual Exercises of St. Ignatius*, 1980, 268 pages.

Series III. Original Studies, Composed in English

No. 1. David M. Stanley, S.J. *A Modern Scriptural Approach to the Spiritual Exercises*, 1967, 374 pages.

No. 2. John Carroll Futrell, S.J. *Making an Apostolic Community of Love. The Role of the Superior according to St. Ignatius*. 1970, 239 pages.

No. 3. William V. Bangert, S.J. *A History of the Society of Jesus*. 1972, 570 pages.

No. 4. Gladys W. Gruenberg. *Labor Peacemaker: The Life and Works of Father Leo C. Brown, S.J.* 1981, 176 pages.

Series IV. Study Aids on Jesuit Topics

No. 1. Ignacio Iparraguirre, S.J. *Contemporary Trends in Studies on the Constitutions of the Society of Jesus: Annotated Bibliographical Orientations*. Translated by Daniel F. X. Meenan, S.J. 1974, 94 pages.

No. 2. David L. Fleming, S.J. *A Contemporary Reading of the Spiritual Exercises: A Companion to St. Ignatius' Text*. 1976, 112 pages; revised, 1980, 112 pages.

No. 3. Thomas H. Clancy, S.J. *An Introduction to Jesuit Life: The Constitutions and History through 435 Years*. 1976, 423 pages.

No. 4. Jean-Yves Calvez, Ignacio Iglesias, Edward F. Sheridan, Carlo M. Martini, Vincent T. O'Keefe, John Correia-Afonso, Cecil McGarry, Francisco Ivern (all S.J.) *Conferences on the Chief Decrees of Jesuit General Congregation XXXII: A Symposium by Some of Its Members*. 1976, 173 pages.

No. 5. Harvey D. Egan, S.J. *The Spiritual Exercises and the Ignatian Mystical Horizon*. With a Foreword by Karl Rahner, S.J. 1976, 198 pages.

No. 6. William V. Bangert, S.J. *A Bibliographical Essay on the Society of Jesus*. 1976, 92 pages.

No. 7. David L. Fleming, S.J. *The Spiritual Exercises of St. Ignatius: A Literal Translation and a Contemporary Reading*. 1978, 272 pages.

No. 8. Thomas H. Clancy, S.J. *The Conversational Word of God: A Commentary on the Doctrine of St. Ignatius concerning Spiritual Conversation, with Four Early Jesuit Texts*. 1978, 84 pages.

No. 9. Anthony de Mello, S.J. *Sadhana: A Way to God. Christian Exercises in Eastern Form*. 1979, 146 pages.